Home Ground

Home Ground

A Collection of Twenty Walks Centred on Pendle Hill

Andrew Stachulski

Published in 2007 by Stamford House Publishing

© Copyright 2007
Andrew Stachulski

The right of Andrew Stachulski to be identified as the author of this work has been asserted by him in accordance with the Copyright, Designs and Patents Act 1988.

All Rights Reserved
No reproduction, copy or transmission of this publication may be made without written permission. No paragraph of this publication may be reproduced, copied or transmitted save with the written permission or in accordance with the provisions of the Copyright Act 1956 (as amended). Any person who does any unauthorised act in relation to this publication may be liable to criminal prosecution and civil claims for damage.

A CIP catalogue record for this title is
available from the British Library

ISBN: 978-1-904985-39-6

Stamford House Publishing

Remus House, Coltsfoot Drive, Woodston
Peterborough PE2 9J

CONTENTS

	Introduction	1
	Walker's Notes	6

The Walks:

1.	An Academic Circle	9
2.	Between Bowland and Pendle	17
3.	Round Cop, Steep Slopes - On a Clear Day	24
4.	Old Man Ribble	40
5.	On The Watershed	49
6.	Breezy Uplands	58
7.	A Border Raid	67
8.	Little Switzerland	77
9.	Earth, Air and Water	88
10.	Heights, Wild and Wuthering	96
11.	A Taste of the Dales	106
12.	Pendle Byways	114
13.	Houses in the Country	123
14.	The Lupine Rocks	136
	On The Way: A Meditation	146
	The Forest of Bowland: An Introduction	151
15.	The Squire's Estates	161
16.	Bowland: Getting to Know You	170
17.	Only By Permission	179
18.	Primeval Visions	189
19.	Deep in the Forest	198
20.	Up, Up and Away: The Hornby Road	207
	Apologia	216
	Acknowledgements and Bibliography	218
	Epilogue: The Shortest Journey	221

TO C.M.H.
We shall not cease from exploration
And the end of all our exploring
Will be to arrive where we started
And know the place for the first time.

T.S. Eliot, Little Gidding (Four Quartets)

Notice
The Countryside and Rights of Way Act and these Walks

Since this book was first written, the Countryside and Rights of Way Act (2000) has given new access to many areas of Britain, including the Forest at Bowland where many of the walks described are situated. In general this is good news for the walker. All the routes I describe are unaffected, and many more new routes and variations are possible. A valuable leaflet, 'Access land: Forest of Bowland Area of Outstanding Natural Beauty,' includes a map which shows the access areas and should be used in conjunction with Ordnance Survey map Explorer OL41 which I make frequent reference to herein. The leaflet is available from many tourist information centres in NW England.

After reflection, I have decided to leave my text essentially unaltered. In the chapters where I refer to the old access situation – much more restrictive! – I refer now to this notice. I repeat that the walks in this book are not affected, and my original comments on the access situation and speculations on new routes opening up (for the situation was already improving for the walker when I wrote in the 1990s) stand as they were. My invitation from the start was that walkers should explore for themselves where possible, beyond the walks described, and they now have far more opportunity to do so.

Remember, however, that the new access rights do not mean we can walk anywhere we like. The act refers to open country (generally high moorland) and acknowledged common land. Even there, access may be restricted during exceptional conditions, and note that it is only access on foot which is referred to. Valuable notice boards are placed strategically through Bowland, and finally I encourage prospective walkers to study the abovementioned leaflet for themselves.

INTRODUCTION

It was in the autumn of 1991, after what had seemed an interminable exile, that I returned to the North of England. During the previous twenty-three years I had lived in Cambridge, Oxford and the Surrey towns of Dorking and Redhill: I had many pleasant memories and made many good friends in all of them. But for one who has loved walking all his life, one crucial question for judging the place where he lives must be, what is the local walking like?

Yes, truly there was something missing! As the years passed I came to understand more and more deeply the true merits of my Lancashire home ground. Although in each place I settled I found enough routes to keep my limbs exercised, those outings were pale imitations of what walking can be. The genuine hills, swift streams, vantage points - and, curiously, the bright and breezy days to enjoy them - lay elsewhere. Long before those twenty-three years were up, and my hand was forced by career developments, I knew it was high time to be heading homewards.

During those years, it was a real treat to walk again those familiar routes in the Ribble Valley, around Pendle, or in Bowland, while on a visit to Great Harwood! Opportunities were few, but all the more appreciated. The walks became trusty old friends, changing little with the years, providing continuity during the uncertainties of life. My wider experience of walking had expanded greatly, taking in the Yorkshire Dales, Pennine Way, Offa's Dyke path, Coast to Coast Walk, Lake District and Scottish Highlands, but I appreciated my home ground nonetheless.

To walk into Downham on a bright Spring day, take in the summit view from Pendle or stroll through the Hodder Woods always gave, and still gives, a special enjoyment.

Just how good is it, then, this section of the British outdoors? A very difficult question to answer - and I hardly feel qualified to answer it. It is a natural human failing to exaggerate the beauties of one's own local countryside: there are too many long-held and personal associations to make an objective assessment. Of course, given the choice, I would sooner be at Hollow Stones admiring Mickledore and Scafell Crag, or scrambling along the Aonach Eagach or Cuillin Ridge. But those are special treats to be savoured occasionally. Week by week, there is so much to enjoy, readily accessible, in the Ribble and Hodder Valleys, South Pennines, Pendle country and the Forest of Bowland. This book is first and foremost a celebration of walking in those areas, and a thanksgiving for the many and varied delights they have to offer.

I offer the walks in this book in the hope that many readers will follow in at least some of the footsteps described. I do not expect that the routes will be followed slavishly: a great deal of the enjoyment in walking lies in discovering for yourself. In fact, I have to say I am rather suspicious of some of the "ways" which are springing up nowadays: this approach to walking can certainly be overdone. A sign saying "Public Footpath" or a dotted line on a map should be enough. My aim here has been to provide enough detail to allow the routes to be followed, but also, by indicating the general character of each walk, to encourage readers to explore further for themselves. At the same time I envisage this can also be a coffee table book, simply giving ideas for places to visit or for gratuitous enjoyment of the walks and scenes described.

Those who are already keen walkers will need no second invitation. I hope they will at least find some new routes here, or new variations on already familiar ones. But I hope I shall be able to address the growing numbers of those who have begun to walk a little, or would like to do so but are not sure how to begin, or even those who have not yet seriously considered it. The great explosion of interest in walking during the last 20 - 30 years, evinced by the new guidebooks, maps and outdoor shops of all kinds as much as by the number of folk you may see afoot, shows no sign of slackening. Apart from its recreational and pleasure value, walking can greatly increase your understanding and appreciation of your locality. The siting of roads and railways, the courses of rivers and watersheds, the ridge-lines and valleys defined by the high fells, the origins of old buildings, settlements and traditional industries - all these and other features become clearer, in a fresh and vital way, as you discover them on foot. Then, supremely, there are the panoramic views from the remote vantage points and summits which are, rightly, the privilege of the walker alone.

Recently I gently chided a friend who described me as a "serious walker". I am sure the remark was kindly meant, but that is not at all how I approach walking, whether in the Ribble Valley, Lake District or on the "Munros". A "serious walker" sounds like one of the species who march grimly along with heads fixed on the ground, apparently oblivious of immediate surroundings, scenery or wildlife, barely able to exchange a greeting with passers-by. If that is "serious walking", then please include me out! To me, if walking is not enjoyment, it loses its point, and if I can communicate at least some of that enjoyment to you I shall be well content.

My condition for including walks in this volume may seem unusual, even arbitrary, but it is clearly defined. Every walk described must be, for at least part of its length (and in most cases wholly) on Ordnance Survey 1:50000 map no. 103 (Blackburn and Burnley). The corresponding old one inch to a mile map, no. 95*, was my first ever OS map - purchased at what then seemed the rather extortionate price of 5s.6d. (read 27½ pence) - and with its help I began my first planning of walks. It is worth pondering for a moment the great variety of scenery encompassed by the map: from Blackburn and its suburbs to Cracoe Fells above Skipton just inside the Yorkshire Dales; from the typical South Pennine scenery of Calderdale to the far-flung, untamed expanses of the Bowland Fells. We are truly fortunate to have such variety on our doorstep.

Most of the walks described, including those already familiar from childhood, were retrodden in 1992/3 with the embryonic idea of this book in mind. At this stage I must come

*Actually the two maps do not quite cover the same area, the new one being slightly "cut off" in the South, but this does not affect the walks described.

clean with my readers and admit that, despite continuing frequent visits to North Lancashire, I currently live in Greater Manchester! It's stretching a point, you will say, to claim them as local walks now. Perhaps, but all the starting-points could be reached in an hour's drive or so, some considerably less; and if they are even closer for you, so much the better.

Aided by a long sequence of fine weekends, I celebrated my "return" by re-discovering those familiar walks, building on them, adding new ones and greatly increasing my knowledge of the area in a most satisfying way. It was a particular delight to deepen my acquaintance with the Bowland area, and a number of walks, arguably the finest, are within that region.

The influence of the late A. Wainwright must inevitably continue to be felt by any Northern guidebook writer. In this area too he has left his mark, as befits a Blackburn man, particularly through his "Pennine Way Companion". I have included sections of the Pennine Way in a few of the walks. Certain of his sketchbooks are also valuable as background reading. Much as I admire A.W.'s work, I have made no attempt to copy his style, which in any case is inimitable.

At the end of this book will be found a full bibliography of sources I have consulted, all of interest in their own right, with brief notes on each. It is a pleasure to thank many friends who have encouraged me in my writings, either by tramping out the miles with me or through valuable comments on the manuscript: they are also acknowledged at the end.

Almost ready to go! A varied programme of walking lies ahead, from pastoral strolls through fields and by noble rivers to striding over windswept summits and rolling high moorland. You will meet varied days of weather, too. But that is an integral part of the picture. Days of rain, mist or cold winds have their own character, and reveal different aspects of the countryside. Even when the distant view is lost, there is usually plenty of interest near at hand. I hope you will enjoy all your walking days, and develop that deep sense of appreciation which is the best foundation for a proper concern for the environment. You will find, too, that instinctive friendship which exists between walkers in many chance encounters along your way, which indeed will often brighten your way.

Before proceeding with the descriptions of individual walks, I have recorded a few general notes which will, I hope, be of particular value to less experienced walkers. These also include some explanation of the scope and difficulty of the walks. Usually the walks are described as circulars based on some particular point for the motorist's convenience, though possibilities for adapting them into "A to B" type walks are frequently noted - and the final one must needs be done in this manner!

WALKER'S NOTES

It is not my aim to discuss any aspect of equipment in these pages. The subject is well covered in many texts. For some of the shorter low-level walks, in any case, the issue hardly arises, though anyone aiming at more than short fair-weather strolls should think about footwear and waterproofs as a minimum. The keynote is always a balance between comfort and adequate protection.

Concerning maps, I have already mentioned OS 1:50,000 map no. 103, and I most strongly advise that you use this as a minimum. Most of my detailed work on routes was done using the appropriate 1:25,000 maps (approximately 2.5inches to 1 mile), which have the great advantage of showing individual field divisions (walls, fences) - provided of course these have not altered. Inevitably 1:25,000 maps cover a rather small area and a number of sheets may be needed to encompass a particular district. The Outdoor Leisure map no. 41 of the Forest of Bowland, first issued in 1996, was a boon to walkers for this very reason, as it covered the whole area. A compass should certainly be taken on walks in the high Bowland fells and the Pennines, otherwise those with no experience of navigating in mist will be in for unpleasant shocks. There are very few cases where precise bearings are essential - but please watch for these in the text.

For the uninitiated in map reading, I again recommend that you acquaint yourselves with a few basic points from Westacott's book (see bibliography) or elsewhere. I think this is something which could be very effectively done through evening classes or their equivalent. One persistent difficulty with maps - and this is said with no disrespect to the superb work of the OS - is the delineation of paths. It is not merely a question of trying to locate the correct line of the path before you - the position of the next stile, and so on - but a matter of sins of omission and commission. Some well used paths, whether because they are not recognised rights of way or for some other reason, are not delineated on the maps; other paths which are so delineated may have fallen into complete disuse, been obstructed, etc. and become useless to the walker. I shall do my best to give appropriate guidance in the text.

I feel bound to say something on the safety issue. Many walkers, I know, set themselves firmly against solo walking, even on relatively short and simple walks. Well, I should not dream of trying to persuade them otherwise. Please remember, though, that a much greater responsibility settles on one who leads a group of walkers, even informally, than on a soloist, who takes responsibility only for him or herself. We are all free to decide for ourselves. Know your limitations; consider the weather and demands of the walk planned; but don't be frightened of walking - the hills are not booby traps waiting to snare you. I find that solo walking and walking with one or a few good friends are equally enjoyable, in different ways. Bear in mind, too, what I call the "Kipling principle":

> Down to Gehenna or up to the Throne,
> He travels the fastest who travels alone.
> *(Kipling, The Winners)*

Well, I sincerely hope my readers will be on the second alternative. But it is inevitable that a solo walker will generally travel faster than a group, and that is a point worth considering when estimating a time for your journey.

Moving on to the individual walks, they range in length between about six and fifteen miles. For nearly every walk, however, there are possibilities for lengthening or shortening the basic route as desired. I have given fairly accurate mileages for each walk, but made no attempt at single-word gradings such as easy/moderate/hard. In my opinion such classifications are too crude - so much depends on the day's conditions, our own condition and personal preferences for type of walk. Rest assured, though, that I have taken pains to summarise the essential character of each walk, usually in the first paragraph or two. Nor have I tried to give estimated times - for the same reasons. Naismith's formula, however, is such a valuable rule of thumb that I quote it here: (see Westacott, op cit., for more detail): Allow an hour for every three miles' horizontal distance and half an hour for every 1,000ft. of climbing. Note that this assumes a reasonable degree of fitness.

Finally, the distinction between paths and rights of way - the latter being marked in red on the 1:50,000 OS and green on the 1:25,000 - should be understood. On the summit plateau of Pendle, for instance, your eyes will detect a large number of well-used paths de facto which on the map are plainly not rights of way. Some are recognised permissive paths. Older OS maps employed thin black dashed lines to indicate paths which, though commonly used, were not rights of way. Note that the Countryside and Rights of Way Act has created new access areas, not permanent rights of way (see Introduction). Nevertheless, the Act has had a considerable impact, notably in the Forest of Bowland where access was formerly much restricted, as lamented by Gillham and other writers. The walks on the high Bowland fells which I describe herein make use of rights of way and permissive paths acknowledged before the Act: they are unaffected and just as satisfying as ever. (Walks 16-20). Indeed, Bowland had been slowly opening up to the walker for some time before the new Act, as I have noted in the text, though that is of mainly historical interest now.

Sketch maps

I have included one sketch map per walk, of appropriate scales as indicated. These are not intended in any way to supplement the OS map for that locale: as noted above, you are most strongly recommended to take one. However, each sketch map will give, at a glance, a feel for the type of walk being undertaken, the heights reached along the way, the amount of climbing overall and the situations of nearby villages, road access etc.

In each case the main route is indicated by a continuous red line, with suggested alternatives in dashed red. Other symbols are fairly self-explanatory - rivers, roads, afforested areas etc. For simplicity's sake, only a few selective contour lines are shown in each case, heights given in feet. Major summit heights are given in both metres and feet.

Enough words! Now let the walking begin.

1. AN ACADEMIC CIRCLE

Hurst Green, Woodfields, Lower Hodder Bridge, Higher Hodder Bridge, Kemple End, Stonyhurst, Hurst Green. 6 miles. Maps: OS 1:50000 'Landranger' no. 103, Outdoor Leisure 1:25000 'Explorers' Nos 287 and OL41 (Forest of Bowland)

* * * * * * * * * *

Background

The river Hodder, which rises in the heart of Bowland Fells above the remote Cross of Greet Bridge and joins the Ribble half a mile from Mitton, will play a major part in these walks. Towards the end of its course, the river offers exceptionally fine scenery between the Lower and Higher Hodder bridges. This section is about two miles in length, and many will find this quite satisfying as a walk in itself. The walk as described here is a circular based on Hurst Green, where there is plenty of parking space and the prospect of something to eat or drink in the village or at nearby Mitton on concluding the walk. It is a delightful easy-going introduction to this series of walks, never too demanding, though with a fair amount of up and down on the riverside section and a noticeable "pull" up Birdy Brow later.

We shall be rubbing shoulders with the famous, too. Stonyhurst College, including Hodder Place, is one of the country's leading Roman Catholic public schools and is well seen along the route. This is an appropriate time to visit Stonyhurst: the four hundredth anniversary of the college's foundation in 1593 was recently celebrated. The present buildings, however, though built in 1592, were occupied by the College only in 1794: the original foundation was in France, the translation to this country occurring only after a more tolerant attitude to Roman Catholicism had developed. Undoubtedly one of its most famous old boys was the author Sir Arthur Conan Doyle, though from his autobiography "Memories and Adventures" it is clear that he was not happy here under the strict Jesuit regime. Although the Sherlock Holmes stories recount no cases of Holmes exercising his crime-solving powers in this area, recent evidence has found some links. The names of Holmes and Moriarty are found in the

Stonyhurst College register at the same time as Conan Doyle, and Baskerville Hall-supposedly in Devon-has features similar to parts of the college buildings and grounds.

Among other literary associations, the poet Gerald Manley Hopkins was also a Stonyhurst student, and the surrounding area is said to have inspired J.R.R. Tolkien's 'Middle Earth', at least in part.

The Walk

From the War Memorial in the centre of Hurst Green walk down the lane past the "Whitehall" - once a cafe and local arts centre - and the cottages beyond, thence over a stile adjacent to a gate and into an open field. Turn left gradually, keeping next to a wall, then pass through a gap in the hedge ahead. Once into the next field, turn sharp right (the tread, both here and throughout this section, is fairly clear) with the hedge now on your right. Leave the hedge and go on past an isolated tree, turning right when you meet the next fence, and keep on in much the same line, through two kissing gates. (A kissing gate is one which turns in a narrow enclosure, admitting one person at a time.) You are going downhill now, through a dip, with spongier going underfoot. A wood approaches on the left, and a sports pavilion appears above the bank on the right.

Tread gently uphill through this pleasant park-like ground, the wood still close on your left, and after the going levels again trend slightly to the right, approaching a fence, leading in a further 300 yards to a gate. Pass through, reaching a lane, when a striking view of the school chapel appears on your left. The Gothic perpendicular style is a conscious imitation in miniature of King's College Chapel, Cambridge, though it postdates the latter.

Turn right along the lane, passing the school observatories, but when you reach a metal gate turn sharp left through a kissing gate into a field with farm buildings on your right. You pass a house and emerge onto a rough lane, keeping the same direction. The extensive college buildings with the famous green domes, visible for miles, continue to afford a fine prospect on your left.

In about a quarter of a mile you reach a minor road by a cluster of cottages (Woodfields) including the former Stonyhurst post office on your left. Almost immediately across the road is another path worth your attention some time: it leads directly to the wooded section of the riverside walk, but misses the enjoyable first section. Instead, we turn right down the road, Pendle Hill now dominating the scene ahead. In about a third of a mile, look for a public footpath sign on the left just beyond a house, cross a stile and descend the field ahead. Keep to the left of a hedge further on and emerge through a gate onto the B6243 Hurst Green - Clitheroe road, then turn left.

Lower Hodder Bridge is reached in another two hundred yards, with the old bridge, "Cromwell's Bridge" by long tradition, immediately downstream - positively not for crossing, but an inviting photographic subject. Whether the bridge really has a direct connection with Cromwell is questionable, though he almost certainly was in this area in 1648 when visiting Stonyhurst, en route to Preston. There are records of a bridge here since at least the fifteenth century.

Turn left off the road at a Public Footpath sign before the (new) bridge and pass through a kissing gate to the right of a gateway, with Riverside Cottage on your left, then walk upstream close by the Hodder. This is a beautiful walk, a stretch for sheer enjoyment at any time of the year, though at quiet moments for choice. Look out for a rich variety of bird life, especially water birds: heron, dipper and grey wagtail are pretty common, and you have a sporting chance of seeing a kingfisher as well as rarer ducks such as goosander. The wooded far bank soon steepens, enhancing the scenery further. About a quarter of a mile beyond the bridge again pass through a gate and keep on the rough, wide track, the river immediately on your right. A fairly new wire fence prevents encroachment into the field on the left.

A long left bend of the river ensues: the large field bears witness to centuries of agricultural use. You pass a curious little

Walk 1: An Academic Circle

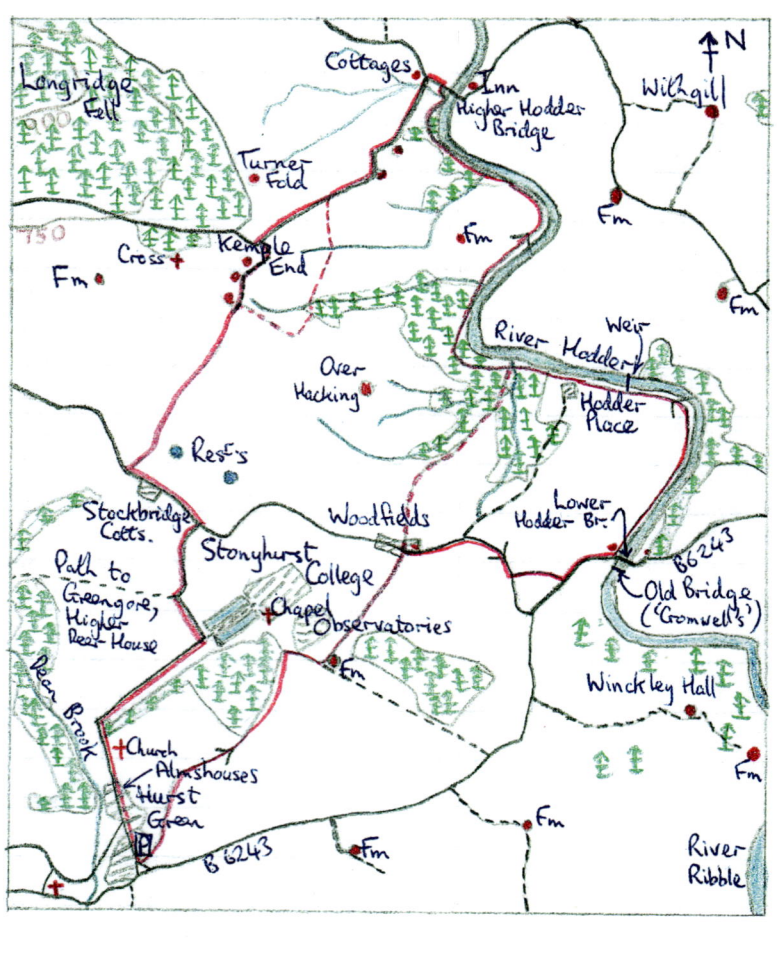

mound near the apex of the bend, and shortly pass a weir, going through a third gate, emerging onto a clear vehicular track.

About two hundred yards on, cross a stile adjoining a gate and climb the steepish bluff ahead, into woodland: soon you are looking down on the Hodder from an impressive height. At the top of the rise you pass a recently refurbished wing of Hodder Place, also part of Stonyhurst; the buildings have been in view for some time owing to their commanding, even idyllic, situation.

Where the "main" track turns back left into the school grounds, go on slightly downhill into the woods. Cross a side stream by a new bridge, reaching a junction of paths: the left branch would return you to Woodfields. The path to follow, up the steep slope opposite, is clearly indicated by a series of wooden steps; the walker feels quite spoilt with such attention! After the first section of precisely 90 steps (note, incidentally, the base of a former cross passed on your right, marking a bathing fatality near this spot), the old path turned right. This is not recommended now: a landslip has turned this section into a slippery scramble. Instead, keep slightly left (observing a waymarker) and ascend a second series of precisely 71 steps. It was somewhere hereabouts, longer ago than I care to remember, that I once "flushed" a startled woodcock out of the undergrowth.

There is a very welcome flat section beyond the steps for recovery of breath, still on a clear tread, a high promenade above the steep wooded slope on your right. After reaching, momentarily, the edge of the wood, turn sharp right down another series of steps, with care - it may be slippery here. In summer this section is redolent with the odour of wild garlic. On the way down there are 101 steps, again in two sets; at the bottom you rejoin the old path and turn left. Proceed downhill through the woodland, nearing the river again, soon turning left over a tidy footbridge and shortly another. By the time you cross a third footbridge, you emerge from the woods onto another section of riverside path.

Pass by a fairly new kissing gate, then enjoy another course of the beautiful Hodder riverside. I well remember walking this stretch once in solitude on a December afternoon, when I was stirred from a reverie by a clear, sharp call. Looking up, I saw a kingfisher speeding by downriver, a brilliant flash of turquoise and orange illuminating the gathering twilight. There is geological interest here, too: note the remarkable rock folding on the far bank. After a 90 degree left bend of the river, pass through a further two kissing gates, then back into a wooded section after a footbridge.

From here, neat and unobtrusive path improvement has speeded progress over what was a sketchy and muddy section: well drained, gravelly going allows you to appreciate the river all the more. After another footbridge, the river bends right: Higher Hodder Bridge is soon in view. The path turns briefly left, away from the river, to a "T" junction of paths, where turn right. Adding to the rich variety of birdlife on show during the walk, you have a fair chance of seeing redstart and woodpecker hereabouts. You cross another footbridge, then drop down to a stone bridge, turning right onto a clear though often overgrown lane. Keep to this, passing through dense shrubbery, with a house on the left shortly. Finally turn right over a footbridge, soon going up stone steps to emerge onto the road adjacent to Higher Hodder Bridge, ending with some reluctance two miles of magical scenery. It really is difficult to tear yourself away and proceed with the rest of the walk, and certainly it seems wrong to press on before taking a last admiring view in each direction from the bridge. Particularly downstream, the combination of the river itself with the rich and majestic trees lining both banks is something quite special, yet remarkably unsung.

We have to get ourselves home, however! By the cottages seen to the left where you emerge onto the road, turn left up Birdy Brow (signposted to Hurst Green and Longridge). A steep uphill pull ensues for the next half mile, with interest afforded by some impressive detached residences passed en route. The simplest continuation is then to turn left and pass by the Kemple End cottages when the road bends sharp right. Alternatively, look for a double footpath sign on the left of the road before you reach the bend, and take the right-hand one, taking fieldpaths which will lead you to the same spot on the Kemple End lane eventually. This requires careful map work, however, and one section of the path is obscure: probably not recommended on a first visit. Whichever alternative you take, don't omit to take in the superb view of Pendle's NW flank. Kemple End is one of the classic stations for viewing the hill - one of the little knolls by the bend in the road is recommended.

If taking the more straightforward route, turn left off the road at Kemple End, soon turning right. At the next path junction, turn left, soon reaching a farm on the right of the lane where the alternative path through the fields would converge at a track coming in from the left. Pass through a gate and continue up a usually rather muddy lane, emerging presently into an open field. Follow the clear vehicular track initially, then cross a stile in the fence ahead between two gates. By now the views have again become expansive, and sunsets hereabouts may be spectacular. You pass two sheets of water below on your left on this stretch, given as reservoirs on the OS. For direction, keep close to the fence on your left, where there is a low bank with a parallel groove: further on, you will need to walk on the right side of the groove, but the going remains good underfoot. Eventually you climb a stile to the right of a barn and emerge onto the road by a public footpath sign. Turn left.

Easy going now: we're on the home stretch, mostly downhill, with the tea already being prepared. You pass the neat group of cottages at Stockbridge, and continue downhill, soon turning right at a junction signed "Hurst Green". Simply follow the (usually quiet) road, with excellent views of the college and grounds, shortly appearing on your left. Note the footpath to Greengore, passed on a corner of the road, which you may consider as an alternative for part of the next walk. Greengore is an interesting old building, thought to have been one of the places which secretly sheltered the fugitive Henry VI around 1461. One of its outbuildings is used as a YHA camping barn.

It is the college, though, which will hold your attention, particularly when you reach the main entrance, with the long driveway and adjacent ponds leading the eye to the buildings with excellent effect. Truly a different world from most of our schooldays! Turn right here, along an unfenced road, then left when you reach the imposing statue of the Virgin at the far end. Soon you pass through the gateway, effectively marking the boundary between the college grounds and the village of Hurst Green. Note the almshouses, passed on your left, another item well meriting an inch of film: on a plaque are displayed the names of the contributing parishes, Aighton, Bailey, Chaigley, Ribchester and Dutton. In a couple of minutes the circle will be complete, and you may satisfy your hunger according to taste from the village establishments.

There it is, our opening course, as it were. The main banquet lies ahead, but I think no walk could afford a better introduction to the area as a whole. It is one of those walks not done for effort or endurance, but for enjoyment. In subsequent expeditions we shall take on many more demanding and high-level walks, but for sheer beauty and endearing nature this one has a special place. A little out of character, you may say, so close to industrial East Lancashire? Possibly. But let us at least be thankful, and give beauty its recognition.

2. BETWEEN BOWLAND AND PENDLE

Car Park, Old Clitheroe Road - Longridge Fell - Walker Fold (Chaigley) - Chaigley Hall Wood - Kemple End - Car Park 6 miles: *Maps*: OS 1:50000 'Landranger' no.103; OS 1:25000 'Explorers' Nos 287 and OL 41.

Alternatives: The final stretch of minor road, though not at all unpleasant, may be removed, at the cost of about two extra miles, as follows. From Kemple End (top of Birdy Brow Lane), take the path leading to the lane above Stonyhurst (Walk 1). From here, either follow the route of Walk 1 into Hurst Green, then turn up via Dean Brook, Greengore and Crowshaw House to the start, or (more directly) take the path leading SW from (683397) to Higher Deer House, thence to Greengore and as above.

Short Alternative: Direct return across the fell from Walker Fold (672418) to Old Clitheroe Road.

* * * * * * * * * *

Background
Certain walks seem to demand a good deal of effort from the walker while apparently giving little reward, in the way of sense of achievement, scenery or wildlife. Others, for an apparently modest expenditure of effort, seem to offer a superlative return in some way or other. Those who know the Lake District will think of Latrigg above Keswick, whose wonderful summit view looking south - encompassing the rooftops of Keswick, the length of Derwentwater and the backdrop of the Borrowdale fells - seems out of all proportion to the very brief climb required to attain it.

Longridge Fell is something of a Latrigg, you might say. At 1150ft. above sea level, its height is very modest by Bowland or Pennine standards, lying indeed only about 600 - 700ft. above the roads to its south and north respectively. Nevertheless, by virtue of its situation and relative isolation, it is a really excellent viewpoint, encompassing a major arc of the Bowland fells,

Waddington Fell, Pendle, a section of the South Pennines and the West Lancashire hills. On a day of reasonable clarity, moreover, you can expect to get glimpses of the Three Peaks area. Geographically, it represents the first high ground to the north of the lower Ribble valley, a ridge of about seven miles in length lying SW to NE; to the west lies the flat country of the Fylde. It is not a watershed, all the water draining from the fell eventually reaching the Ribble estuary beyond Preston; the walking is generally easy, with little exposed rock or steep slopes; yet it has special significance among this set of walks. Those with even a little ambition to explore this area further will have their appetites whetted by the views en route. Between Pendle, with the South Pennines further afield, and Bowland in the opposite direction, Longridge Fell is a half-way house. The walk to be described is straightforward, a pleasant afternoon stroll, but remember that the north side of the fell (which is much steeper) may be slippery underfoot after heavy rain or ice.

The Walk

Longridge Fell is quite heavily afforested, a point to be borne in mind by those looking for clear views all the way: there is a multiple choice of routes across the fell, some through heavily forested areas, especially on the southern slopes. From the small car park on the Old Clitheroe Road at (664396), the simplest route will be found on proceeding about 150yds. along the road to the left, then through a gate into the forestry area on the right. Note that this path is given on the 1:50000 map, but not the 1:25000.

Forests are difficult, even potentially embarrassing places, for the walker: it is remarkably easy to become quite disorientated. In this particular case, where neither the 1:50000 nor the 1:25000 map gives sufficient detail on the first section of the walk, the following instructions should be carefully followed. Remember that the pattern of forest roads, firebreaks and afforested areas may change with time, in which case one hopes waymarkers will be provided. Or you may prefer the "forest-free" alternative given later.

Walk 2: Between Bowland and Pendle

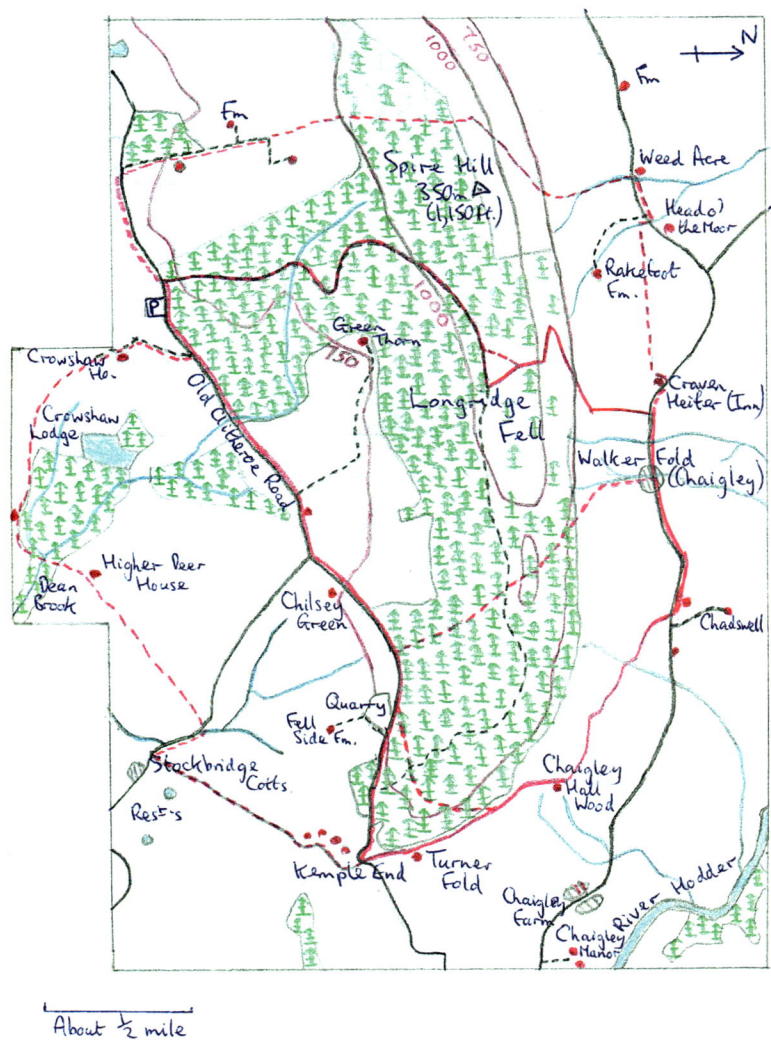

As usual with heavily afforested areas, new plantings and felled areas vary with time. The above indicates which areas are currently relatively sparse where they affect the given route.

About a third of a mile along the main forestry track, keep to the main track as it bends left, ignoring a branch to the right. Pass a firebreak on the left some quarter of a mile later, and about two hundred yards further on ignore a major branch on the left. The place to turn left comes in another quarter of a mile, going uphill where the "straight on" track contours. Shortly you will climb to the summit of the track, with the true summit of the fell - Spire Hill on the 1:25000 OS map - close by on your left, due west. Keep your eyes about you, though, while taking care over the route! There is plenty of interesting bird life about - I have seen and heard owls, and fairly certainly caught a glimpse of a buzzard. Before the fell was so heavily afforested, there were grouse on the summit plateau, more especially on the west side, though I am not sure whether any remain.

At the very summit of the track, you have a choice: either follow a clear path going straight on where the track turns right, or swing right with the track, which in about another three hundred yards is intersected by another clear path (actually a bridlepath) at a cairn. Turn left onto the path (there is a substantial clearing opposite) and, a little way further on, you meet up with the earlier alternative path at a large cairn. Keep on (right) and very soon the steep northern slopes of the fell begin to drop away in front of you, revealing a splendid view. The suddenness of the transition is dramatic, imparting quite a different character to the next phase of the walk. Is it too much to ask that the Forestry Commission will leave a sufficient unplanted strip to allow future generations of walkers to enjoy this panorama? From Beacon Fell right round the sweep of the Bowland fells to Waddington Fell, with Ingleborough (if you're lucky) as a backdrop, and the pastures of the mid-Hodder valley seemingly below your feet, it calls for a leisurely appraisal.

The path, very clear hereabouts, breaks into zigzags now to negotiate the steep descent. Turn right after the first section of "zig" (straight on down the grooved track is an alternative, leading to the road beyond Rakefoot). Continue to the end of the "zag", negotiating a wet section with care, then turn briefly left, turning right again before the little stile. Finally turn left straight down the hillside - watch your step if it's wet or icy! Cross a stile to the right of a gate and continue in the same line, with a hedge on your left, eventually crossing another stile with a clear footpath sign onto the road from Higher Hodder. The Craven Heifer, just to the left along the road, affords an opportunity for a detour. Our route turns right, however, reaching in a few hundred yards the hamlet of Walker Fold, the population centre of the parish of Chaigley, and a pleasant mix of old houses and "conversions". A plaque set into a wall on your right, at the old school and chapel, gives an intriguing insight into the religious history of the place - an unexpected link with the Church of Latter Day Saints.

To your right, the fell slopes look impressively steep: did we really come down there? In fact, a shorter alternative return over the fell leaves almost immediately, turning right up the lane past the manse. This is very steep, however, and inferior in views to our route. Continue down the road beyond Walker Fold, and in a little over a quarter-mile, just past some buildings on the left, take a public footpath signed on the right. Pass through a gate and a rather muddy enclosure, then take a rising diagonal line across the pasture ahead. There is a fine prospect of Pendle here, with Weets Hill to its left, and in retrospect the Bowland fells make a lovely backdrop. Before long the buildings of Clitheroe are also prominent ahead.

This section of path appears lightly used, but fortunately route-finding isn't difficult. Pass through a sharp dip, crossing a little stream in a gully, then go over a stile ahead (this has no "crossbar" but its location is fairly obvious, thanks to a non-barbed wire strand). Go on through a gap, keeping a fence-cum-hedge on your left, soon crossing another stile while maintaining the same line. By now you can sense the end of Longridge Fell approaching from the line of the heavily afforested slopes on your right. Once, passing this way on a long summer evening, I was struck by the haunting cry of a lone curlew breaking the prevailing silence.

The next stile is a bit further to the right, away from the field corner. Keep a fence to your right afterwards: Chaigley Hall

Wood farm, long ruinous but currently being restored, soon comes into view ahead. Cross the fence to your right by a stile, then ford a small stream, climbing towards the building through an area of rough, wet pasture. Climb over a stile in a fairly new fence (aim for a prominent raised post) and pass to the right of the buildings ahead, crossing a little footbridge. Turn roughly half right here, newly waymarked, proceeding with a wall/fence to your left on a clearer tread. Downhill on your left the extensive buildings of Chaigley Farm and Chaigley Manor are visible.

Keep on roughly the same line by a wire fence and cross a wooden stile, going ahead by the edge of the extensive plantations. You could investigate a path leaving uphill through the wood shortly by a stile on the right: this cuts off some road walking, and is sporadically waymarked, but involves hard going on a steep and overgrown path. I was once rewarded by a close-up view of a startled owl along here. The main path continues through a broken fence with a superfluous stile, becoming much easier and wider. Hereabouts you pass a memorial seat (1969) to an Alan Forbes, donated by Liverpool Ramblers' Association and beautifully situated, with an extensive view including the remote Cracoe fells. A few hundred yards further on, cross a stile adjoining a newish gate and keep along the lane with the former barn at Turner Fold, now a large and impressive conversion, on your left. You are now on a rough vehicular track: a gate may be bypassed on its right, then bend left, very soon reaching the road at Kemple End, whose attractive little heathery hillocks afford notable views of Pendle, as noted in the first walk.

From here, the simplest return involves turning right along the road and following it to the starting point - about 1.75 miles. It's usually quiet here, along "Old Clitheroe Road", making for pleasant walking, especially (I shall end up saying this often) on a summer evening. You remain at a considerable altitude, and the views, from SE to SW, remain far-ranging: Pendle and its satellites, a section of the South Pennines, right round to the West Lancashire Moors, with the greenery of the Ribble Valley nearer at hand. If you wish to explore field paths to take you off the road, at the expense of extra distance, I have made some suggestions in the introduction. Whatever you decide on, the walk offers a compact circuit in itself, with splendid views and prospects of many other areas we shall be exploring in later and more ambitious walks. It's difficult not to fall under the spell of Bowland fells, in particular, after seeing that superb prospect from the north side of Longridge Fell.

Finally, as promised, that "forest free" alternative to the first part of the walk. From the car park, walk up the road past the forestry gate. Continue to point (657394) and turn right up a clear lane, passing outlying farms. Keep on in the same line, with a fence on your right, then cross a stile at (655404), emerging onto the open fell with a clear tread ahead. In clear conditions the sea is visible to the west from here. In about a quarter-mile you reach the summit of the path, with the highest point of the fell a short distance away ENE. Once you begin to lose height, the track turns right to make a very clear diagonal descent of the fell.

Emerge at a stile at (658414) and go straight down to the road near Weed Acre. The final section to the road may be very wet. Turn right, when you can shortly make use of a W-E path that cuts off a long loop of road and emerges in the car park of the Craven Heifer. This is best joined via the public footpath sign at (661419) opposite Head o'th'Moor. Meet the main route on the road some hundred yards east of the Craven Heifer.

3. ROUND COP, STEEP SLOPES

Pendleton, Wymondhouses, Nick of Pendle, Spence Moor, Pendle Summit, Fox's Well, Pendle Road, Hook Cliffe, Little Mearley Hall, Pendleton. 10 miles. Maps: OS 1:50,000 'Landranger' no. 103; 1:25,000 'Explorer' OL41; 'Paths around Pendle' © Duncan Armstrong and associates.

Pendle stands "rownd cop, survaiying all ye wilde moore lands." (Rev. Richard James, 17th cent.)

Short Alternative A very good circular of the summit plateau, minimising loss of height and re-ascent, can be made from Nick of Pendle. Reach Pendle summit as on the main route, then head NNE, following the escarpment, to the wall. Cross this, follow the ginnel track (usually clear, bearing 270 degrees in very thick mist), till the N escarpment is reached. Follow the line of cairns to the main one (Scout Cairn) at the head of Mearley Clough. From here, follow a rather faint path, bearing 225 degrees, skirting Turn Head (map) until a ruined wall is reached. Follow this left (ESE) until you pass Howcroft Brook (head waters of Ashendean Clough), then simply take a line due S, picking up the outward track, returning over Apronfull Hill to the Nick. Five miles. For the popular ascents of Pendle from Barley and Worston, see Iddon in Gillham (op.cit).

* * * * * * * * *

Background

During my years of absence, there was one feature above all whose reassuring form was lacking from the landscapes I surveyed. A bold, commanding form, an immediately recognisable shape which, surely, no-one who has grown up in East Lancashire can ever forget. Despite the sinister associations with the activities of the "Lancashire Witches", their subsequent trial and execution, most locals will, I suspect, join me in regarding Pendle as a familiar friend, albeit one of the strong silent type. The fact that it has its own folk song is a tribute to the affection in which this fine old pile is held.

The truth is that Pendle Hill cannot be ignored. It dominates the surrounding countryside in all directions for many miles, in a manner that puts far higher fells to shame. From most of the other walks in this volume, it is readily visible, often commandingly so; you expect the old "lion's head" to come jutting into the sky at any appropriate viewpoint on the way. Pendle's splendid isolation is, indeed, its strong point, and many writers have commented on the way that its height was frequently exaggerated, often grossly so, in olden days. Even at its true altitude of 557m (1829ft.), there is no higher ground before Fountains Fell (20m due NNE), Ward's Stone (17m approximately NW) or Black Hill (30m approximately SE). Walk round the streets of Clitheroe, and sooner or later an alleyway opens up, revealing those sweeping moorland slopes, seemingly no distance away. From the keep of Clitheroe Castle you can pick up much detail, on a clear day: the Sabden Road leading up through the shallow "pass" of the Nick of Pendle, the prominent indentations of Mearley and Ashendean Cloughs, and for the sharp-sighted, or those with binoculars, the "Scout Cairn" at the head of the route up from Worston is fairly clear. From Downham, particularly on emerging from St.Leonard's into the churchyard, Pendle's presence is overwhelming: it seems to fill half the sky.

Inevitably, the hill has acquired its fair share of mythology - and misunderstanding. I do not propose to relate, again, the story of the crimes attributed to the Lancashire Witches, the course of their trial, or their eventual execution at Lancaster in 1612; in the bibliography I have included what appear to me the most valuable texts for consultation. As to precisely what, if anything, the accused were guilty of, who can say? At this distance of time, beyond the thin stratum of recorded facts, all is speculation. It is probably fair to say that a mounting body of opinion would now hold that Chattox, Devize, Nutter and the rest were most likely victims of an unholy alliance of frenzied puritanism, misogyny - and fear. Others would maintain that there was no smoke without fire; crimes were undoubtedly committed. What is certain is that these centuries-old happenings still have their reverberations today; the atmosphere of Pendle and its environs is definite enough and still fascinates the tourist and the local alike. Those with a lively imagination will have ample opportunity to exercise it when caught on the upper slopes in swirling mist!

Geographically, Pendle is certainly *not* (as often incorrectly supposed) a part of the main Pennine chain. It is an outlier standing well to the west of the main watershed of Northern England, all the streams draining from the hill ending up in the Ribble estuary. To the SW, the Calder valley divides the hill quite sharply from higher ground beyond; to the NE, a lowish ridge extends, rising again to the summit of Weets Hill (1350ft.) before a final descent to the Vale of Craven, a branch of the Aire Gap, one of the principal breaches in the Pennines. Millstone grit and older strata of limestone are the staple rocks of the Pendle area; it is to the W and N, particularly in an arc from Clitheroe to Worston and Downham, where most of the limestone has been exposed, and this is reflected in generally lusher, greener pasture hereabouts. On the other hand, on the Burnley side (Forest of Pendle) the aspect is rougher and wilder.

In the Pendle area the Ordnance Survey have some competition, and the map "Paths Around Pendle", which I cited in the introduction to this section (at the unusual scale of 7.5 cms. to the mile), can be warmly recommended. There is much valuable local information and history here, as well as more detail of footpaths than you will find on the OS. *Please note*, however, a potentially dangerous feature of this map: top of the map is *not* North but about 30 degrees E of N, and this must be borne in mind when calculating bearings.

There is some confusion and uncertainty about Pendle place names, too. To take just one, but fairly significant example: I have always referred to, and thought of, the steep defile leading up the hillside from Little Mearley Hall to the Scout Cairn as Mearley Clough. Phil Iddon (in Gillham's book) uses the same name; interestingly, Alan Lawson in "Walks in Pendle Country", names it on a map as Mearley or Brast Clough, while using only "Brast Clough" in his text. The "Paths Around Pendle" map gives it no name at all, but uses "Brast Clough" for another clough rising from Angram Green at (781424). To complete the confusion, the old 1:25,000 OS (Pathfinder 669) names the latter as "Burst Clough" and, again, does not use the name Mearley Clough at all. Ladies and gentlemen, take your choice! In this description, I have used "Mearley Clough" which seems to me a logical and consistent name.

Now, after allowing myself a much longer digression this time, on to the walking, with the summit of this grand old hill as our goal. Probably the direct route from Barley up Pendle's "Big End" is the most commonly used; it is certainly the most straightforward, particularly if you come from the Burnley side. I cannot, however, recommend it as a walk to enjoy: it calls for a very steep, short climb and shows you very little of the hill's more interesting features. On the other hand, the Ogden Clough route from Barley, while offering an excellent, adventurous scramblers' route - and avoiding the crowds - is a bit tough as an introduction to the hill. If you start from the Clitheroe side, the ascent from Worston via Mearley Clough is a fine climb, but again very steep. To do justice to the hill, it would be rewarding to explore all these routes, building up your own Pendle portrait.

The route I describe here is inevitably a reflection of my Great Harwood origins! From that angle, the Nick of Pendle approach is a natural one. We Harwooders enjoy a rather special view of Pendle, quite different from the flank aspects known to Clitheroe and Burnley folk. It is a particularly satisfying view, the bulk of the main hill being flanked by Wiswell Moor (left) and Padiham Heights (right), giving a balanced picture reminiscent in miniature of the southern aspect of the Skiddaw massif in Lakeland. I like to spend a few seconds in contemplation of Pendle whenever I walk through the War Memorial Park wood, especially in evening light: brooding, mysterious, yet mellowed by the sun's last rays, awaiting the next ascent.

A total of some 1700ft. of ascent is called for on this walk, allowing for some reascent, and the going underfoot is tough in places, with peat bog and tussocks to cross. Nevertheless, none of the climbing is particularly steep - it's a well-graded climb - and, on a clear day, you will be thrilled by the extensive and inspiring views. Finally, note that the first mile or so from the 'Nick' is on an exposed ridge, vulnerable to strong winds, and those with sensitive skin should take precautions.

The Walk

At Pendleton, the car park adjoining "The Swan With Two Necks" is open to the public, though the amount of space available is fairly limited. From here, walk up the main street of this pleasant unspoilt village, divided by Pendleton Brook, one of the many clear, swift streams flowing down from the hill. Take the left (Sabden) fork at the road junction, and before reaching the church take a signed footpath on the right, shortly passing through the right hand of two gates into the field beyond, the stream close on your right. Keep close by the stream (there is no visible tread), passing a little copse, then after a hut on the far bank go down to the stream and cross it by an FB (white marks).

Go diagonally across the field ahead, climbing steadily on a faint tread, again noting a conspicuous white mark on a tree. The hotel of Wellsprings is very obvious above on this stretch, as indeed it is for miles around. On reaching the fence, go uphill by it, crossing a scattered line of trees, and when you arrive at a junction of fences turn sharp right over a stile. Cross the next field alongside the fence on your left, probably in the company of many sheep, and after climbing another stile turn sharp left. Go up now by a line of hawthorns, approaching the isolated farm of Wymondhouses. This interesting and historic building has its origins in the growth of Congregationalism (that is, the form of Church constitution which rests on the autonomy of each local Church): Thomas Jolly founded a chapel here in 1667. It is somewhat exaggerated to claim, however, that this was the first Congregational chapel (as implied in "Paths Around Pendle"), as the movement was well established during the reign of Elizabeth I. Have a look at the plaque over the door, commemorating the last service held here (1954).

Cross stone steps in the wall to the *left* of the house, then a stile, and cross rough ground, reaching a track coming from the house. Go over this and climb approximately ESE, steeply,

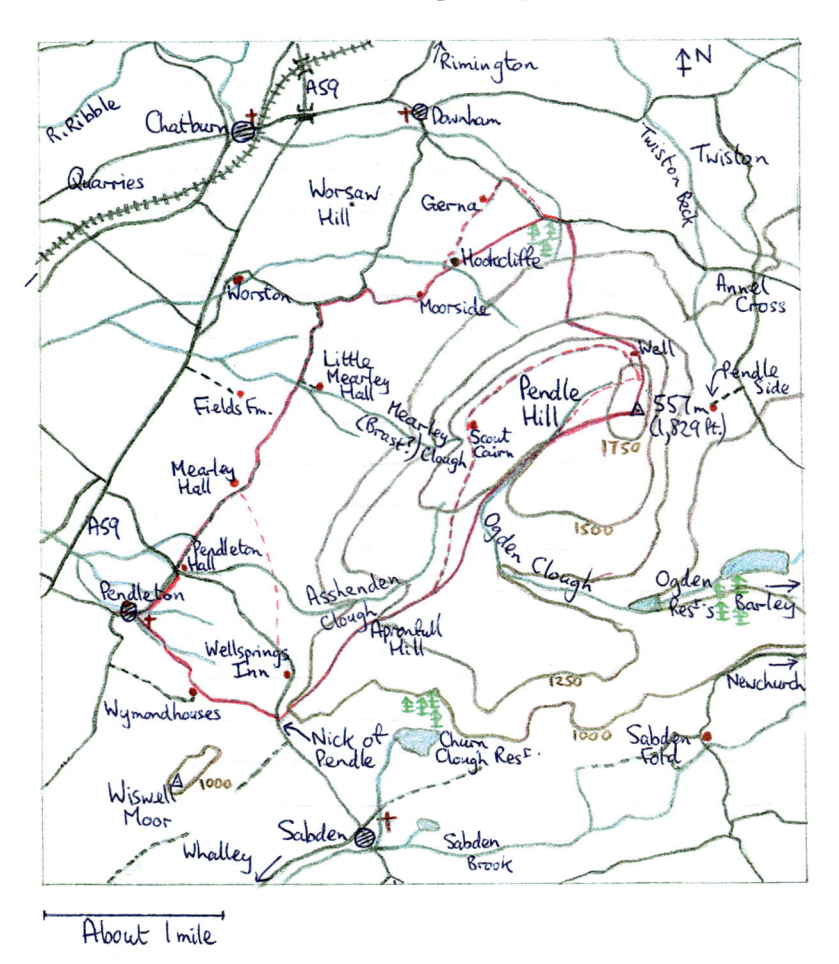

Walk 3: Round Cop, Steep Slopes

Pendle from Kemple End

Pendle from Abbot Stone, Boulsworth Hill

towards a prominent gap in a wall above: here pass through a gate and emerge onto a well-worn track. Turn uphill on this, by the wall, climbing steadily. You are now close to Wellsprings and its artificial ski slope, with the upper slopes of Pendle soaring behind around Ashendean Clough.

By the time you reach a more level area you will probably be glad of a breather, being already at the 900ft. contour: indeed the retrospect is already excellent, the Craven mountains visible on a clear day as well as extensive prospects of the Bowland and Waddington fells closer at hand. Cross a wet patch, go through a gate and climb more gently, initially with a wall on your right, but bending left on a clear track to emerge in a few hundred yards by a gate (PF sign) onto the road at the "Nick of Pendle". This prominent notch in the main SW to NE ridge of the hill is the natural crossing point for the road, and is clearly seen for miles around.

Turn right up the road for just a few yards, then cross it - carefully! - and turn left up a broad stony track. Follow this, turning, the views improving with almost every step as you join the ridge proper: from W to NNW there is a whole skyline of fells stretching from Beacon Fell round to the Dales. Initially the view on the right is restricted by a shallow gully and low ridge, but before long this also opens up to reveal prospects of the South Pennines with Churn Clough reservoir, Sabden and Padiham Heights closer at hand. As noted earlier, this ridge section is a noted wind trap, so don't expect to feel warm along here. The going is easy, at any rate, a steady rise on a clear track to the top of Apronfull Hill, where there is a simple cairn. It becomes clear now that this is scarcely a "hill" in its own right, only an interruption in the ridge to the main summit: a fine viewpoint, though, at around the 1250ft. mark and a likely place to watch hang gliders perform.

More level going ensues for a time, still on a very obvious track heading ENE. The diverging track heading for the Scout Cairn turns off more into the N in about a quarter-mile, actually following an old parish boundary; not easy to spot - an area of marshy ground with reeds just to the left of the faint path is the best clue. I should not recommend it on a first visit or in mist. On the main route the going continues straightforwardly, though heavier, through a muddy dip past the declining head of the clough (left) and shortly reaching another cairn. Hereabouts another track heads down on the Sabden side: we bend slightly left, climbing slightly, and soon the deep defile of Ogden Clough comes into view, an invaluable landmark. The aspect of the walk has profoundly changed, the distant views temporarily lost while we stride through an extensive plateau.

This is as likely a spot as any on Pendle to observe grouse: my general impression is that there are fewer around nowadays, but with the greatly increased volume of foot and mountain bike traffic one must admire their surviving at all. Drop down towards the headwaters of Ogden Clough, as it turns N then NE, on a thinner track after a boggy stretch. Only once, in the remarkable summer of 1976, have I known it truly "dried out" up here. Keep close to the left of the stream for some way now though initially well above the watercourse: a fine vigorous flow in wet weather or thaw, even at this height.

After about half a mile, the track - still quite clear - goes right down by the stream, offering in all likelihood a sheltered place whatever the wind direction. This is an ancient district boundary, as evinced by the ruined wall and boundary stones, one bearing prominent letters: W A. Soon a cairn on the opposite bank (ford) offers a choice of routes. You may keep straight up to the very head of the stream, soon meeting a wall, which should be followed onto the summit plateau as it bends round to just a few degrees N of E. When you reach a gate in the wall just before the ground falls abruptly away, turn sharply into the SSW for the final 350yds. to the summit trig. point.

However, I usually take the more direct alternative: formerly, the next section was very boggy but it is now a simple walk over recently laid stone flags. Cross the stream by the cairn and go up the side gully ahead. Turn left and climb a few feet onto the summit plateau, then in mist take a bearing of 080 degrees; in the clear, just keep heading along the stones. After about a third of a mile, the artificial surface ends - mercifully, some of us would say - and you reach a peat-free area of stones, grass and moss. Then, that moment which always provides rare satisfaction: the summit at last! - sitting on a distinctive little platform.

For centuries this airy, windswept point has been a magnet: beacons have been lit here, friends have rendezvoused, walkers of all ages have been proudly photographed, religious pilgrims have gathered. I have visited the summit in all moods and weathers; days of pellucid clarity, with the views seemingly for ever: days of heavy windless mist, clinging and silent: days of hard frozen ground and bright winter sun, the Dales peaks looking truly Alpine: days of biting gales and wind chill, the effective temperature far below zero. The enjoyment has never paled, above all for the sake of the views, and anyone who has seen them at their best will appreciate the great advantage of an isolated situation in enhancing a summit's panorama. Here for once I have broken my promise not to attempt to write 'a la Wainwright', by including a breakdown of the summit view put together by photo-montage (p37). I hope this will at least inspire you to see what you can spot yourselves, and for me it represents a personal tribute to Pendle.

We still have to return! After a final lingering glance round (if you're not quite frozen), turn into just E of N on a clear tread above the eastern escarpment and reach the wall mentioned earlier in just under a quarter-mile. From the gate (cross and turn left here to return to the "Nick", see earlier) turn briefly right down the wall-side and soon cross stone steps in the wall. The direct descent to Barley goes off to the right, steeply downhill, at this point. Here is a striking bird's eye view of the Annel Cross and Barley-Downham road area: indeed a direct, very steep descent down the wall to the road is possible but watch your step! A notice planted in the ground here some years ago now discourages this direct route. I suggest instead a much quieter, but interesting descent on the hill's N flank, long known but only recently recognised as a permissive path. From the wall, go straight across on initially a fairly clear contouring path which soon begins turning left, descending gently, then more steeply.

Here you meet an ancient well, long associated with a visit by the Quaker founder George Fox in 1652. Snow may drift deeply here in winter, and all along this section the views into the Dales remain inspiring.

Beyond the indentation by the well, a faint tread continues, steadily descending and turning left with Clitheroe now back in view. As the track becomes faint, keep a contouring line above the steep slopes to the right, then a more definite track joins from above left. Descend quite steeply now on a clear rutted track to a hairpin bend, the Fair Snape ridge of Bowland fells seen strikingly in the distance. At the hairpin, observe a marker on a stone: here you may break up the sharp gradient with a right-left zig-zag, or go *cautiously* straight down the slope (it may be dangerously slippery when wet or icy). There is a suggestion of another faint path going up towards the Scout Cairn hereabouts, but this is unauthorised.

When you reach a second stone with a waymarker, continue down the hillside, initially turning slightly left, then right - aiming for a stile seen in the fence below. A retrospect will show both the efficiency of our descent and the daunting steepness of the upper slopes. Cross the good new stile and proceed in the same line, the going eased by some laid stones and drainage ditches. Another old boundary-type stone is passed, and when you pass to the right of Hookcliffe plantation Downham is clearly in view. Cross a little stream, then stone steps in a wall, dropping steeply now to a new wooden kissing gate in a fence. Here is a Forest of Bowland waymarker and a notice acknowledging our route as a concessionary footpath to Pendle. I consider it a superior route in descent, however.

Turn left along the road just below, moorland roughness now exchanged for pleasant greenery, but our summit still soaring proudly above. Where the road bends right, you have a choice to make. If you intend to complete the walk in Downham, simply follow the road downhill for about a mile; you may also combine a visit to Downham with the present circular by taking a field path from the lower end of the village that leads below Worsaw Hill to the road near Angram Green, rejoining the main route. However, the present walk will be demanding enough for most, leaving an exploration of Downham for another day. The main route, almost a mile shorter, proceeds through a gate just below the Hookcliffe plantation as the road bends right. Note that this track is not actually a right of way but has been recently recognised (2003) as a permissive path. Or, you might prefer to use the right-of-way that turns off the road a little further down (FP sign), proceeding via Gerna Farm. Consult the OS map!

Go on below the plantation, then pass through another gate and keep on a clear track above a wall, passing scattered trees. Where the track turns uphill, leave it and keep closer to the wall, soon passing above Hookcliffe, and turning right through a gate into the rough lane beyond the farm. You pass the attractive deep hillside clough of Rad Brook, and soon leave the lane where it dips, turning half left through a gate onto a green lane. On approaching Moorside Farm, circle left, then turn right over an FB by a little waterfall, and through a gate into the farmyard. Trend right, picking up the farm lane and following it down a tree-lined avenue.

Easy going now, time to relax a little after the earlier demanding miles on Pendle. Note Worsaw Hill, on the right, a striking example of the limestone outcrops in this part of Pendle country. You are very close, here, to some of the locations used in filming 'Whistle Down the Wind'. Once over a cattle grid, there is another choice, either following field paths to Mearley (signed on the left) or - more easily - turning right to reach the Downham-Worston road in about 200yds. Turn left along this quiet lane, but after it bends right look for a PF sign to Mearley on the left. Go through a gate and cross a little stream, then go ahead by the fence.

Cross a stile and keep the same line in the next field. Views in the western arc are still extensive, over the Ribble valley to Longridge Fell and the Bowland fells, and it is hard not to keep glancing eastwards towards Pendle's summit. Over the next stile you join a metalled surface pro tem: go straight on, bending left after a cattle grid, and after passing a thin copse on the left Little Mearley Hall comes into view. Beyond the next cattle grid the metalled lane soon turns left towards the Hall: we keep straight on along a rough lane. The Hall cuts a fine figure as you look towards it up the tree-lined brook: it features an ornate window transferred at one time from Whalley Abbey, and has associations with the Nowell family of the Lancashire Witches story.

Beyond the next gate, we join a green lane. Almost unconsciously our pace seems to quicken over this pleasant, easy-going stretch of outlying farms and meadows; I have often had to quicken hereabouts for a more practical reason, namely fading light! Bend right, go through a gate and pass a farm, again on a metalled surface. Turn with the lane ahead through a little copse, where I once had a somewhat eerie twilight encounter with a tawny owl, and soon pass more farm buildings on the left and right ahead.

You will keep a brisk pace along the lane, the traffic on the A59 Whalley-Clitheroe by-pass very obvious on the right across the fields. In a quarter-mile you pass through a gateway, usually open, and in a further quarter-mile you reach Pendleton Hall, the last of the farms passed. Go through a gateway and past buildings, finally turning left then right past the main farmhouse. Howcroft Brook, another fine stream, is crossed by a bridge, then you go up to the Clitheroe-Sabden road where there is a PF sign. Just up the road (left) is a junction with a clear sign, Pendleton 1/2; follow it, soon reaching the village and completing the circle with the outward route just below the church of All Saints.

In truth, despite the pleasantness of the latter miles, it is our encounter with Pendle - whether for the first or the hundredth time - that will dominate the day's memories. Always a worthy opponent, always a reliable friend! Paradoxically, Pendle's simplicity is its attractiveness: there are few hidden recesses, nearly all is clear and open, soaring powerfully skywards, casting its shadow over a whole district and across the centuries too. There are few times during this collection of walks when it will stay hidden for long, rightly so, for it sums up so much of our wanderings.

Walk 3 (Supplement) The Summit View From Pendle Hill

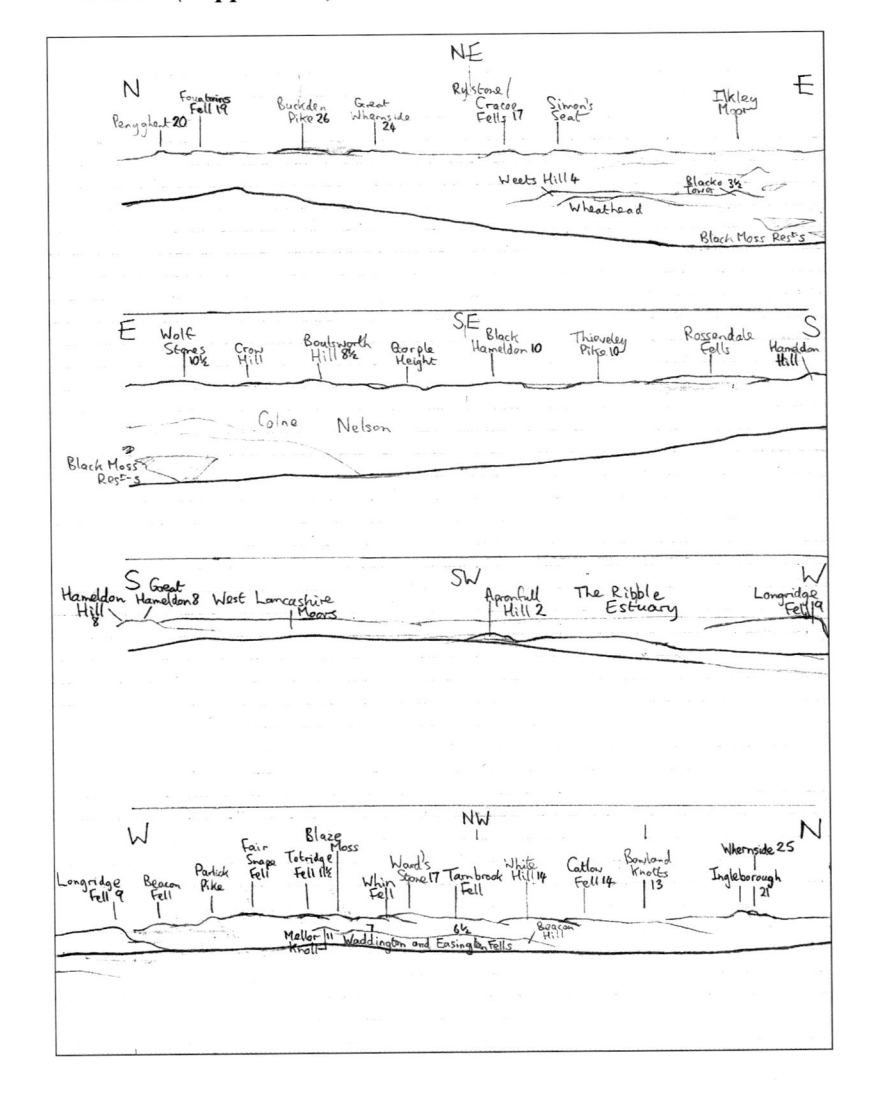

On a Clear Day . . .

The compass-point sketch, in the Wainwright manner, indicates all the main fells that may be seen from Pendle Hill's summit on a very clear day. The thick line, or lines, in the near ground indicate Pendle's visible boundaries and the numbers accompanying the fells give distances in miles.

There are some important differences between this panorama and that observable from many Lakeland summits. Pendle is relatively isolated, and the grandest peaks visible, notably those in the Dales, are twenty miles away or more; typically, from any central Lakeland summit, most of the interest will be concentrated within a ten-mile radius. There are many compensations, nevertheless, notably the most attractive grouping of the Bowland fells in the NW arc and the distant but unmistakable grandeur of Ingleborough and Penyghent, especially in winter. To the SW, the prospect of the Ribble estuary - inevitably, often softened by afternoon or evening sun - is most soothing.

. . . and even clearer

There is a real satisfaction, on crystal-clear days, in catching a glimpse of the Lakeland peaks above the Bowland fells! They are concentrated between 35 degrees and 70 degrees N of W: from Scafell Pike to Pendle is about 55 miles as the crow flies. The Haweswater fells are possibly the most likely to be seen - and in reverse, I have seen Pendle quite clearly from High Street.

More distant prospects open up in the Dales, too. Look between Ingleborough and Penyghent, for instance, almost directly due N: you may see the sharp edge leading down from Wild Boar Fell to Mallerstang Common (36 miles). Almost diametrically opposite, look down the gap between Black Hameldon and Thieveley Pike, far down the Pennine chain to Black Hill (29 miles).

I am assured it is possible, on the clearest of days, to catch a glimpse of Snowdonia; I look forward to confirming this personally one day! The direction is almost exactly SW and Snowdon's summit is about 95 miles distant.

4. OLD MAN RIBBLE

Dinckley, Suspension Bridge, Marles Wood, Ribchester Bridge, Stydd, Dewhurst House, Clough Bank, Suspension Bridge, Dinckley. 6 miles. Maps: OS 1:50,000 'Landranger' no. 103; OS 1:25,000 Explorer no 287.

Alternatives The detour to Stydd church may be omitted, leaving a circuit of five miles. Or you may like to take the opportunity of visiting Ribchester for exploration, adding both distance and time.

* * * * * * * * * *

Background

If Pendle is the undoubted monarch of the hills on our map, there can equally be no doubt that the Ribble is the most significant river. Although the Hodder has considerable influence, especially in Bowland, it is after all only a tributary of the Ribble, whose course runs a full eighty miles from its origins in the Dales to the estuary beyond Preston. It is indeed an odd man out among Dales rivers, heading for the Irish Sea rather than the North Sea. Many would consider the Ribble to be the most important river draining into the Irish Sea between the Mersey estuary and the Solway Firth. For a most readable and entertaining account, see "The River Ribble" by Ron Freethy (bibliography).

The Ribble Way offers the walker the opportunity to trace the course of the river from source to sea: it is a fairly recent creation, and some parts are still disputed by local landowners. Booklets giving the route in detail are available at many local bookshops, and a number of signboards give the story in outline: we shall pass close to one today, in a car park off the Dinckley - Ribchester road. As is often the case with rivers, there is some dispute as to which stream forms its true beginning. Gayle Beck usually gets the nod, and indeed the official beginning of the Ribble Way is at Gayle Wolds, barely half a mile NE of the Pennine Way where it crosses Cam Fell (OS 1:50,000 no. 98). It is probably unkind to query whether some other minor streams in the vicinity might provide an even longer passage to the sea. Just to the south, Cam Beck is also a significant feeder.

For the purposes of today's walk, those lonely upland stretches of the Dales are only a diversion, but they are grand walking territory in their own right. The great railway viaduct at Ribblehead is a justly famous monument to nineteenth-century engineering, visible for miles around: here too are views of the Three Peaks as giants close at hand, not as distant glimpses. If anyone collects watersheds (well, why not?) this high plateau would be a happy hunting-ground: here are lateral watersheds between Wharfe and Ure and, further west, Ribble and Lune as well as the main northern England watershed (Ribble-Wharfe, Lune-Ure). Yes, an area well worth exploring. After completing the present volume, of course.

The lush greenery of the lower Ribble Valley where we shall be walking today is in complete contrast, the river being wide and majestic on this stretch, and tremendous in spate. As well as the riverside stroll, there are pleasant woodlands and some elevated banks from where the distant view is already remarkably good, but the walking is easy. From Ribchester Bridge it's only a short detour, or pilgrimage, to the remarkable little church of St. Saviour's, Stydd, happily still used for worship. Without the detour the walk would total five miles.

The Walk

You may turn down the little lane adjacent to the former Tanner's Arms, Dinckley, lately demolished, at (688356): about 200yds. on, a clear sign says "No Parking Beyond This Point". Out of the car and get going, then! Walk down the road, ignoring a major branch to the right, passing a pleasing variety of scattered country houses. Bend right, going through a narrow stone stoop by a gate saying "Private, Footpath Only". Here a loop of the Ribble comes into view, more prominently through bare trees, with Hurst Green and the slopes of Longridge Fell behind.

Pass through an open gateway, now on a rough lane, and go down through scattered woodland, turning left. When you abruptly reach the riverbank with Dinckley Hall farm on the right, turn sharp left through a gate (FP sign) with the suspension

Walk 4: Old Man Ribble

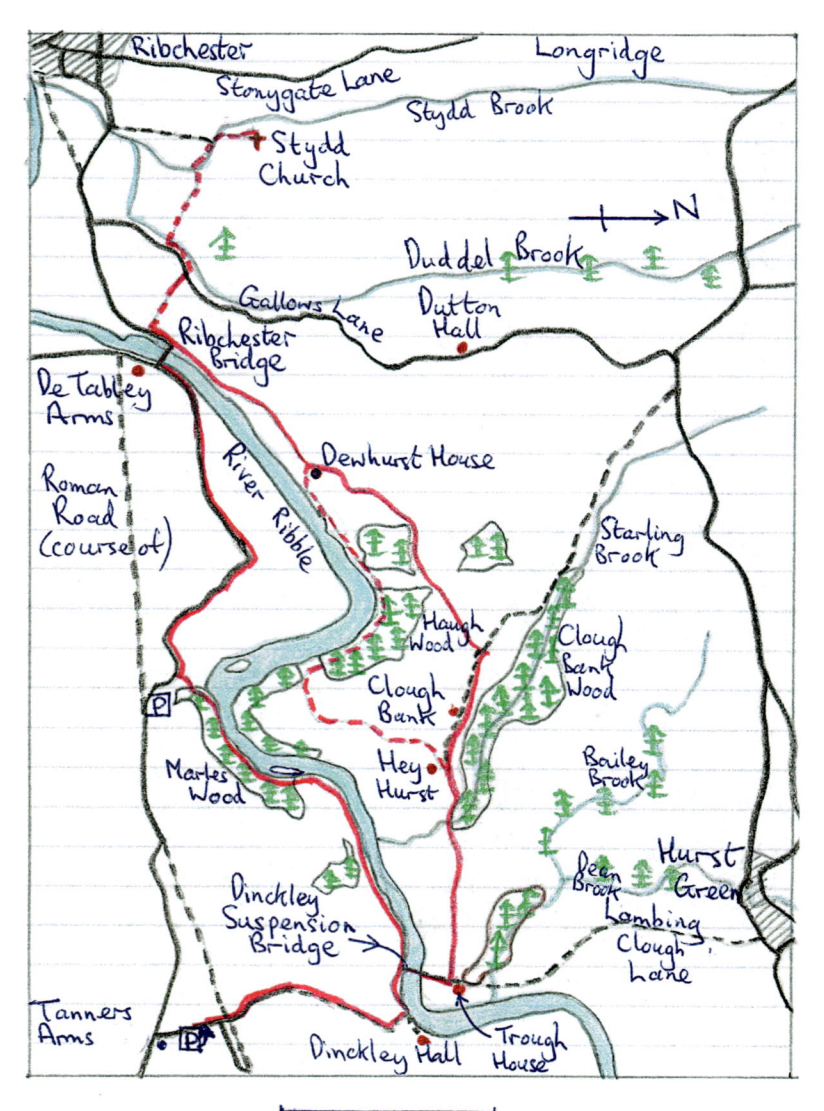

River Ribble, Mitton Bridge, looking towards Pendle

Ribble at Ribchester Bridge

bridge now in view. Proceed through another small gate, keeping near the riverside and soon crossing a stile. Fording the little side stream ahead may not be trivial after heavy rain! Once over, though, you come to the suspension bridge, built in 1951 and repaired after extensive flood damage in 1982: the Ribble, I repeat, is a force to be reckoned with when in spate. Before the bridge pedestrians could be ferried over at this spot for a modest fee: there was another ferry upriver by Hacking Hall.

For the moment we leave the bridge and keep downstream on the left bank. During summer, when the river is low, a line of rocks goes well out into the stream at this point making an ideal picnic spot: it is naturally an excellent location for bird-spotting, too, with herons in particular often seen. There is no obvious tread to follow at first, but the going remains very easy. Soon you enter an area of scattered trees, and cross a simple wooden stile about half a mile below the bridge. The river bends left ahead, entering a delightful area with wooded banks on both sides and an enhanced current. I once witnessed canoeists around here, pitting strength and skill against the fast-flowing winter stream; fascinating to watch, but I was happy to stay on the bank!

Beyond the stile we soon enter Marles Wood (often referred to as Sale Wheel Wood, though this name does not appear to be recognised by the OS). The tread is now quite obvious, and we keep close to the river which goes into a narrow, rocky, rapids section followed by an abrupt right bend. Here the waters emerge from the narrows into a wide, deep pool that may be several hundred feet wide in spate, afterwards turning into a more sedate course. This is a truly enchanting spot, a place to linger and - almost - forget about the walk. On foot, we turn left up a bank, whence a new concessionary FP turns up to the car park referred to earlier. Our path drops to an FB over a side stream, then turns left and goes uphill to the Dinckley-Ribchester road, over a stile. At the time of writing the sign was in need of repair.

Turn right down the road (the car park, a substantial one, is about 150yds. left) and keep going for about one mile of road walking. It's rarely a busy road, and there is no convenient footpath alternative - unless you wish to try the one leaving the road at (675356), heading SSW, eventually meeting a crossing path and reaching the De Tabley Arms by a long detour. The road dips to the level of the river meadows and winds along pleasantly, with retrospective views of Pendle, ENE. When you reach Ribchester Bridge, the De Tabley Arms is just down the road (now the B6245) on the left.

We turn right over the bridge, a fine three-arched structure but with tight entry and exit which demand motoring precision. If you intend the direct return to Dinckley, take the BW (signed Ribble Way) on the right immediately over the bridge. However, now that we are so close to Ribchester it seems a pity to pass over the opportunity of a visit to the town itself or the Stydd. I suggest the latter, as to do justice to Ribchester itself - Roman museum, parish church and a stroll round the town - would take some time, and might well be reserved for a separate visit.

For the Stydd, turn left after the bridge but look for an FP sign on the right in about 150yds. Cross steps in a gate and cross the field ahead: be warned, these low-lying meadows are apt to be waterlogged in winter - in which case the stile to be crossed next may be under water. In that case, it is easier to keep to the left side of the field and cross gates. Either way, on reaching the minor road (Gallows Lane, heading to Hurst Green) turn briefly left, then right over a stile by a PF sign and down some steps. The pasture ahead may again be very wet; cross it as well as you can, go over another stile, then rise a few feet to mercifully drier ground and proceed with the fence on your left.

Cross two more simple stiles and another potentially wet area, then go over a small FB. The next little section of linking path is not actually given as a right of way on the OS, but it is clearly extensively used by locals. After the FB, turn slightly right by some scattered bushes, where I was once entertained by a close-up view of a party of long-tailed tits. Cross a stile and again trend right by a hedge, then cross a further stile and go along by the hedge on the left. You soon reach a rough lane, with a newish Roman Catholic church on your left and the Stydd church (St. Saviour's) about 200yds. on your right. If you are fortunate it may be open - or the key may be requested, most readily from St. Wilfred's, the Ribchester parish church. There is real beauty of simplicity here, both in the setting and the construction of the church, which was built in 1136 during the reign of Stephen.

There is a great sense of peace and seclusion inside, and it is heartening that the building is still used occasionally for worship, indeed monthly in summer. The paved stone floor is rudimentary but clean, and the fine octagonal font (conspicuous 'IHS') and Jacobean pulpit would grace many a larger church. Behind the altar acreen, in addition to the altar, there are the grave of a Roman Catholic bishop and a sarcophagus. Above all this is a place for a few minutes' quiet and meditation, a worthy object of our short pilgrimage, nothing of ostentation but a quiet witness to centuries of Christian worship.

Retrace your steps to Ribchester Bridge, and take the BW by the riverside (left to us, but true right, and clearly signed Ribble Way). Walk along easily in the Ribble's company for nearly half a mile to the farm of Dewhurst House, where in the farmyard a clear sign gives you the choice of the Ribble Way or keeping on the BW. If you like to stay close to the river as long as possible you will opt for the former, but the alternative high level route is well worth the effort, offering more varied walking and good views. To do this, turn left in the farmyard and go uphill through a muddy area to a gate. Here, with a strip of woodland on your left, turn right, keeping atop a fence. Leave the fence and go through a little copse, turning uphill and crossing a brook on the right. Continue uphill, crossing a second brook and aim for the top of the wood (Stewart's Wood) seen ahead.

Pass through a neat new waymarked gate and go on, keeping by the wood on your right, with the Ribble seen strikingly below from some height as it turns a major bend. Where the enclosing fence turns away right, turn half left, picking up a faint tread and losing height to cross an FB (waymarked). Here you could turn right, keeping close to woodland, when you would rejoin the Ribble Way more quickly, but the BW climbs diagonally across the field ahead. Further on a field division given on the OS seems to have disappeared, but keep the same line and reach a double metalled gate, emerging onto a lane serving outlying farms. Cross the gate - somehow! - and turn right down the lane.

You pass a little pond on the left, and the views from this modest height are quite extensive. Pendle soon bulks large ahead, and the ridge terminating in Whalley Nab stretches away on the right. Go through gates (usually open) at Clough Bank and down the lane, the river now seen again winding below. Watch carefully for the point (signed) where the Ribble Way is rejoined: follow it to the left, leaving the lane which descends to Hey Hurst. Go gently down the field with a fence on your left, and plenty of Ribble Way markers to help on this last lap of the walk.

Bear right, now adjacent to a wood, and descend more steeply to cross an FB. Observe a waymarker here and bear right, keeping close to a fence: we contour along here, on a slight promontory above the river flood plain to the right. Climb a stile next to a waymarked gate, with the suspension bridge now in sight, and proceed over another stile (narrow) by a metal gate. Go through an open gateway, then be careful not to slip up close to home! It is tempting to make a beeline for the bridge, but there is no way through there. Instead keep ahead over another stile and meet a vehicular track: follow it briefly left, but before reaching Trough House leave the Ribble Way, making a sharp hairpin to the right and crossing a stile. Go along a narrow enclosed lane with a newly afforested area on your right and come to the bridge. Once across you will rejoin the outward route, of course, but the day's last sight of the river is a moment to savour, and the view downstream is worth an inch of anyone's camera film: lighting effects may be dramatic, if you time your visit. Return to the starting point in half a mile of fields and lanes.

Only a gentle stroll today, but plenty of memorable scenes and an intimate portrait of a fine stretch of a noble river. We shall revisit the Ribble in a later walk, and I imagine many will wish to explore it more extensively: understandably so, for it makes an excellent companion. In the pages of this book we must move on, ranging widely across our map, but from many vantage points on subsequent walks we shall glimpse a long verdant strand stretching across our view, and appreciate it the more for having seen the Ribble's grandeur close at hand.

5. ON THE WATERSHED

Car Park, Laneshaw Bridge to Haworth Road - Wycoller - Turnhole Clough - Spoutley Lumb - Boulsworth Hill - Gilford Clough - Trawden - Wycoller - Car Park. 8 miles. Maps: OS 1:50,000 Landranger no. 103; OS 1:25,000 Explorer OL 21, South Pennines.

* * * * * * * * * *

Background

For many walkers, the walk itself is the thing, and I say amen to that. To be out for a few hours on a fine day, enjoy some impressive scenery and perhaps observe interesting wildlife, in company with good friends, is all that we ask or reasonably can ask. The fine details of geography or geology of the actual ground we pass over probably seem dull or irrelevant by comparison. Nevertheless, there are occasions when some particularly interesting feature of the terrain makes us stop and think; and this may well happen spontaneously if we start to essay longer and more ambitious walks with the aid of a map.

Boulsworth Hill is clearly in view from my native Great Harwood, though I doubt whether many residents could put a name to it. Turn from Church Street into Queen Street on a clear day, and there it is on the skyline ahead of you, some twelve miles distant. It cuts a rather shy figure, in comparison to the bold outline of Pendle Hill, and has been generally ignored; indeed it is only in recent years that the hill has become legal to the walker, with the creation of a permissive path to the summit. In no sense is it a pretty hill; it is largely raw, bleak moorland, with little shelter to offer in rough weather, the true stuff of the South Pennines. Though the walk described here is not long, it should not be underestimated: 1,500ft. of climbing are called for, and the going is frequently heavy underfoot. Yet this unprepossessing hill has an interesting distinction, namely: it lies squarely on the main watershed of Northern England, the water flowing from the hill ending up in either the Ribble or the Humber estuaries.

Walk 5: On The Watershed

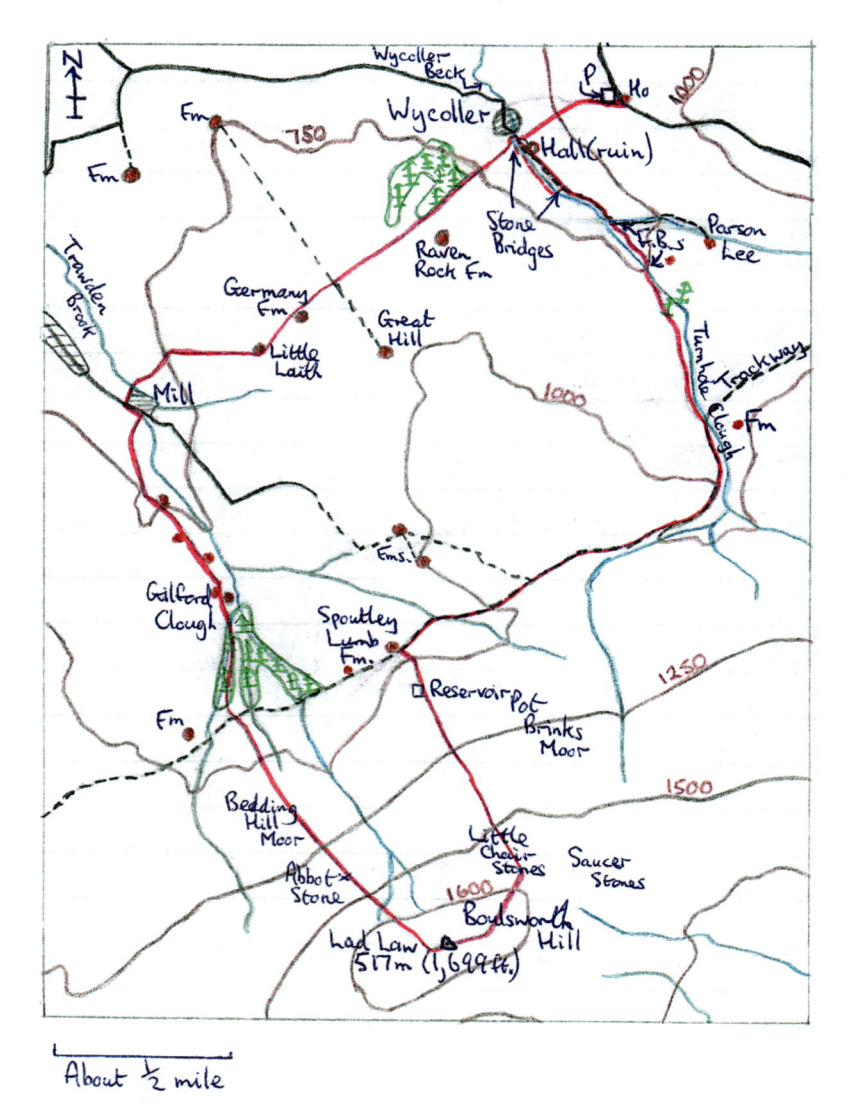

Wycoller

Winter sunset near Trawden

In truth, Boulsworth is a much more typical Pennine summit than Pendle Hill itself, which (as already noted) lies well to the west of the main watershed. One might expect the Pennine Way, logically, to pass this way: in fact it runs some miles to the east, though with good reason, namely to visit the Bronte country. In passing, we might note that the PW seems to shun the main watershed quite often! Wainwright accused it of turning soft at one point. If I have been rather hard on Boulsworth earlier, let me say that, on the right day, you will certainly enjoy this walk. The summit cone rises distinctly and in some isolation from the main Pennine chain, creating a far-reaching viewpoint. Elsewhere on the walk are steep, wooded cloughs and streams, plus an introduction to the attractive village of Wycoller, which gives us our 'Bronte connection' after all.

The Walk

Wycoller is served by a minor road from Trawden, but please don't try to park in the village, which is patently unsuited for much traffic. A convenient starting point is the car park and picnic site (Wycoller Country Park) at (936394) on the minor road from Laneshaw Bridge to Haworth and Oakworth. From the car park, proceed quite steeply downhill on a clear path towards the village, after noting the useful information displayed on the board. Initial steps give way to a steep grassy path: trend right, downhill, through a kissing gate and onto a grassy lane. Turn left with this and proceed downhill, ignoring branches to right and left. Upon entering the woods ahead, you may use either branch of the track: the left branch swings back to the right later, through the grounds of the old Wycoller Hall. This is generally accepted to be the model for Ferndean Manor of "Jane Eyre", though the usual cautionary note about such a glib equation applies - see also the observations in Walk 10.

What is undeniable is that Wycoller is a delightful unspoilt village, and on a pleasant day you could be in some danger of forgetting all about Boulsworth and simply paddling in the beck. The more resolute will, after crossing the stone 'clapper' bridge perhaps (you may initially go up either bank of Wycoller Beck), turn left and go upstream. Here on an evening walk once, I was delighted to see a small charm of goldfinches enjoying the profuse supply of weed-seeds hereabouts.

Turn left over a bridge, assuming you had crossed the stream earlier, and proceed initially up a metalled road. A glance up on your left will reveal the striking rocky outcrops of Foster's Leap. Ignore the next clapper bridge, right, over the stream, but where the road bends left, take a path going straight ahead, signed "Bronte Way: Gawthorpe Hall". You continue close by the stream, on its left (true right). Following a grassy stretch, find a waymarker near the stream, then cross a footbridge and proceed up the far bank, on which side we now remain. Stone flags and steps are laid hereabouts, though the tread in any case is perfectly clear. Climb up and pass through a gap, then cross a fence by a stile: do *not* recross the stream by a bridge here (though this is clearly a used route, leading up to Dean House atop the far bank). Instead just keep on upstream on a thin but adequately clear path, through the pleasantly wooded confines of Turnhole Clough, with waymarkers to assist. At the edge of the wood, cross a stile to the right and go up through bracken, the view now opening out impressively.

When the fence on your left bends away, there appears a choice of routes, but these actually merge quite soon: either way, you drop to a stile nearer the stream and climb it. Regain height on the right (true left) of the stream, still following a made path with stones, waymarkers proclaiming "2 Walk". Would it seem churlish to complain that there are almost too many footpath signs hereabouts? Too many can be almost as confusing as too few - as witness the excess of cairns in some popular Lake District spots. A glance at the map - which walkers need to get in the habit of doing anyway - would be just as informative, and guard against lapses of concentration.

Cross a stile by a gate next, with the slopes of Crow Hill and Jackson's Ridge (a long spur of Boulsworth going roughly SW-NE) ahead of you, SE. Go straight on at a path junction (signed "Witches Way"), very soon joining a clear and venerable trackway coming in from the left, which we now follow to the right, keeping the stream on our left as a welcome companion.

The direction here is just E of S. Typical water-birds may be seen along the stream, even at this height (900 - 1000ft.): I have seen dippers here, and you can consider yourself unlucky if you don't spot at least one of these attractive, chubby, white-breasted birds during the walk.

As Gillham notes, the rocky outcrops on Boulsworth belie its grassy nature as implied by the 1:50,000 OS, and you will begin to spot many of them along the summit ridge soon, the Great Saucer Stones first. The walk hereabouts is a very agreeable promenade above the deep brackened defile of the stream. Many flags continue to be seen underfoot, again tending to suggest the centuries of existence of the route. Beyond a slight dip and subsequent rise, the stream left behind now, the lonely outpost of Spoutley Lumb is seen ahead. On a bright summer evening, the light coming across imparts a warm, mellow look to the normally gaunt slopes above. Indeed, the whole walk is eminently suitable for such a time, though in a sense it does then seem somewhat out of character.

Go through a kissing gate adjacent to a five-barred gate, joining a rough vehicular track: ignore a branch to the right. Snipe, as well as more familiar moorland birds, are liable to be flushed out of the long, reedy grass adjoining the track hereabouts. Proceed to Spoutley Lumb, where on your left you will find a clear sign indicating the permissive path ("Boulsworth Hill Concessionary Access: NW Water"). The path is uncompromisingly direct - short but not sweet, you might say - with no attempt at zig-zagging to ease the slope, though in truth it isn't exceptionally steep. Up you go, no wavering! Initially the surface is concreted, to a little covered reservoir, then a waymarked path (poles) ensues. Spare a moment to look left for an impressive profile of the Wolf Stones on the nearby stretch of the Pennine Way.

After passing through a gate, the way steepens a little, though remaining pretty firm underfoot in all but the very wet spells. The tread is thin, but serviceable, at a general bearing of 160 (SSE). You pass through a flatter area, followed by the final rise to the ridge at Little Chair Stones. Turn right along the ridge, with some boggy patches in evidence now. The summit rocks (known as Lad Law) and trig.point are reached in about a quarter-mile, where the ground is firm and you can enjoy the panorama, which is extensive. Pendle inevitably dominates a whole arc of horizon (WNW) with more distant glimpses of, among others, the Bowland fells and Three Peaks. The long outcrop of the Dove Stones stands to the SSE, and beyond to their left are lengthy vistas into West Yorkshire: too lengthy, the native Lancastrian will doubtless consider.

The way off is not quite clear for the first few yards. Take a WNW bearing (300 degrees; a few degrees west of Pendle, if visible) and you soon pick up the waymarked track again, though this section is not so well marked. Turn a little right and pass the Abbot Stone, another fine outcrop, then lose height more steeply, with care needed in wet or icy conditions. Aim for a right-angled wall junction ahead and go down with the wall on your right through some heavier going until you rejoin the earlier trackway. Initially turn left, but in about forty yards cross stone steps in the wall on your right. In the field ahead, go to the edge of the stream (Gilford Clough) and follow it downstream, initially atop the bank. These steep, wooded cloughs are an attractive feature of the hillsides in these parts. Soon drop towards the stream on a more defined track; the stream should be easily fordable when reached, but the footbridge might be needed in spate. Ahead, do observe the Public Footpath sign which leads you, *not* straight on by the house above but through a gate to the R of the main track. Keep the fence just on your left in the field ahead, and soon turn sharp left by the wall of a house (footpath marked). Emerge through a gate, turning right to rejoin the lane, proceeding straightforwardly down through the southern outskirts of Trawden.

Beyond Meadow Bottom Farm (simply "Bottoms Farm" on the OS 1:25,000), go right, sharply downhill, and reach a road by a mill (Hollin Hall), turning left past its front. After the mill, turn right: there is a Public Footpath sign, unfortunately hidden from your direction initially. Go down a concreted surface, still adjoining the mill (how incongruous it seems, compared to the rest of the walk!), over a bridge and cattle grid, then turn left uphill on a clear track. Bend round, continuing uphill through a gateway with another cattle grid. A little care is needed here: do not turn onto the crossing path, but leave the track altogether and go up, turning slightly right, on a thinner path, by a fence. You are quickly into open country again, a pleasant grass pasture flanked by scattered hawthorns. By the time you pass to the left of a small copse, Boulsworth is again very prominent on your right. Keep to the right edge of the field, soon climbing a stone stile, passing the building of Little Laith to its right. Look for another stone stile to the right of a gate, cross it, then turn left and go up by a fence (a waymarker again gives "2 Walk", as seen earlier near Wycoller). There is an adequate tread here now for confidence, and the path has more or less levelled out, giving you the chance to appreciate the surroundings - the view is still quite extensive - on this last lap.

Before reaching Germany Farm, long ruinous but lately restored, swing to the left, turning right again to rejoin the track after the building. You pass through a decidedly narrow stone stoop next (admitting only sylph-like hips in comfort, as A.W. once remarked), then go straight on at a subsequent crossroads of paths. Keep the same line, over a wooden stile with a fence on your right, then (after a stone stile) a wall. Raven's Rock Farm is now clearly seen, right: you bypass it, crossing a wooden stile, then going ahead through a gate and over a stone stile, reaching an attractive area of mixed woodland (alder, birch, conifers, rowan) with apparently ongoing planting. There is a waymarker here too. You begin to descend on the right-hand edge of this woodland, gently at first, then more steeply, eventually over a stile and onto wooden steps leading to a lane which reaches Wycoller in a few hundred yards further. All that then remains is to cross the clapper bridge and reverse the outward route to the car park in under half a mile. Naturally you might decide, with good reason, to explore Wycoller further, but if feeling peckish note that the village cafe closes at 5 p.m. A good, satisfying walk, very varied, and an introduction to some of the more demanding walks later in the book.

Now what? Oh. Not long enough for you? Well, you can easily extend it, you know! For instance, you could consider taking in the Coldwell Reservoirs (above Nelson) as suggested by Gillham. As I said before, self-exploration is of the essence: nothing about walking should be carved in stone. I fancy I hear another, pedantic, voice in addition. Yes, quite right! After all the fuss about the main watershed, very little of the walk was actually on it: Lad Law itself is on a jutting spur out to the west. The ridge running down from Weather Stones to Warcock Hill, and on to Dove Stones, is the true main watershed: therefore our walk was only on that invisible line for a few hundred yards. Apologies to those who feel deprived, but we shall return to the Great Divide in later walks.

6. BREEZY UPLANDS

Barley, Wheathead, Coal Pit Lane, Weets Hill, Admergill, Roughlee, Barley. 11 miles. Maps: OS 1:50,000 Landranger no. 103; OS 1:25,000 Explorer OL 41, Forest of Bowland; "Paths Around Pendle" (See Walk 3).

Alternatives: The section NE of the A682, including Weets Hill, may be omitted as follows, making a much shorter circuit. From the path between the two summits of Wheathead, walk S towards the higher summit, then turn E on a clear path downhill. At (843427), meet another path which runs almost due S to reach the Blacko-Annel Cross road (Wheathead Lane). From here you may follow the road E until you meet the main route at Admergill Water, or follow field paths more directly back to Barley, via Brown Hill and Offa Hill (respectively, six and five miles). Additionally, 'The Weets' may readily be climbed separately from Barnoldswick.

* * * * * * * * * *

Background

Some walks seem just right for certain days. I enjoyed this one first on a bright, fresh Spring day of long clear views, the time of year when the breeze can chill but the sun is already warm. Curlews and lapwings seemed to abound, and there were glimpses of less common species, notably redshank. Those who would, perhaps, be reluctant to forsake their favourite spots in the Ribble Valley for these parts should think again. This is grand walking country, mostly over rolling uplands with springy turf underfoot, visiting windswept heights which have a remarkably remote feel about them - and have excellent views to boot. Inevitably Pendle dominates the country to the W very strongly - Barley is just one and a half miles from its summit - but the views up Ribblesdale to the N are superb, leading the eye for miles. The return section, via Admergill Water and Pendle Waters, offers a fine contrast with sparkling streams and wooded hillsides; the recently created "Pendle Way" shows good taste by coming this way.

It is difficult to get away from that Lancashire Witches story in these parts! At Roughlee, you will have the chance to see the Old Hall, former home of Alice Nutter and still an imposing building (dated 1536). Malkin Tower, where the witches were supposed to have gathered, is within a mile of Admergill Water at one point. * However, the tower on the hill just N of Blacko is not, as sometimes erroneously thought, connected with the story: it was built for a man named Stansfield in the late 19th century.

Geographically, the walk explores the millstone ridge continuing NE from Pendle which was alluded to in Walk 3, and it is for this reason that I have included Weets Hill, the natural terminus of the ridge, even though it is often regarded as a separate hill - being quite some distance from Pendle itself. By including 'The Weets' I had to make use of a short stretch of main road in designing this walk, there being no natural path from Wheathead to Weets Hill. However, it should not prove too unpleasant: the distance along the A682 is under half a mile, and it isn't a trunk road. Even if you cut down to the shorter alternatives, you will derive a good picture of the general character of this area. Yet another possibility, granted transport, would be an 'A to B' walk, dropping NE from the summit of Weets Hill along the Pendle Way and into Barnoldswick.

The Walk

Whichever route you decide on, the large car park in the village of Barley, where there is also a refreshment kiosk, makes an ideal starting point. Enjoy Barley, too: though quite different from Downham, it is a very pleasant and typical Pendle country village. Walk up the Downham road, over the bridge and past the Methodist church, until the road turns sharp left. Here keep straight on, up a lane signposted to Blacko: almost at once you pass through a gateway saying "Black Moss", turning right

There is some uncertainty here. The "Paths Around Pendle" map (see Walk 3) places Malkin Tower in the pastures SW of Newchurch, near Sabden Brook.

Walk 6: Breezy Uplands

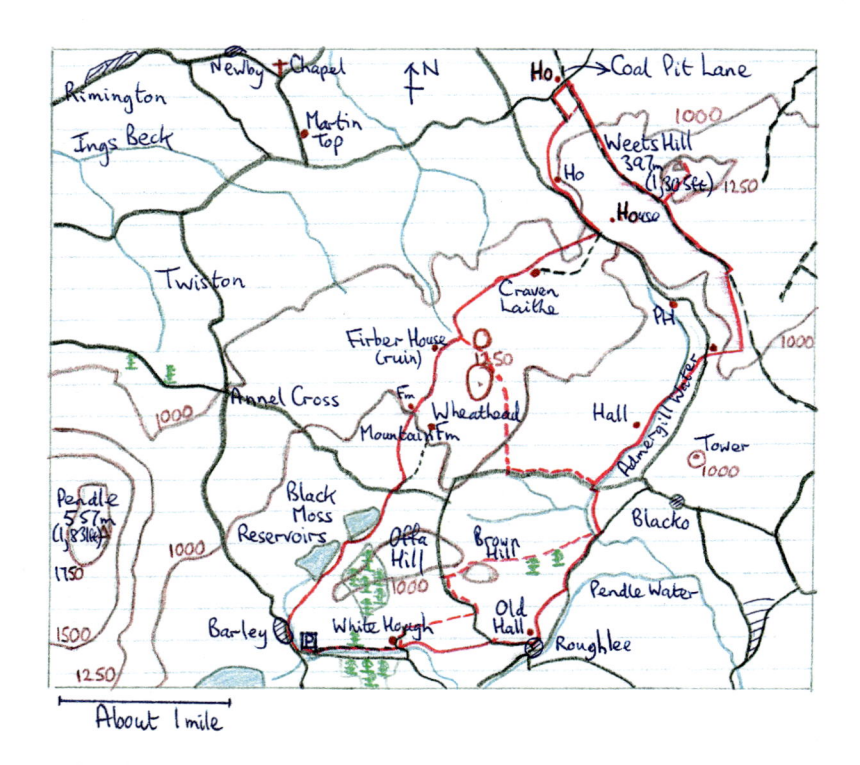

along an initially well-surfaced lane running between walls. Climb steadily for a time, then pass the first of the Black Moss reservoirs on its right, having negotiated a gate. When you reach a wall ahead, turn right, then veer left around the end of the second reservoir, going through a kissing gate (embarrassingly narrow) adjoining a main gate, now on a much more primitive track. Here I once peered over the wall to examine the reservoir's bird life - there were many swallows around - and was quite startled when a heron rose silently from a few feet away, having been concealed by the wall.

At the top end of the second reservoir, cross the inlet stream by a bridge. Throughout this first section Pendle is powerfully dominant to the west. Continue up a clear winding track and reach the Annel Cross - Blacko road at Lower Black Moss: go straight across the road ("Public Footpath" sign both ways) and through a gate. Initially, follow a clear vehicular track, but when this turns away half right, keep straight on with the small stream on your left, soon crossing a wall ahead by a stile to the right of a gate. Once over, trend towards the wall on your right and follow it uphill. You are in an extensive area of upland pasture here, nearing the 1,000ft. contour, and often excellent bird-spotting country. I have seen redshanks, those attractively marked and neat but noisy waders, in this particular field: their triple call-note is distinctive.

At the top of the field you reach a ruinous farm in a little dip with a wood (Helliwell Wood on the 1:25,000 OS) on its left. Pass through the yard (or you could bypass the buildings altogether on the left) and continue uphill with a stream on your right. Keep atop of a bank here for easier going, trending left when the fence cuts in, then uphill again, the summit of Wheathead now very close on your right. Dip down right, briefly, to cross a stile, then turn half left and go up once more, aiming for another sad ruin, Firber House, on the skyline. Just to the right of Firber you will pick up a disused, but still discernible, 'green lane': go up this, adjacent to a wall, to the north summit of Wheathead. The actual top would involve a slight detour - unless you intend the alternative walk (see earlier). No matter, the view is excellent from here: Pendle seen almost end on, not quite so dominant now, then a whole sweep of high moorland from Longridge Fell to Waddington Fells and right up Ribblesdale. A suitable point for a break: the route turns left over a stile when you meet a wall ahead, making it possible to find shelter either side, depending on wind direction.

During the next section we steadily leave Pendle behind, even out of sight on occasion, and the different feel to the walking is very obvious. Once over the above-mentioned stile, go briefly downhill with a wall on your right, but soon go through a gate in this wall. The line to follow in the next field of rough, sloping pasture is not obvious: trend half left, with Weets Hill now clearly in view, and cross the wall ahead through a gap by a wall junction. Continue along a roughly East-West wall, aiming for the buildings of Craven Laithe, but when you meet a fence ahead there is no trace of a stile or gate. The best solution is to go downhill by the fence, reaching a farm track by a gate. Follow the track to the right, pass in front of the neat farm buildings and through another gate, trending left, still on a clear track. Bird-spotters will find this is good wheatear country. Turn sharp right with the track, passing a ruin (also "Craven Laithe" on the map), then turn sharp left. There is no discernible tread on the ground: the simplest approach is a beeline for the road, as suggested on the 1:25,000 map, and you should converge with a lane by a gateway onto the A682.

Here is the rub! Weets Hill, the next objective, is only half a mile or so away as the crow flies, but there is *no* right of way up the lane to Cold Weather House or onto the moor beyond. Instead, turn left along the road, turning right in nearly half a mile onto a lane signed "Public Footpath: Coal Pit Lane" - slightly misleading, as the said Lane is not met till later. Pass left in front of the buildings ahead, then through a gate, and turn half right. Go over a stile, and follow a wall on your right, passing next through a decidedly narrow stone stoop. Here turn half left away from the wall; ahead, pass right through a gate onto a track (there is a stile a little lower, but this has been surmounted with barbed wire). Once on the track, proceed with a wall on your left: in clear weather you will appreciate, on this stretch, a rather fine prospect of the Cracoe Fells several miles ahead. When the wall turns away, turn slightly left, keeping well above Newfield Edge Farm, and cross the field to a stile. Pass over this and turn left by the side of the house ahead onto a lane. Here, I have not been able to locate the path which should go straight across to Coal Pit Lane (according to the 1:25,000 OS); therefore turn down the lane, turning right onto another lane by a double 'cycle' sign, this being a recognised minor road (Brogden Lane). Once past the house at Lane Side, turn sharp right onto Coal Pit Lane itself, a recognised ancient trackway from Gisburn. Proceed along this clear track in a SSE direction; the next junction with a crossing lane from the left is the point where the earlier path should have come straight across the field from the right - should you have succeeded in locating it. We continue uphill, keeping a straight course, soon passing through a gate, again over the 1,000ft. contour and climbing, with a wall on the left.

About a quarter of a mile beyond the gate, pass through another gate on the left before the wall does a sharp right-left zigzag. You remain on a perfectly clear track, but now open on both sides, in the midst of a rough pasture which seems very remote. Half a mile of this going, becoming quite a steep climb, brings us to the road end by Weets House, which has been visible on the skyline for some time. Should you wish to visit the summit of 'The Weets' or go on to Barnoldswick, turn left here, but to continue the main route pass through a gate and proceed down the ensuing lane, a better-defined section of Gisburn Old Road.

You have now passed the highest ground encountered on the walk, though in clear weather the distant views remain good for some time. On the descent, we soon begin to pass some outlying houses. Once past Star House on your left, turn into a field on your right at a "Witches' Way" sign; no, that Pendle influence will not be gainsaid! About half a mile of easy going, following a dyke of sorts to the left of a wall, ensues. One stile is crossed; after passing Peel's House (on your left, at the roadside), look for a waymarker and cross a stone stile in the wall on your right, then march straight downhill to the road A682. A succession of wall stiles on the left of the main track, with further waymarkers to guide you through the farm of Admergill Pasture, makes this section easy. Once through the farmyard, trend left beyond the final wall end, soon dropping down a steep bank to meet the A682 again.

This time we go - carefully! - straight across the road, over another stile, and continue to lose height steadily until we meet Admergill Water, which makes an agreeable companion for the next stage of the walk. Cross it first by a footbridge and proceed downstream on the far bank (true right) after crossing a waymarked stile (here, and for some distance ahead, are 'Witches Way' signs). Stansfield's (Blacko) Tower, referred to earlier, looms above from a hillside on the left and becomes a watching sentinel for quite a way ahead.

A fence lies between path and stream at first. Turn a little infield to cross a stile, then proceed downstream, going over a stile adjoining a gate (signs again). Here we join a metalled lane - rather, one paved with bricks - and a wooden table and seat offer themselves for a picnic stop. Go down the lane and pass Admergill Hall, a fine old building with stone mullions. Bend left with the now roughened track, turning off to the right where you observe FP signs: a newish building lies ahead. Go through a small gate by a larger one and cross the bridge, then cross the field ahead diagonally and cross another footbridge. Turn left on reaching the field ahead.

Keep on the right bank of the stream, cross a stile and bend left, crossing another stile by a gate (again waymarked). The path ahead is clear: go down and over a simple stile. By now the stream is delightful. Cross an FB over a side stream and go up some steps to the Annel Cross-Blacko road, where a decision must be taken. More in keeping with the 'Breezy Uplands' theme would be a return to Barley via Brown Hill, Offa Hill and Whitehough, beginning at an FP sign on the near side of the bridge over Admergill Water. However, that would entail the third significant climb of the day and would make the inclusion of Roughlee an awkward detour, so it might well be left for another day.

Instead, the main low level route should see you comfortably back in Barley within an hour. Cross the road bridge and immediately go right down some steps and over a stile, then proceed along a clear path with FB and steps on the left bank. Cross a stone step stile in a wall near the stream (signs) and soon go over another stile, bearing left with the stream, a steepish wooded bank on your left. Soon you reach Blacko Bar Road, meeting it over a stile and turning right. A quarter-mile of easy road walking follows: where the road turns sharp right, take a narrow stile (surmounted by a gate) on the right, before reaching North Farm, and go up the field with a barn on your left, subsequently keeping close by a new wire fence, turning gradually left.

At the end of the field, pass through a stone stoop ahead, ignoring a gate to the left. Go straight along by a hedge, trending left onto a lane as the going levels out, then go over a stile to the right of a gate. Pass along a lane between farm buildings, then turn left with the lane, descending past more buildings. You are now on a metalled lane: lower down you come to a crossing of ways (Witches' Way sign here). Go straight on into a narrow lane, ignoring a lane branching left (returning to the road) and a path to the right. In a few yards you pass the front of Roughlee Old Hall, still a sturdy and very well-kept building, though now divided into separate properties. Continue up a narrow ginnel and pass more houses, reaching the road again at a junction.

From here you could simply return to Barley along the main road, but the route through the fields is pleasanter. Turn right up a minor road, going uphill, soon turning sharp left and passing a caravan site. Look carefully on the left for a path through the hedge, just above the caravans, and follow a clear tread through a succession of six narrow fields linked by stiles and an FB. Before you cross the seventh, a minatory notice tells you to beware of the bull! I have yet to meet 'El Toro' here, but such notices need to be taken at face value lest the walk degenerate into a headlong sprint.

Bear more to the right in this last field and locate a stile, cross it into a wood and go steeply downhill to a stream (White

Hough Water). A tread is visible, but you need to negotiate some tree-trunks on the rather awkward slope: lower down, pass through a gap (there is an FP sign on a tree, more obvious in reverse) and turn right on nearing the stream. This is a lovely tranquil spot on an evening walk, and you may well have an accompaniment of owls from the neighbouring woods. Go over a stile, and proceed upstream with a bank or dyke (artificial?) on your left. Soon you emerge from a gate onto a lane to the right of a bridge over White Hough Water.

Go straight across here, initially on a metalled surface (a sign says "White Hough Outdoor Education Centre"). Pass a number of buildings, with many new conversions, and in about 150yds. come to a junction of road and rough lane. Go straight along the latter, the stream still on your left: two gates at an interval of about a quarter-mile may be passed on their left. You come out at Narrowgates, part of Barley, and go briefly along a cobbled street past stone cottages. Beyond the cottages keep on in the same line, now a wide lane with stone chippings (also a BW) and soon reach the car park.

The easy-going nature of the final section disguises the demanding up-and-down nature of the walk, but emphasises its variety, in common with all this Forest of Pendle area: lonely airy heights alternating with wooded streams and charming settlements. It is an immensely appealing, homely area, and I think your feet will inevitably wish to turn this way again, for in truth today's walk has only scraped the surface. A whole host of paths may be explored hereabouts, and on days when we may not wish to explore the highest or most remote parts of our district this region will always satisfy.

7. A BORDER RAID

Long Causeway, Holme Chapel, Thieveley Pike, Green's Clough, Portsmouth, Black Scout, Long Causeway. 7 miles. Maps: OS 1:50,000 Landranger no. 103; OS 1: 25,000 Explorer OL 21, South Pennines.

* * * * * * * * *

Background

If I were a Yorkshireman reading this book (what a thought!), I fancy I should have eyed the recent expedition on Boulsworth with some disquiet. "This Lanky lad", I would say, "is pushin' 'is luck 'ere. When 'e comes over t'border, we'll be ready for'im!"

Yes, on the summit ridge of Boulsworth we were only half a mile inside the Lancashire - West Yorkshire boundary. It is an inescapable fact that our home map includes considerable areas of North and West Yorkshire (though less than before the 1974 boundary changes), so that in order to do justice to the whole sheet we must sooner or later enter the Tykes' domain. The vicinity of Todmorden seems an appropriate place to take the plunge: not only cricket afficionados will know that Todmorden supply the only Yorkshire team in the Lancashire League. To be frank, no-one around the A646 seems to worry just where the border lies: life goes on, the demarcation between the counties does not even coincide with the watershed hereabouts. Yet the border is there, with its inevitable evocation of turbulent history and ongoing rivalry.

Doubtless Southern readers will regard all this with incredulity, as puzzled as Neville Cardus's mythical Londoner watching a Roses match. Sadly, those matches no longer merit television time, but scrape the surface and that old rivalry soon emerges in other ways. Recently, when the Wensleydale cheese factory at Hawes had to close down, the proprietor's scorn at the prospect of the famous cheese being made in Lancashire could hardly be expressed. Back in 1974, the annexation of Barnoldswick and Earby by Lancashire caused a furore more appropriate to a military coup. At a still deeper level, however, I believe something more profound emerges, namely a burying of rivalry in an admiration of each others' good qualities: industry, determination, humour, hospitality, nowhere better seen than in those communities who have won a living from this tough Pennine country, on either side of the divide.

Back to the walking! Today our excursion into West Yorkshire will be brief, and passports are not currently required. The walk takes the form of a down-and-up-again trek, twice over, exploring the moorland and ridges to either side of the Calder Valley A646 road. A measure of Lancashire-Yorkshire *entente* is seen in that both rivers (the road crosses the main watershed) share the name of Calder. After totting all the ups and downs, major and minor, around 1,500ft. of climbing are called for - some steep - and though much of the walk takes place on high open moorland, there is some valley walking among park-like surroundings and some interesting stream scenery thrown in. Some of the upland stretches involve rough and boggy going underfoot.

We begin on the Long Causeway, that ancient high-level route between Burnley and Hebden Bridge, by the car park at (894288). This is not marked on the South Pennines OS map, but is shown on the latest 1:50,000, with the intriguing legend "The Limestone Trail". The car park is a good base for exploration, for as well as the two paths we are about to employ there is a path leading away to the north, where the old mineworkings in Sheddon Clough are only half a mile away. Houses are very few and far between on this section of the road: half a mile towards Burnley lies the solitary Causeway House, while a mile and a quarter in the other direction lies Stiperden Bar House, which features prominently in views throughout this area.

The Long Causeway itself makes an interesting subject of study, its age being hinted at by its indication as an antiquity on the OS. Though references to its present-day name are fairly recent (Whitaker in 1801 was the first), there seems no doubt that the road began as a medieval trackway. A number of medieval crosses are encountered *en route,* and one working hypothesis (from Bennett's "History of Burnley") is that the trackway was used by monks taking wool from Whalley Abbey to Halifax or vice versa. The causeway, it is suggested, may refer to some sections having been paved by the monks. Improvements in this and other local roads were recommended by an Act of Parliament in 1759 - "almost impassable for wheeled carriages" was a previous comment! Of the old wayside crosses, those still extant include the Stump Cross near Mereclough at (877300) and the Mount Cross near Shore at (915272), the latter possibly as early as the seventh century, and presumably moved from the roadside at some time.

The Walk

From the car park at (894288), cross the road and take the right-hand footpath sign from the point where two paths and a track diverge; head initially WSW across rough moorland with tussocky grass. The windmill farm, adjacent, is not to be ignored. Well, at least they're fairly silent! Certainly a number of visitors come this way to view the strange sight, getting used to the shape of energy generation of the future perhaps - who knows? However, I suspect most walkers will be relieved to get them out of sight quickly. Curb your impatience though, for the going is rough at first with only a faint tread. Don't head too far to the right: locate a wooden, waymarked post by a ruined wall corner and continue in roughly the same line, fording a little stream, and continuing close to the wall through thick grass and reeds.

Where the wall bends slightly right, keep straight on, crossing a vehicular track and soon climbing a waymarked stile in a fence ahead. The short-cropped pasture ahead will be welcome after the earlier rough going. Keep the same line, WSW, with a most impressive view of the whole frontage of Thieveley Scout now, its cliffs and bounding wooded cloughs showing to advantage: often a little dark and menacing, facing NE away from the sun as it does. Go on under a power line and soon cross a waymarked stile in a fence.

Watch carefully ahead: turn slightly to the right, aiming for a stile in a newish fence not given on the 1:25,000 OS, then drop

Walk 7: A Border Raid

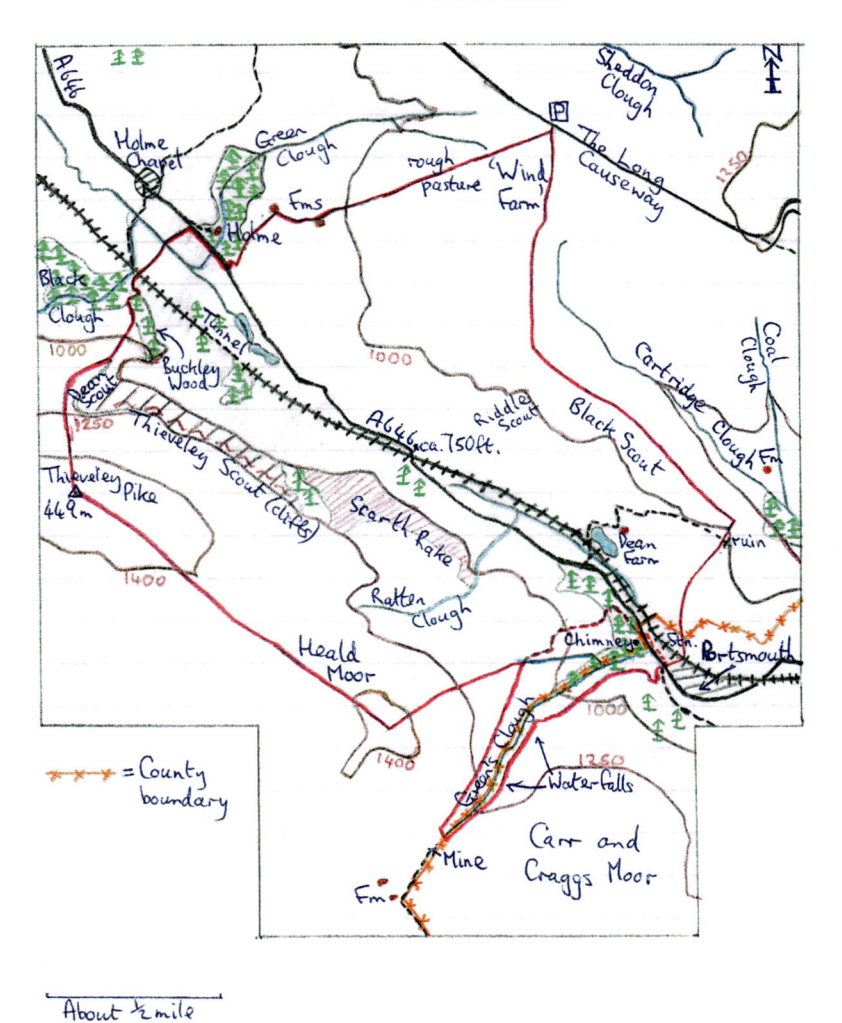

down slightly to the left through a gateway (a waymarked stile is adjacent), keeping to the right of the farm below, unnamed on the OS. When you meet the farm lane, follow it to the right initially. As I passed this way once in late autumn a party of fieldfares flew by, their characteristic sharp calls breaking the prevalent quiet.

Cut through the apex of a hairpin in the lane (which turns away left here), soon passing through a gate as you near the next farm. Before reaching the buildings, turn left through another gate, then cross a stile, subsequently going quite steeply downhill with a wall on the left. Pass through a gate at the bottom of the field, then continue your steep descent through bracken, the wall now on your right. You are soon down to valley level: after going through a swing-gate, turn right then immediately left, reaching the road by a gate with a waymarker. Turn right.

The A646 has a reputation as a slow and tortuous route for the motorist - vulnerable to flooding, too, during heavy rain. Our encounter with it is fairly brief, about 200yds., but note the old residence of Holme, passed on the right and now a nursing home. This dates from around 1600 and was built for one Whitaker, a former Dean of St.Paul's. Certainly the feel of a country park domain has survived locally to this day.

Watch carefully for the point of departure on the left by a signed footpath, easily missed, in green railings. Go across the level meadow ahead, with a fairly clear tread, along a line of scattered trees and crossing a little runnel by a footbridge. Stone flags briefly mark the route here. Turn slightly more left, passing through an area of rhododendrons then taking an underpass below the railway (on the East Lancs. - Hebden Bridge - Leeds line). Intricacies of route are eased by numerous waymarkers hereabouts, and echoes of past living are all around: signs of an old station, remnants of nineteenth-century mineworkings, and - less pleasingly - the dirty stream issuing from the aptly named Black Clough.

Beyond the railway, turn round between walls and cross a stile into woodland. The lane to Buckley Kennels is on your left: join this very briefly, leaving it in about 50yds. by a fenced path on the right. Now the steep climb out of the Calder Valley begins, still on a well marked path with the deep defile of Black Clough on the right. On emerging from Buckley Wood, keep up the obvious steep path, aiming for a ruin (Thieveley Farm) seen above. Pausing for breath, you can admire the retrospective panorama between N and E, Black Hameldon and Boulsworth being prominent. The ruin is situated to the right of a little plateau, formerly used for entertainments as recorded by Gillham.

The climb continues, aiming for the summit of Dean Clough with its craggy outcrop, behind the ruin. The deep clough effectively marks the terminus of the Thieveley Scout cliffs which stretch away SE from here. Take a clearly signed path climbing to the right of the gorge, over a stile, steadily overtopping the gritstone outcrops. Above the gorge, where the gradient eases, turn more into the south. Todmorden is tucked out of sight from here, but Stoodley Pike is prominent to the ESE : indeed our eyes will start to explore the distant view here, the latter stages of the climb seeming rather tame after the initial pull out of the valley. The area of open mineworking noted on the 1:25,000 OS has left its scars, most obviously in a broad stony track crossed just below the summit. The isolated Stiperden Bar House mentioned earlier is very prominent from here, looking ENE, in a situation that will fire the imagination of lovers of solitude.

After crossing the track, a cairn marks the beginning of a brief steeper section, but the trig-point of Thieveley Pike is quickly reached, still on a fair tread. Sadly, we have to cross a stile in a barbed wire fence to attain the spot. Here we have reached a new watershed for these pages, that between Ribble and Irwell: indeed the spring regarded as the source of the Irwell is barely a half mile away, SW, and the outskirts of Bacup are nearby to the south. Instinctively, the hillwalker's gaze will tend to the northern arc, where Pendle stands up boldly, and further afield Ingleborough and Penyghent are well seen when it's clear.

After our survey from the trig-point (in truth, not one of the more inspiring summits) we move on again. Leave the fence, taking a bearing of 130 degrees, aiming for the summit of Heald

Moor if clear. Pass through a gateway in a ruinous wall, then go over a waymarked stile, keeping the same line. The ridge is reasonably well defined: don't lose height to left or right. Views into Calderdale, ESE, become more extensive as we proceed. When the wall on the right bends away keep the same ridge line, on a discernible tread, the going underfoot quite reasonable: cross a track in the dip (for quarrying originally?) then rise slightly for half a mile to Heald Moor's top – 'summit' would be too ambitious. A few cairns mark the way among some peat and cotton grass.

The top carries a waymarker post, and here we turn into the ENE (bearing 070 degrees), following a less well defined tread across the moor now. Portsmouth, a frontier post of Todmorden and our next objective, comes into view hereabouts. Locate a wall running across your course, roughly SSW-NNE, and aim to cross it in a little dip, where you will find a waymarked stile: just 50yds. ahead you reach a clear rough track which may be followed right or left. The latter gets you down more quickly, (see the notes at the end of this chapter) but the extra effort involved in the right detour is worth it for the sake of the scenery in Green's Clough and Beater Clough. Turn right, then, following the track easily for about half a mile among the excavations and debris of old mining operations. On reaching a fence by an area of open spoil-heaps, go down a few yards to the stream and cross a plank footbridge.

That was it! Yes, the stream provided the border, unannounced. Turn left now, downstream, on a developing path. The clough becomes spectacular, remarkably narrow and deep, spoilt only by the dirty water it carries: there are some significant waterfalls. Lower down the clough enters a greener stretch among trees and bracken, very pleasant in summer, still extremely steep-sided. There is a prominent chimney on the far bank. Eventually cross a stile adjacent to a gate, then bend right, going steadily downhill now, presently taking a sharp left hairpin down to the road. A stile and sign inform you this is the Bearnshaw Tower Forestry Estate, and that Bacup Road is two miles distant. You have reached Portsmouth, and the Roebuck Inn opposite provides an excuse for a detour.

Turn right, then left down Station Parade (a PF sign says "Kebs Road ½"), crossing the railway with care at a level crossing. Here, with twilight drawing on one November afternoon, I had one of those pleasant chance encounters with a local man walking his dog. He guided me on the way up to my next objective of the Black Scout ridge, and his company proved so agreeable that it would have seemed impolite to comment on his pronounced West Country accent - but how it struck the ear, in these parts! Time and again these fortuituous meetings cheer the walker on his way.

Go along the lane over the crossing, pass a building (B.R. property) and turn left off the lane through a yard. Turn slightly right up a path and through a gate. Ahead, keep by a wall on your left initially, but when it bends away further left follow a thin path which turns uphill and re-enters Lancashire. A zigzag tread (not as given on the OS 1:25,000) may then be followed, still gaining height and keeping a wall section on your left. Look at the ridge above - you will detect a pronounced cleft in the escarpment, which we have to pass through shortly.

The original line of the path ahead (OS) appears to have been obstructed, but simply follow the visible tread to the right, crossing a broken wall, then turning sharp left onto a clearer tread through a little delph. Go uphill, over another broken wall, into lusher pastures where you soon approach a ruin. Pass it, joining converging tracks from both left and right and meeting a waymarked post. Go ahead to the cleft in the ridge, now immediately above, and turn left onto the SE-NW ridge of Black Scout at another waymarker.

Here is another trackway thought to be of some antiquity: signs announce "South Pennine Packhorse Trails". Packhorse routes, many of them stone-flagged, are very characteristic of the Calderdale area. Black Scout affords relief in the shape of a near-level promenade, after the climb from the valley, and the views soon open out nicely. To the N the wind farm is all too obvious: to the SE, Stoodley Pike towering above the roofs of Todmorden forms the backdrop, with Blackstone Edge just seen, further right and more distant. Pendle's summit peeps over the intervening ridges occasionally in the NNW.

Keep the wall on your right initially: beyond, to the NE, the defile of Cartridge Clough is quite prominent. When you reach a gate ahead, there has been a little re-routing (clearly marked): turn left for a few yards, then right through a newish, waymarked gate, subsequently resuming your NW line along the ridge. Stiperden Bar House is prominent, in the NNE now, and as the escarpment on the left converges with the path there are striking views down to the valley road. Thieveley Scout comes back powerfully into view, and there is a sizeable millstone outcrop immediately to your left where a side clough bites deeply into the ridge.

Pass through a gate, continuing NW between a gate and a fence in a wetter section. Bend very slightly right, recrossing the wall and keeping the same general line. Where another craggy outcrop bites in from the left, cross the fence by a stile near the perimeter of the windmill farm and head N, leaving the escarpment. You cross a fairly level moor now, rough and wet in places, only a faint tread visible, but from here it's impossible to go wrong as you must hit the Long Causeway road soon. Keep the stream valley (much shallower now) on your right, turning a few degrees E of N and crossing a line of fence posts.

Moorland scenery very definitely replaces valley scenery again on this home stretch. Once over a little bank, you soon encounter the rough road serving the wind farm, but it is probably not recommended to follow it. Look for waymarkers, indicating where this track should be crossed, and resume a virtually due N course across the last section of moorland, reaching a stile with a P F sign in the very corner of the field. The car park is then directly opposite.

Not one of our more spectacular or beautiful walks, I grant, but one offering interesting insights into the use of moorland and valley, natural resources and ancient trackways, over the centuries - quite apart from that 'border business'. Driving back initially on the Long Causeway you will have time to reflect on the many ages of travellers who have passed that way, and in what manner, recalling medieval times long before those of the warring Roses.

Alternative descent to Portsmouth

A more direct descent may be made from Heald Moor to Portsmouth, crossing the county boundary just as surely but missing the impressive ravine of Green's and Beater's Cloughs. On reaching the rough track about half a mile NE of Heald Moor's summit, turn left where the main route turns right. On reaching a ruin, cross a stile on the right (marked with a "B") and pass the ruin, then go through a gap (stile adjacent) and turn right, going downhill by a wall/fence. A tread develops; pass a waymarker post and go down half left to a stile below. You meet a rough vehicular track: follow a hairpin bend, left then right, and go down past trees. The county boundary sign is passed on the road below; go through a gate and drop to the roadside where there is a PF sign. The fine wooded cliffs ahead, to the right of the road, look striking from this vantage. Go down the road for about100yds., passing the Roebuck Inn and rejoining the main route. This is about one mile shorter.

8. LITTLE SWITZERLAND

Whitewell, Middle Lees, Mill Brook, River Hodder, Buck Thorn, Browsholme Hall, Spire Farm, Crimpton, Whitewell. 8 ½ miles. Maps: OS 1:50,000 Landranger no. 103; OS 1:25,000 Explorer OL 41, Forest of Bowland.

* * * * * * * * * *

Background

An ambitious title, indeed, for this walk! Yet no-one who knows this part of the district will begrudge the name given by locals and admirers to this fine stretch of the Hodder valley. Indeed, the gorge of the Hodder for a mile or so downstream from Whitewell is well worth seeing even if you intend to go no further: there is, strictly speaking, no right of way along the river bank, but the view from the road is quite satisfying. The combination of mature trees, steep hillside and swiftly-flowing stream makes for possibly the finest river scenery in Lancashire, and I would include the 'Pudsay's Leap' section of the Ribble in that assessment.*

Our walk, however, though never far from the Hodder, offers plenty of variety as we also take in a moorland section rising to around the 1,000ft. contour, with fine views deep into Bowland, up to the Yorkshire Dales when clear and retrospects of Pendle and the Ribble valley. You will also have the option of visiting a fine stately home, Browsholme Hall, the ancestral home of the Parker family, for centuries important landowners and once Bow-Bearers in the forest of Bowland. Add to that the creature comforts on offer at Whitewell and (just off route) at Bashall Eaves, also the useful bus service linking those two places, and a large number of possibilities for spending a pleasant and varied day are opened up. The walk involves roughly 1,000ft. of climbing but with no particularly steep sections.

*Note that, under arrangements in place at the time of writing, the 'Pudsay's Leap' section is not accessible to the walker. See Walk 13.

Whitewell, though a very small village, is a popular spot, particularly at weekends when the inn does a brisk trade - and what better place to enjoy your meal, particularly in the back dining room, overlooking the river? However, one practical difficulty may then present itself, namely lack of parking space in the village. It is normally possible to go down the little lane past the church (going away from the inn) and park on recently improved and levelled ground near the river. Or you may prefer to use the parking space adjoining the road on Hall Hill, thence walking down to the village (alternatively, join the route at (666468), turning left off the road at a gate). Wherever you decide to park, you should certainly not miss the view from Hall Hill, one of the highlights of the district: indeed I would consider it one of the best in Northern England. The sweeping lines of the Bowland fells combine with the prospect up the Hodder and Dunsop valleys and the nearby limestone knolls in a beautifully balanced picture, particularly attractive - though arguably somewhat out of character - in mellow evening light.

The Walk

Assuming a start from the centre of Whitewell, walk a short way up the Hall Hill road (viz. towards Cow Ark). Go past the cottages on the right and reach a row of stone steps leading up on the right, surmounted by a gate with a neat hand-painted sign saying "Foot Path". What more invitation could the walker ask for? Pass through, following a fairly clear tread, past what appears to be a covered well, then turn right on an obvious track in front of the house ahead. Here, and for some time to come, you are in a stretch of limestone country which has greatly influenced Whitewell's scenery. Your eyes will inevitably be drawn to the right, where the view up the Hodder valley is glorious, and beyond it, in a line northwards, the much narrower, steep-sided Dunsop valley (*not* the Trough of Bowland).

Bend first right then left with the track, thus avoiding a stone watercourse, and keep on, soon passing a small disused quarry on your left and climbing slightly. When you reach a gate in the wall ahead, don't go through, but turn left and shortly go through another one, then turn right. Continue just topside of the

Walk 8: Little Switzerland

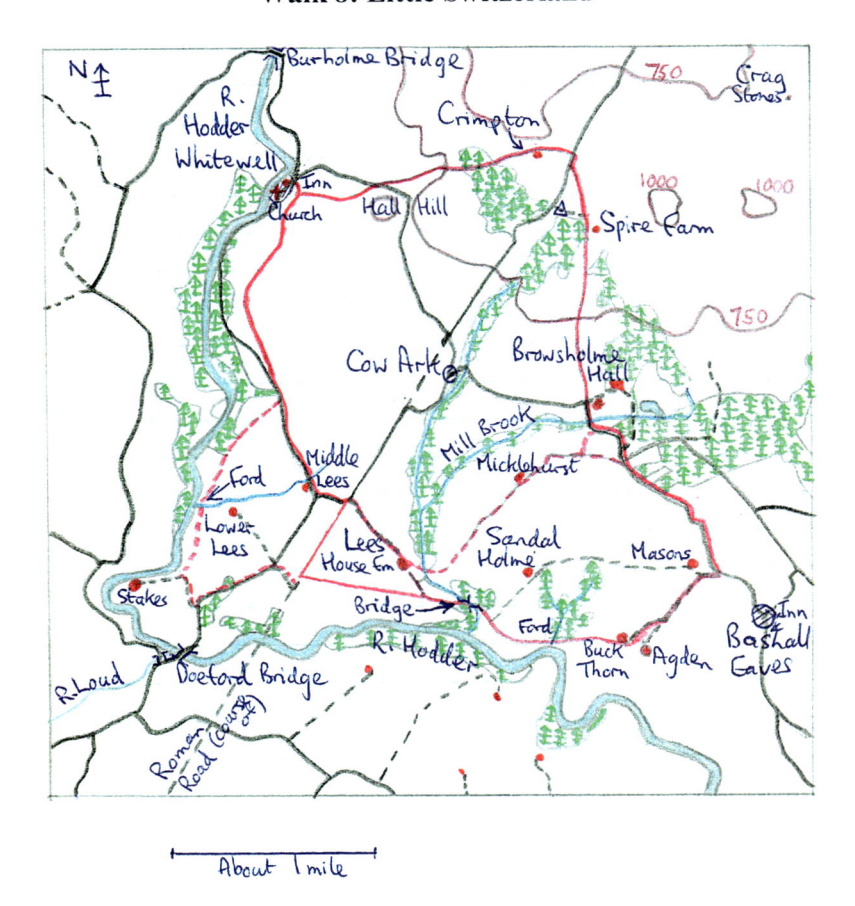

Grounds of Browsholme Hall

wall, going through a tall iron kissing gate, then continuing in the same line. The shapely little cone of Parlick Pike is now visible ahead, terminating the long Totridge Fell - Fair Snape ridge which will become very familiar after a few walks in this locale. Below on your right is the richly wooded Hodder gorge.

Go over the fence ahead in the corner (new stile), and keep the same line in the next field. Curlews seem particularly common on these upland pastures, in spring and summer. In about 300 yards, turn slightly left and pass through a gate, keeping above the fence; a broadside view of Longridge Fell has now appeared ahead. You pass another little quarry, turning more left, soon going through another iron kissing gate. In the field ahead, trend slowly right towards the roadside - but *not* for the first gate seen there; aim for the wood jutting towards the far side of the road ahead. Pass through a fairly new gate, then in about 50 yards, on the right, through a much older one (stiff!) admitting you onto the Whitewell - Chipping road by a footpath sign. Turn left.

Here, very soon, you have a choice: after passing the little wooded strip on the right, another public footpath sign leads away on that side. You may either explore that path (adding about a mile and half to the distance, but visiting another pleasant stretch of the Hodder) or proceed along the main route via the road past Middle Lees.

On the main route, then, simply keep on the minor road, passing out of the limestone belt as we approach the pleasantly shaded buildings of Middle Lees, one of which till recently had an outside stone staircase. The traffic on this road is usually light, with the possible exception of Sunday lunchtimes! Beyond Middle Lees, turn left at the road junction (for Clitheroe and Whalley). In about 200 yards, you join a section of the Roman Road between Ribchester and Burrow in Lonsdale (see also walk 20). Here again you have a choice of routes. For the shorter alternative, turn briefly left along the metalled road but almost at once turn right down the farm lane to Lees House. When you approach the last building along the lane, look carefully for a footpath sign on the left and follow a rather steep, usually muddy descent to a footbridge over the very attractive Mill Brook. Once over follow signs to Micklehurst, thence onto the road near Browsholme Hall where the main route is rejoined.

For the main route, however, we press on to enjoy another beautiful stretch of the Hodder. Turn right at the point of meeting the Roman Road and follow it (here just a rough track) for about three eighths of a mile. Watch carefully for a footpath sign on your left: here cross a stile, then cross the usually wet field ahead to a pleasant wooded dell by a stream. Atop the far bank you will see a stile: ford the stream (not wide), climb the bank and cross the stile into a large field, now in open country with a fine view of Pendle, some miles away ESE, now opening up. Aim for the left hand edge of a narrow strip of woodland across your path and cross a succession of three stiles, the first two close together (recent pipelaying here). Further on cross a fourth stile, then turn right where you meet a fence enclosing woodland ahead. Go along by the fence, but where the fence kinks slightly to the right, cross a stile into the woodland. The next section of the path is lush and overgrown, though the tread is pretty clear, and until the way is more popular again - I have every hope! - you will need to force your way through, certainly in high summer. But it's worth the effort. Certainly the scenery in this deep little gorge cut out by the Mill Brook is most attractive, well wooded, steep and sheltered. The going eases as you drop to a clearer stretch by the stream, then on your left appears a fine new footbridge, crossing Mill Brook at quite a height, which has replaced a dilapidated old stone bridge.

Over the bridge, turn right on a clearer path and continue slightly uphill. This is a delightful spot for a halt; keep an ear and eye open for woodpeckers, and enjoy the stream and its valley. Ahead, after a stile, cross a small stream (a dry-bed in summer) by another new footbridge. Soon the path diverges; we keep close to the fence on the right initially, while the left branch aims more directly for Mason House and the Bashall Eaves - Whitewell road. Ahead, the path is a bit sketchy: the fence turns sharply away on the right, but don't drop towards the river too soon. Go on into the field, initially roughly parallel to the river, while contouring, and cross two new fences (close together) by stiles, then drop to a clearer path across the bank, with the extensive flood plain of the Hodder below. When a wood comes in from the left, drop towards the lower end of it, ford a small stream and cross a neat stile. The river is met again - at last! - and a much clearer path develops on the next section. Here the Hodder is in a tranquil mood, flowing fairly sedately over rocky slabs interspersed with deep pools, a popular anglers' stretch. On a sunny day you will find a real reluctance to leave this spot.

Proceed near the water's edge, entering woodland again, noting a welcome waymarker (fence on right), then cross a good new stile. The river turns away here in a graceful, long right-hand bend. Wishful thinking, no doubt, but what excellent prospects for walkers could be opened up hereabouts by a new footbridge! There is no crossing-point between Higher Hodder and Doeford Bridges, otherwise one could envisage connections between this route and the Longridge Fell paths. Just a thought.

Leaving the river, cross a side stream from the left at a ford, but as I once found to my embarrassment (January, 1993) this can be dangerous in spate. Never underestimate stream crossings! Once over, climb the steep bluff on a clear, waymarked but possibly muddy path. After this stiff pull, emerge from the wood and cross a stile (waymarkers inscribed "The Forest of Bowland"). A redundant stile in a non-existent fence follows, then cross the field ahead diagonally left, eventually passing a little overgrown pond on your left. In the very far corner, you meet another waymarker: cross another, narrower field, aiming for a stile by an isolated tree, Pendle prominent ahead.

Cross the next field in the same line to a gate, nearing the farm of Buck Thorn on your left. From here you may like to try the footpath given in the OS, over a stile tucked away on the right, through the next farm of Aigden and on to Bashall Eaves. However, that would be quite a detour from our next objective of Browsholme; it is simpler to turn left beyond Buck Thorn onto the farm lane (sign for anglers here). Follow the track for about half a mile to near Mason House, then turn right on another lane to reach the road by a little copse.

Feeling a bit peckish at this stage? Well, some sustenance may be at hand. A short detour to the right brings you to Bashall Eaves, where there is the Red Pump Inn. Equally, if that feels like enough walking for the day, you may be able to catch the Clitheroe - Slaidburn bus from the village back to Whitewell - if the time is right. There are few Sunday services, though.

The more resolute will press on and turn left along the road, following it for about three-quarters of a mile. Here again, it's not usually very busy, though timing is all, and both the immediate, well-wooded surroundings and the longer views continue to please the eye. I have seen sparrowhawk and tree creeper hereabouts, in addition to commoner species. You may then either continue on the road to the main entrance of Browsholme or, at (685446), turn down a lane signed "Micklehurst", opposite a road junction. After the lane bends left, take a gate on the right and aim for the house seen ahead. Trend right near the end of the field, dropping down a bank opposite an impressive garden and back onto the road by a sign. Turn left and go up to Browsholme Hall lodge in about 200 yards.

It is a matter of some astonishment that only the most recent editions of the OS have recorded Browsholme Hall as an antiquity. The building is Tudor in origin, having an Elizabethan façade with significant additions in the Queen Anne and Georgian styles. As a period piece it certainly merits a visit, combining fine interiors and artistic treasures with stylish external architecture and a lovely setting. The influence of the Parker family actually extends back well before the building of the hall: they have been major landowners in Bowland for many centuries. At the time of writing, the hall is open to visitors on certain weekends from Easter to the end of August, also to pre-booked parties. It used to be permissible to walk through the grounds at any reasonable daytime hour, but I am not sure if this is still the case: you should politely enquire.

Leave the road by the lodge, turning right initially as the road bends left, then left through a gate, going uphill on a vehicular track. Simply follow this for a quarter-mile, with a little wooded stream on your right, but when the track turns sharp right for the farm (Crow Wood), pass through a gate and go straight up the field ahead, aiming for the right-hand edge of the mixed woodland above. Pass over a stile by a gate here, but observe how splendidly the retrospective view has developed: Pendle, Longridge Fell, the South Pennines and West Lancashire Moors are ranged beyond the greenery of the mid-Ribble valley. A good spot for a tea-break. Doing this myself once, I was almost deafened by a screeching pheasant just behind me in the wood.

Go up the short lane and through a gate, noting Spire Farm, your next objective, on the skyline. Trend slightly right in the next field, with a fine prospect of the Bowland Fells on your left. Cross a stile, keep left of a little pond (not on the 1:25,000 OS) and turn left over a stile in the fence. Go up past the copse on your right, but when it ends turn half right in the field ahead, aiming for the forestry just below Spire Farm. Keep near the forest's edge on reaching it, passing to the left of Spire: note the remarkable (and non-functional) castellated wall, said to have been built to improve the view from the hall below.

Cross a rudimentary stile, still close to the forest, pass through an overgrown area, and over another waymarked stile. You have reached the summit of the walk at about 1,000ft., and on reaching the farm road there is a wonderful view ahead: Whin Fell and the Dunsop Valley are prominent among the nearer fells with the Three Peaks and other Dales summits visible if clear. You may now turn left and shortly join the road, or go straight across the farm lane into rough pasture. Trend slightly right, soon crossing a stile into a fairly new afforested area (given on the new 1:50,000 OS) then down an overgrown path, over a stile and onto the road lower down. Turn right, but almost at once turn left at a public footpath sign, down the farm lane to Crimpton to start the last lap.

Forestry is obviously a key word, hereabouts: one must hope that the plantings will not start to obstruct the view eventually. Ahead, the path has been diverted away from the farm buildings - a series of waymarkers guide you to the right, below the farm, then circle round to regain the track behind. Continue on roughly the same line, close to the fence on your left, through two more new gates with further extensive plantings on your left. Beyond the last gate, trend slightly left through a rough and neglected pasture, aiming for the right-angled corner made by the forest. Cross a waymarked stile and proceed along what was formerly a wet, boggy section but is now stony and well-drained. In about 300 yards, emerge from the forest and cross a stile, then a wall, with beautiful views of the Hodder valley and the fells suddenly appearing.

Go down the field on a very faint tread, passing to the right of the first copse encountered: you are suddenly back in limestone country. In fact that little copse encloses a recognised pothole, and on your right a dry valley deepens into a collapsed cavern - examine with care! Malhamdale in miniature. Turn more to the left now, passing left of the large, walled wood ahead (Raven Scar on the OS). Keep on a faint tread, follow the wall round to the left and cross a high wall stile. Ahead, contour, keeping above the gorge on the right, and meet a rough vehicular track which is followed onto the road at a gate, where there is a new footpath sign.

If you turn right down the road, you will return to Whitewell in under half a mile. Alternatively, go straight across through a gate and follow a light vehicular track with rocky outcrops on your left. Lose only a little height initially, then join another track from your left and turn more right, locating a gate with a wood to the right. Pass through and go downhill, with glorious views again ahead, a fitting end to the walk: the mid-Hodder and Dunsop valleys, Whitewell and the Bowland fells, including the secluded recess holding the isolated, superbly situated farm of Whitmore, nestling below Totridge. Aim for the buildings below, passing to the right of them and crossing the track met on the outward journey. Simply reverse your initial steps now, past the covered well, through the gap in the broken wall and through the gate onto the road with the inn immediately downhill on your left.

A varied and fascinating walk, encompassing many different kinds of scenery, and with numerous variations to explore on future visits. Indeed, of the walks that do not reach a true summit, I rate this one of the best: the sudden dramatic views, changes of underlying rock and first-rate river scenery are a feast for the eye. But remember, we are still only on the fringe of the true Bowland here! The deepest delights are still to come.

9. EARTH, AIR AND WATER

Widdop Reservoir, Gorple, Hare Stones, Black Hameldon, Long Causeway, Dukes Cut, Noah Dale, Reaps Cross, Graining Water, Widdop Reservoir. 11 miles. Maps: OS 1:50,000 Landranger no. 103; OS 1:25,000 Explorer OL 21, South Pennines.

Alternative: Another good circuit incorporating Black Hameldon, though of very different character, may be made from Worsthorne. Take the Gorple Road from the village (clearly signed) and follow it until you join the main route by the Gorple Stones at (915321). Continue on the main route to the Long Causeway road; from here, after some initial road walking, you may make use of a variety of paths in the Sheddon, Mereclough and Hurstwood areas to return to Worsthorne.

* * * * * * * * *

Background

Today those who have waited patiently for the rectification of our previous omission, or at least inadequacy, will reap their reward. Back to the main watershed of Northern England we go, indeed to a longer and better-defined section of it than we met on Boulsworth Hill. The dividing line runs quite sharp and clear, almost directly N-S, over the substantial slopes of Black Hameldon until we reach the true summit, Hoof Stones Height, where it turns away West. To complete the walk we make use of a variety of paths and tracks, some ancient travellers' ways, others relative newcomers - like the Pennine Way. Wide-open moorland, generally between 1,000 and 1,500ft., with no shelter from the elements; gaunt blocks of millstone grit, encountered at intervals; numerous well-stocked reservoirs, with one or two greener stream cloughs at the margins - these are the truly elemental features of today's walk.

I have no doubt that many walkers who habitually turn their footsteps to the lowlands would be rather dismayed by such a prospect. Bleak moorlands, they might say: nothing attractive or interesting up there. We'll leave that sort of thing to the Pennine

Way boys, the enthusiasts. Fair enough. I have always said, walk where you enjoy your walking: there is no attempt at conversion to other grades of ambulatory activity in this book. Perhaps I should make it clear, though, that no rebate will be offered for those walks you may consider uninteresting. We sell the whole package.

The fact of the matter is that what we see on a walk depends on how well-trained our eyes are: and, indeed, any walk may often be seen on quite different levels. On one level, this circuit around Black Hameldon is just earth, air and water - with maybe fire too, if they are burning back areas of heather moor. But look again, and you will see all kinds of evidence of human activity, ancient and modern. This is no primeval landscape such as you may encounter in the Bowland fells. The reservoirs, obviously enough: the ruins of Gorple, and other high moorland farms: the ancient trackways used by travellers, evinced particularly by the Reaps Cross passed en route. Even on the very summit of Black Hameldon you are not far from old mine workings, some - in the Sheddon area - worked as recently as the turn of the $19^{th} - 20^{th}$ century. Then, on the roads, old wayside inns such as the Pack Horse, which has tempted many Pennine Way walkers to a minor detour. Finally, and most obtrusively, the modern windmills, generating power, looking like a 'Dr. Who' set.

More traditional walkers' rewards are on offer, too, in particular the fine and extensive views from Black Hameldon, as befits its main watershed situation. There is a fair amount of heavy peat bog to cross - in fact the main summit is hard work indeed during a wet spell. However, the going underfoot is generally not bad. On the return section, you will be pleasantly surprised by the attractive Noah Dale, the upper reaches of Colden Water. The whole walk is fairly elevated, so that only about 800ft. of climbing is called for. Yes, give it a try! Not superficially an attractive walk, I grant you, but full of interest to those who look deeper, and a satisfying walk to complete.

Walk 9: Earth, Air and Water

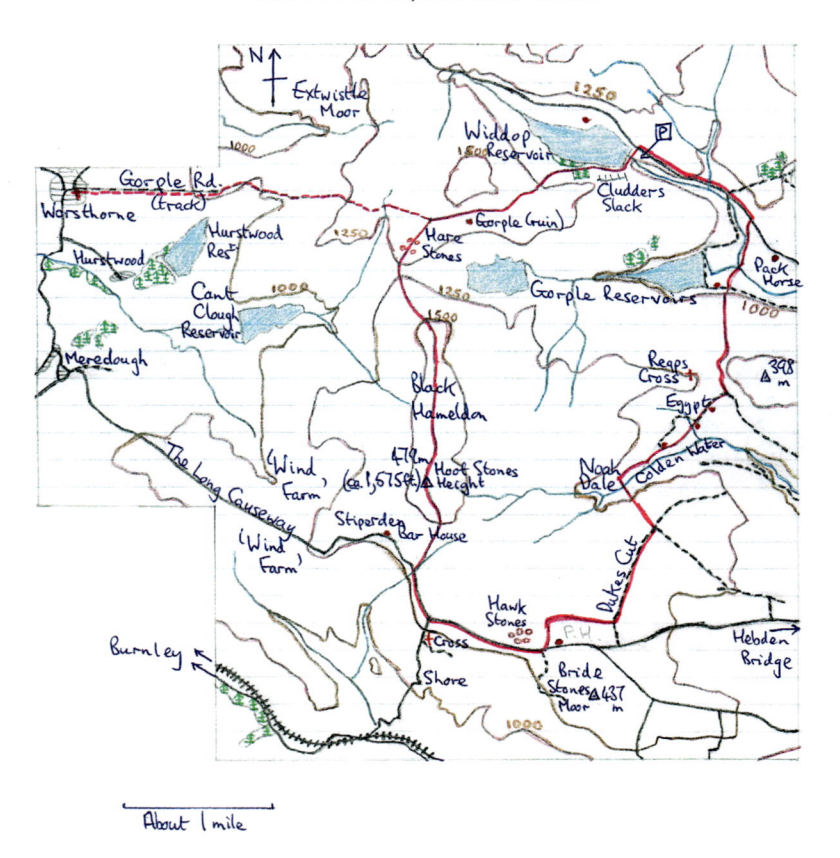

The Walk

The recommended starting point is by the Widdop reservoir on the minor road to Hebden Bridge at (927328). Parking is somewhat limited here, however, so a slight detour may be called for. Begin by crossing the reservoir dam on a clearly-marked path (there is a recognised short-circuit of the reservoir), then turn W by the water's edge under the impressive rocks of Cludders Slack, a climbers' playground. Continue along a rough track by the water's edge, evading oncoming cyclists as best you can, soon passing a small plantation. Looking around, you will see how Widdop is set in a profound hollow, its rim sporting many millstone grit outcrops, Cludders Slack being merely the most prominent.

The track soon leaves the reservoir, climbing the hillside, and trending right after passing a disused quarry. When you reach a path junction, turn sharp left (sign-posted "Gorple Ruin and Worsthorne"); the right fork is merely to complete the reservoir circuit, but a pleasant evening stroll. Continue with the main track, still very clear, where a side path (much fainter) goes off left, climbing uphill through a little gully and emerging onto open moor around the 1400ft. contour. The view opens up pleasingly hereabouts, the lower Gorple reservoir (left) coming into view first, then the upper, with the peaty mass of Black Hameldon rising like a substantial pudding behind it. At the next junction, take the right fork, for Worsthorne. You are on the main Gorple track, which becomes broader and better-defined all the way until it enters Worsthorne as a road.

Where the track bends very slightly right, you are very close to the Gorple ruin: as well as obvious fragments of wall, the old field divisions around the house are palpable. In fact the house is not ancient, having been built by the Towneleys (of Towneley Hall) in the 19th century, but its setting is still some cause for wonder. A few hundred yards further on, the track bends definitely right and dips, by a wooden sign saying "Bridleway Only". Here turn left on a faint tread, aiming for the Hare Stones, a prominent millstone grit outcrop just above the col between Gorple Upper and Cant Clough reservoirs. You have hit the watershed now, and the going underfoot becomes boggy, with cotton grass: keep to the height of land to avoid the worst areas. In very thick weather, a bearing of 220 degrees will bring you to the Hare Stones, an agreeable stopping place situated on firmer ground. Try to find the large millstone lying here on the W side.

Beyond the Hare Stones, swing round to a more southerly point, through a dip with a stone shooting butt, then begin the final rise up Great Hameldon itself, still on a fairly clear tread, bearing now 170 degrees. You are on a triply-distinguished boundary - Lancashire/West Yorkshire, access land and watershed - but through excessive modesty, perhaps, not even a fence post marks the fact. After about half a mile of fairly steady pull (keeping to the height of land, but avoiding the swampier patches) the climbing is nearly done. Look around you: the view is very good from hereabouts on a clear day, though not quite equalling that from Boulsworth. Pendle dominates to the NW, with the ridge of Parlick, Fair Snape and Totridge behind and to its left; to its right the Craven mountains are impressive, though Boulsworth (NNE) shuts out a significant arc. The dark tower of Stoodley Pike is prominent in the SE, and indeed a long sweep of the Pennines shows up; to the E you look a long way down Calderdale into the West Riding, mainly a prospect of long horizontal lines, Dales-like. Near at hand, the highly obtrusive windmills work industriously at their power generation, something quite outlandish.

You encounter a kind of shallow groove hereabouts (artificial?), along the line of the walk, after which the going underfoot is generally better. There continues to be a pretty clear tread, though the ridge is sprawling and rather ill-defined. About 300yds. short of the summit, you may spot a particularly obvious boundary stone in the groove. The summit itself, Hoof Stones Height, at just under 1,600ft. boasts a trig.point and is firm underfoot - no Black Hill! - if a little cheerless. Admire the view for a moment, with the windmills now looming close and menacing below you, the most obvious artificial element in the Pennine moorland scene.

Beyond Hoof Stones Height, the tread is less obvious at first. Take a SSE course, aiming for another prominent rocky outcrop, the Wolf Stones. Soon a thin path develops: after passing the Wolf Stones, turn into a SSW direction, more definitely downhill now, and in a little over a quarter of a mile you meet the "Long Causeway" road, an ancient high route from Burnley to Hebden Bridge, (see Walk 7 for more details) by a little stream. You are still some 1300ft. above sea level here. Looking across SW, there is a good prospect of the long line of moor topped by Thieveley Pike, with the cliffs of Thieveley Scout below. Turn left along the road here and follow it for about one and a quarter miles: normally a pleasant high-level promenade along a quiet minor road, with good views to your right into the developing Calderdale, and further rocky outcrops along the way, notably the Hawk Stones passed on your left.

Just before you reach the Sportsman's Arms (or on returning?), take a signed public footpath on the left, along a fairly clear tread, waymarked initially. When you reach a wire fence (with a marshy area and much cotton grass beyond), turn right, following the fence through a little dip, then over a stile. You pass two small ponds - the first on your right, the second on your left: only the second is shown on the 1:25,000 OS. When you meet a fence ahead, take a few paces to the right and cross it by a stile. Go ahead with a fence now on your right and a telegraphy mast of curious design beyond it. A little way ahead, pass through a small gate adjacent to a five-barred one, turning left onto the rough lane running at right angles ahead. This is Dukes Cut, another trackway of considerable age, running initially through a shallow cutting. Follow it for about three-quarters of a mile.

You are now on the fringes of Calderdale, more obviously so as the track rises above the surrounding fields. Though this is not such prime bird-watching territory as some parts of the Pennines, there are plenty of curlew and lapwing about, and you have a sporting chance of sighting golden plover and snipe. When you reach Four Gates End, a distinct crossroads, turn sharp left (90 degrees) and go down by a ruinous wall, while the main track bends slightly right. This stretch of upland pasture is rough and wet at first: avoid the worst areas if you can, keeping somewhat away from the wall, and eventually cross a stone bridge at the bottom of the field, onto drier going. Go up to a T-junction of walled routes and turn right: this is Noah Dale, in effect the upper reaches of Colden Water, and in the stream's company the going is pleasanter - and easier. You dip towards the stream and pass some ruined outbuildings ("Colden Water" on the 1:25,000 OS). Beyond, the wayfinding becomes a little more intricate. Go through a gate, then climb a little, bypassing the house of Hoar Side on its right. This requires passing through a wicket gate before the house and, after passing it, trend slightly right (waymarked), soon crossing a wall by a stone-step stile. Beyond the next field, turn half left, now on a clear tread with some stone flags to assist, then as the ground dips, turn more definitely left and cross a side stream by a little footbridge.

Above the far bank you pass the ruined building at Rough Hey, whereupon a broad farm track ensues: follow it, soon passing Egypt, long ruinous but recently restored. About 200yds. further on, pass through a gate at the end of the farm track and turn left onto another clear track, signed "Lower Gorple: Pemissive Bridleway", the beginning of the final stretch, with the view soon opening out again as you surmount a slight rise ahead. On your left hereabouts, by the angle of a wall, are the remains of Reaps Cross (only the base can be seen now), a further reminder that these barren moors have been crossed by a network of tracks for centuries.

Going downhill now, you turn sharply right, then about 300yds. after turning back into the North again, the Pennine Way is met at a gate. Go straight on here, noting the sign "Bridleway: Lower Gorple", with the reservoir indeed very close on the left. Soon you reach another crossroads of paths, adjacent to Gorple Cottage. While it is possible to turn left here and proceed via the reservoir dam, it is pleasanter to keep ahead on the Pennine Way (signed "Pennine Way: The Ridge"). You go downhill, gently at first, then more steeply with a right turn, passing a striking gritstone outcrop on the far bank and crossing two footbridges.

Turn left after the second and walk up the deep little valley of Graining Water, a feeder of Hebden Water. Soon you begin to climb out of the valley on the clear path, with many stone flags again in evidence, very characteristic of the Calderdale area. Once atop of the bank, you have the option of crossing the stile on your right to indulge in the 'Pack Horse Detour', one of the recognised inn diversions off the Pennine Way. The main (teetotal) Pennine Way goes straight on, over a stile, then crossing to the other side of a ruinous wall. A little way ahead, turn right up a narrow walled lane to the road. Here turn left and regain the starting point by about a mile of road walking.

It is the same elemental mixture as before: perhaps you will have grown to like it a little more by now! Moor, scattered trees, deep stream cloughs, the odd wayside house, yet in its own way, on the right day, a satisfying conclusion to a fine walk. On this final stretch - and not quite where the 1:25,000 OS indicates - the Pennine Way leaves us, striking off for points North. Are you developing a curiosity to see where it goes next? Very good! In later walks of this volume you will have the opportunity to see some more, and perhaps even develop a wish to do the whole walk.

10. HEIGHTS, WILD AND WUTHERING

Slack, Hardcastle Crags, Wadsworth Moor, Walshaw Dean, Withins, Bronte Waterfall, Leeshaw Reservoir, Stairs Lane, Crimsworth Dean, New Bridge, Hebden Water, Slack. 14½ miles. (13½ if done from New Bridge). Maps: OS 1:50,000 Landranger nos. 103, 104; OS 1:25,000 Explorer OL21, South Pennines.

Alternatives: For those prepared to make the necessary transport arrangements, two excellent through walks based on the above long circular are recommendable. For one: take the Gorple track from the centre of Worsthorne and follow it to the road by the Widdop reservoir dam at (937328). Go down the road, join the Pennine Way and follow it till you join the above route by the middle Walshaw Dean reservoir. From the Bronte bridge, leave the above route and take clearly marked paths to Haworth. For the second: take the main route from Slack or New Bridge, leave it by the Bronte bridge and go on to Haworth. Logistically, the second alternative is easier - there is fairly good transport from Haworth back to Hebden Bridge, even on Sundays. This is also a shorter walk than the main route.

* * * * * * * * * *

Background

While you can undoubtedly take this walk just as it comes, a long and vigorous tramp through the heart of the South Pennines, there is no doubt that the literary associations of the area add much to its interest. Many who habitually take little interest in literature are nevertheless fascinated by the work of the Bronte sisters, the remarkable range and intensity of human experience which they portrayed. To make a pilgrimage to their old locale is then a very natural inclination. Even if we leave aside the difficult question of whether Top Withins really is 'Wuthering Heights', there is no doubt at all that these windswept moors were, as you may say, the sisters' back garden, where they walked often. In combining these moors with the streams and wooded hillsides radiating from Hebden Bridge, I have made up a circular walk of contrasts, and those who have not yet discovered Hebden will find ideas for short walks in that area which are very satisfying in their own right. The two through walk possibilities both end at Haworth, where transport is relatively easily arranged.

If the full circular route is taken, the walk becomes the second longest in the book, though it is not an exceptionally demanding one - the going underfoot is generally good, with only a few boggy patches, on well-defined paths and tracks. However, the open high moorland sections are rather vulnerable to hill mist, making some navigational skill desirable: it is remarkably easy to lose paths in such conditions! A good deal of up and down is involved, around 1500ft. of climbing in all, but without any particularly steep gradients: through the woods and by the reservoirs you will easily keep a good pace. We shall again be making use of a section of the Pennine Way, and a well-used one at that, to the North of the Heptonstall Moor section of the Pennine Way used in Walk 9.

The Walk

There is no reason why you should not begin the walk at Hebden Bridge, in which case the logical start would be the car park by Hebden Water at (988293). However, this car park may well be overcrowded, especially during holidays, and it comes at a price. At the cost of a little extra walking at the beginning and end, you may use instead the National Trust car park at (969298) on the minor Colne to Hebden Bridge road near Slack. From this upland spot, signed "The National Trust: Hardcastle Crags", take a made track at the rear of the car park and follow it down to a lane (which may be reached directly from the road). Go downhill alongside a pleasant stream and through a gate into the wood ahead. Simply follow the lane initially: in fact, you may follow this all the way, taking a large hairpin bend later. A more direct route is offered by turning left off the lane on a thinner path (the first one met, after the lane bends right). Initially this keeps parallel to the lane, but then turns left again down stone steps, descending quite steeply towards Hebden Water. You emerge directly at a bridge, with stepping stones just downstream. Cross

Walk 10: Heights, Wild and Wuthering

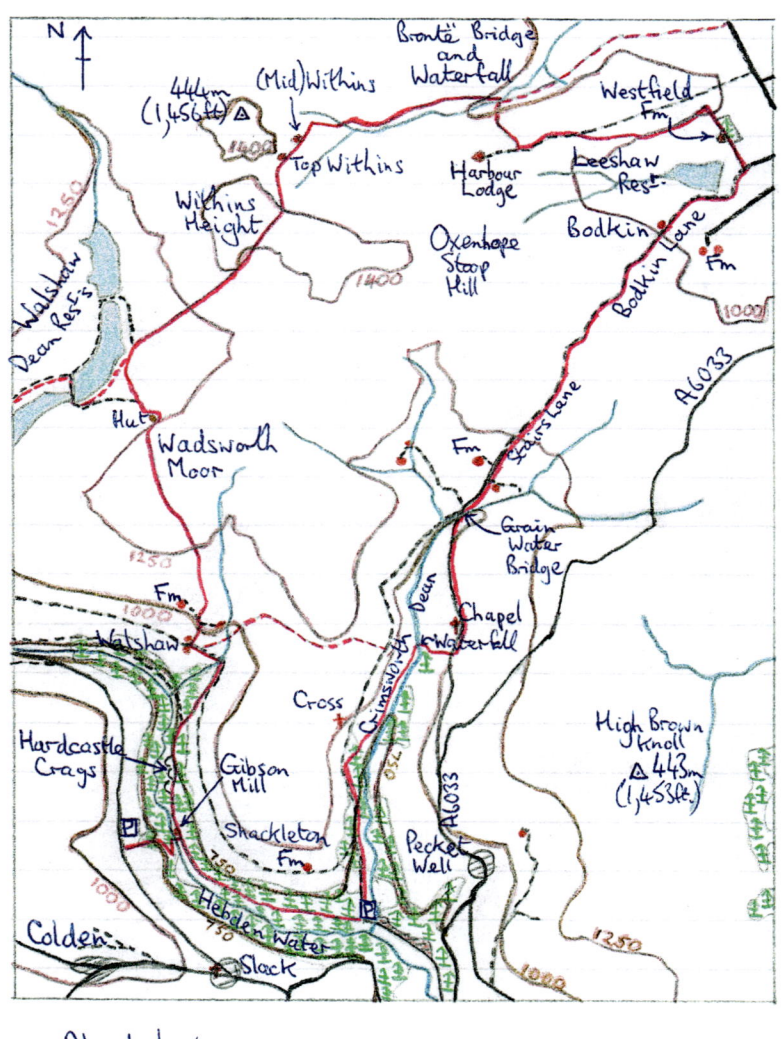

Hebden Water and Woods

the bridge, admiring the fine stream, and go past the interesting remains of Gibson Mill, an early (1800) cotton mill. A plaque in the wall gives you a fascinating insight into working life, and entertainments, of the 19th century. Bend right with the track, then turn sharp left onto the main track coming up from Hebden Bridge. This spot is just over a mile from the New Bridge car park at (988293) if starting from there, on a broad and easy track.

Stroll along through the very pleasant mixed woodland, an idyllic spot indeed on a bright Spring day. These richly wooded dales are much more characteristic of streams to the East of the main watershed, relatively sheltered situations. The woods frequently seem alive with chaffinches, and you may hope to spot other less common species, blackcap and woodpeckers for instance. About three-eighths of a mile uphill after leaving the mill, you pass the prominent, vegetated, rocky outcrops of Hardcastle Crags. A little way beyond, keep right where a nature trail branch goes left. Soon you emerge from the National Trust area, continuing to climb, and turn left when you reach a signposted junction at the edge of the woodland, on a lane initially metalled. The lane presently turns sharply left, approaching Walshaw Farm. Here I once heard a distantly-remembered, rather plaintive, mewing sound and looking up I was delighted to see three buzzards circling above. Just visiting, or are some resident hereabouts? It would be interesting to know.

Before reaching the main farm building, turn right to join the permissive path over Wadsworth Moor (a board gives an explanation and says "Savile Estate"). Before leaving the farm, you may note that a path goes East from here, traversing to join with Crimsworth Dean and offering a pleasant, much shorter circular. Keep left where the private track to Horodiddle goes off to the right, but very shortly leave the farm road, going uphill at a sign ("Permissive Path: Walshaw Dean"). You will be pleased to note this is for walkers only! Go up through a gate, then climb on a track with a copse on your left. Keep left, crossing a stile by a gate, and further on cross stone steps in a wall (or just use the gate, alongside) reaching the open moor.

The ensuing crossing of Wadsworth Moor should not pose a problem, granted any reasonable sort of visibility; the tread is pretty clear nowadays. In thick weather, the general direction is NNW; a broader track (initially turning left, then doubling back) soon peters out. You reach the summit of the moor (about 1380ft.) in about half a mile, and the view by then is extensive: the back of Boulsworth, the Widdop and Gorple Reservoirs, and further round to the South, a long sweeping line of Pennine moors, with Stoodley Pike prominent. To the SSE, you can look far into Yorkshire, beyond the hills and into the plains. A less welcome sight (though compelling in a bizarre way) is provided by another set of windmills - Black Hameldon doesn't suffer alone! - to the ESE, though these are thankfully invisible from the very top. Generally the going remains good underfoot, with just a little cotton grass, the botanical danger signal of the peat moors.

Soon you begin to descend, and a few hundred yards beyond the summit the tread turns into the NNE briefly, reaching two shooting huts. From here all three Walshaw Dean reservoirs are clearly visible, and inevitably I think of that baking hot day in 1976 when we passed this way on the fourth day of our Pennine Way trek. In that remarkable drought summer all three were reduced to small muddy puddles.

Turn left at the huts by a further permissive path sign and follow to the middle reservoir (you may follow a fainter right-hand branch later, passing through a gate onto the main track by the reservoir). Here you join the Pennine Way coming in from the left; rhododendrons are profuse hereabouts. The going is easy here, through a little dip and up through another gate, keeping the reservoir wall on your left. The point where the Pennine Way turns away uphill is marked by a clear sign: a benchmark (331m, nearly 1100ft.) is at hand, also a large flat stone, a natural stopping point. Ahead, the gradient up to Withins Height is not severe, and while the path has been well-blazed I cannot help feeling - not uncharitably, I hope - that the repairs performed here are disproportionate. There has been much local rerouting of the path and laying of stone flags, though the erosion - compared to, say, some major Lake District routes - looks very slight. I may not make many friends, but I will say it anyway: the problem of footpath erosion has been greatly exaggerated.

The general direction up the rise is NE; you pass through a flatter area in half a mile or so, then the view opens ahead to offer a prospect of Haworth and Keighley beyond the intervening moors. Beyond the boundary (roughly on the line of the local watershed), Top Withins comes into view (no top on the OS maps), and the tread, still very clear, turns towards it, more northerly. On a very clear day, you can catch a fine glimpse of the distant Great Whernside from here, and the nearer Cracoe Fells. Press on eagerly, over more stone flags and bending through a ruined wall, coming to 'Wuthering Heights' - or is it?

The plaque in the wall of the semi-ruinous building, placed by the Bronte Society in 1964, can seem a little deflating! If you can't wait, Wainwright gives the text in full in "Pennine Way Companion". In truth, though, it is fitting that the answer is ambiguous, for that is of the essence of fiction. You cannot say that Top Withins 'is' Wuthering Heights, any more than Dorchester 'is' Casterbridge or Bowes 'is' Greta Bridge. What we have is a certain situation and atmosphere, a base on which the fictional structure is built: and anyone who knows the spot will feel, I think, that in the isolated setting of Top Withins, with the two straggling trees at the rear, miles of open moor around and the descent to the distant lights and buildings of Haworth before, we are as close to Wuthering Heights as we are likely to get. Beyond that, all is imagination, and Emily had plenty of it.

Pass on below the building, then, perhaps after a little meditation, and keep on a clear path NNE; the more direct branch to the right given on the OS is not apparent on the ground. Soon you reach another ruin, Mid Withins, and here leave the Pennine Way, on a path signed "Haworth 3.5 miles, Bronte Waterfall 1 mile". Drop down to the stream (South Dean Beck) on this nice firm path, and follow it, going straight on at the next path junction, soon climbing a little. About a quarter of a mile on, cross a high stile, beginning a more intricate stretch of path-finding. Pass a yellow waymarker on a stone, then go through a narrow stone stoop-cum-gate. After the next wall gap, turn gradually downhill (right) and back towards the stream. At a signpost marked "Bronte Way", turn right, the stream and falls now immediately ahead: again the situation on the ground does not quite seem to tally with the 1:25,000 OS map.

This is a pleasant watersmeet, popular with children and families. Cross the 'Bronte Bridge', a sturdy pack-horse affair. If going on to Haworth, the simplest route is downstream (well signed) from this point. Check current bus times if you plan a return from Haworth to Hebden Bridge or to the Burnley area.

Our main route goes straight across, quite steeply up by the right (true left) of the little waterfall. After a brief climb, you emerge onto open moor again on a faint but adequate path.

Look for a sign, "Bronte Falls/Stanbury: Public Footpath, Haworth". Take the latter direction, over a footbridge, and you soon meet the farm road to Harbour Lodge. From here it is now possible to take the path to Oxenhope Stoop Hill, then follow the wall SE to join Stairs Lane at (004338), near its summit, taking advantage of the new access situation. This would reduce the walk's length by about two miles.

The main route proceeds more circuitously, though if you enjoy this kind of moorland trek you will not object, I'm sure. Turn left down the farm road ("Public Footpath: Haworth") and follow it for about half a mile. When you meet a further sign (retrospective) for "Bronte Waterfall and Top Withins", turn half right off the track down a thin path, with one boggy stretch to negotiate. Turn left when you meet a wall (for Haworth: again, Oxenhope Stoop is indicated to the right). The going is still easy and pleasant in its wide-open way. At the next path junction, turn sharp right (90 degrees) over a stile and go down a field, passing scattered trees and then Westfield Farm. The farm lane turns left at its terminus, onto Lee Lane: turn right here, passing below the dam of Leeshaw Reservoir and up to the far end of the dam wall. Here on a spring day I was once presented with an unusual close-up of a redshank pacing along the top of a wall: normally they are most easily alarmed.

Proceed initially due West along the lane to the South side of Leeshaw Reservoir. Where the track turns left, away from the reservoir, take a deep breath or two and gather yourself: this is the last serious climb of the day as we turn definitely for home, along what was once a recognised road from Haworth to Hebden Bridge. This section is Bodkin Lane: climb with it to the skyline, passing the lonely habitation of Bodkin Farm on your right, later Bodkin Top, a ruin. The walled lane, now called Stairs Lane, remains perfectly clear: cross a conduit, turning left, and soon right again. Go through a gate, then a curious little gully over a stream. Soon you reach the summit, Top of Stairs, at around 1400ft; nearly all downhill from here! The modern road from Haworth to Hebden Bridge is clear on your left during this stretch less than a mile away, and the panorama has opened up in fine style once more, particularly of the South Pennines in the forward arc. Around here you also pass a wall going NW towards Oxenhope Stoop Hill (Deep Nitch on the OS), with a stile and apparent tread: see the earlier note. This is another section of moorland where you should keep an eye (and an ear) out for the attractive golden plover.

The route bends a little left by the Deep Nitch wall and soon begins to descend steadily; half a mile on you pass through a gate, after which you are definitely among the outlying farms. After passing Thurrish on your right, you meet a metalled surface. Further down you turn sharp left then right, crossing a stream at Grain Water Bridge followed by a slight rise. In another half mile you pass the remote, delightfully situated, former Crimsworth Dean Methodist Church. Look for a public bridleway going down right from the road in a further quarter mile and follow it, down a stone-paved path to the attractive Lumb Hole waterfall, the high spot of Crimsworth Dean's scenery (not 'Grimsworth Dean' - an unfortunate howler on the 1:50,000 OS).

Cross the bridge just above the waterfall, then double back to follow the stream downhill on its true right, turning left off the green lane when the latter goes uphill. The path here is thin but easily followed. In about half a mile, cross a wall by stone steps, soon passing a conversion property onto a much clearer vehicular track. Drop down left off this before reaching a gate ahead, soon entering a pleasant wood. Do *not* cross a bridge going off to the left ahead, but keep right, slightly uphill, on a tread. When you come to a Public Footpath sign some quarter of a mile on, trend more to the right, briefly rising quite steeply to a broad lane; follow it left. At the next junction, go straight on (downhill). This is another likely area for spotting a woodpecker or two, and the views across the wooded valley to the East are impressive, typical of the Calderdale environs.

After passing Hollin Hall on your left in a clearing, you soon re-enter the wood and main car park by Hebden Water: journey's end if parked here! If you began at the National Trust car park near Slack, just follow the road through the car park round to the right, then walk out of the car park area and up the wide track through the Hebden Water valley and woods. A mile or so of this pleasant going will return you to Gibson Mill where you cross the bridge and retrace your steps to the starting point.

Indeed a long walk, but a rich and varied one, hopefully providing something for everyone: ever-changing surroundings, literary associations, long views, varied wildlife. On a first visit, only the surface of this fascinating area can be scratched: many visits and explorations of alternatives will be called for to get to know it well - and that, to my mind, is a definition of a fine walk.

11. A TASTE OF THE DALES

*Rylstone, Rylstone Fell, Embsay Moor, Embsay Reservoir, None-Go-Bye, Sandy Beck, Rylstone. 11 miles. Maps:*OS 1:50,000 Landranger nos.103, 104; OS 1:25,000 Explorer OL 10.

Alternatives: Through routes from Rylstone via Embsay Moor to Bolton Abbey and Barden Tower.

* * * * * * * * * *

Background
We have been making ever-bolder forays across the Lancs. - Yorks. border in these walks, but the present venture is the most ambitious yet. Not only is every step within North Yorkshire, it is wholly within the Yorkshire Dales National Park - yet all but half a mile lies on map 103. It is probably unkind of me to suspect that many would be unaware that our map contains any of the National Park at all. True, the area is not great, some forty square miles lying N of the A65 road in the top right corner of our familiar map. The character of this walk, though, is already quite distinct from the South Pennines or Pendle country, the nearest approaches in these walks so far. Even though the 'limestone dales' as usually defined are still some miles away, there is an expansiveness about the moorland slopes and a lushness in the pastures which mark the area with true Dales character. It is a fine and varied walk, not too demanding, and I warmly recommend it to those wishing to extend their usual walking horizons.

We are once again to the East of the main Northern England watershed here, by a few miles, and the weather too can feel quite different over this way. On showery westerly days, noticeably fewer showers are likely to penetrate this far inland (compared to Bowland, say) and the higher ground to the NW, culminating in the Three Peaks, also has a sheltering effect. Having said that, there is no recommendation to leave your waterproofs at home! Geographically, we shall be exploring a sizeable wedge of moderately high fell and moor lying between the Aire and the Wharfe valleys and North of Skipton. Indeed, through walks based on the present one and ending by the Wharfe at Bolton Abbey, Barden Tower or elsewhere would be feasible and pleasant, as noted earlier. However, I feel that to describe such routes in detail would take me far beyond my map remit - and there is no shortage of Dales guidebooks. This walk calls for about 850ft. of climbing in all, with just one steep section, and the going is mostly good underfoot.

The Walk

There is a fair amount of off-road parking available at Rylstone, both in the village and just before it. You will enjoy the village itself, too, with its pond and well-maintained stone cottages. Take the lane just N of the road junction, signposted "Rylstone Church and Manor House Farm". Pass the manor house on the right and go up the lane, past the parish church, turning right immediately afterwards at a sign, "Sandy Beck Bar/Barden Moor Access Area". Route-finding on the section ahead has lately been much simplified. Turn initially right, then left through a gate, and simply follow the broad track, keeping a wall on your left. Further to your left, the aspect of Watt Cragg with its war memorial obelisk is dramatic, standing above the steep slopes.

Continue easily through the lush pasture, soon passing a narrow wooded strip on your left (the path used to go through this), then through a gate. Keep following the track, gradually turning more to the right with the B6265 road now clearly not far away. Eventually you meet a gate, signed to Rylstone church in reverse. Pass through and turn left along the lane ahead, signed in this direction for Barden Moor and Sandy Beck Bar. Not surprisingly, these wide-open spaces and the nearby fell host a good deal of varied wildlife: I have heard redshank here, and seen snipe, in addition to the commoner waders.

Go along the lane, still signed to Barden Moor, but keep on where the original access point departed on the left - again this is clearly indicated. The access (bridleway) now turns off about a hundred yards further on, at a useful board and map display. Note that the access arrangements allow you to explore the summit

Walk 11: A Taste of the Dales

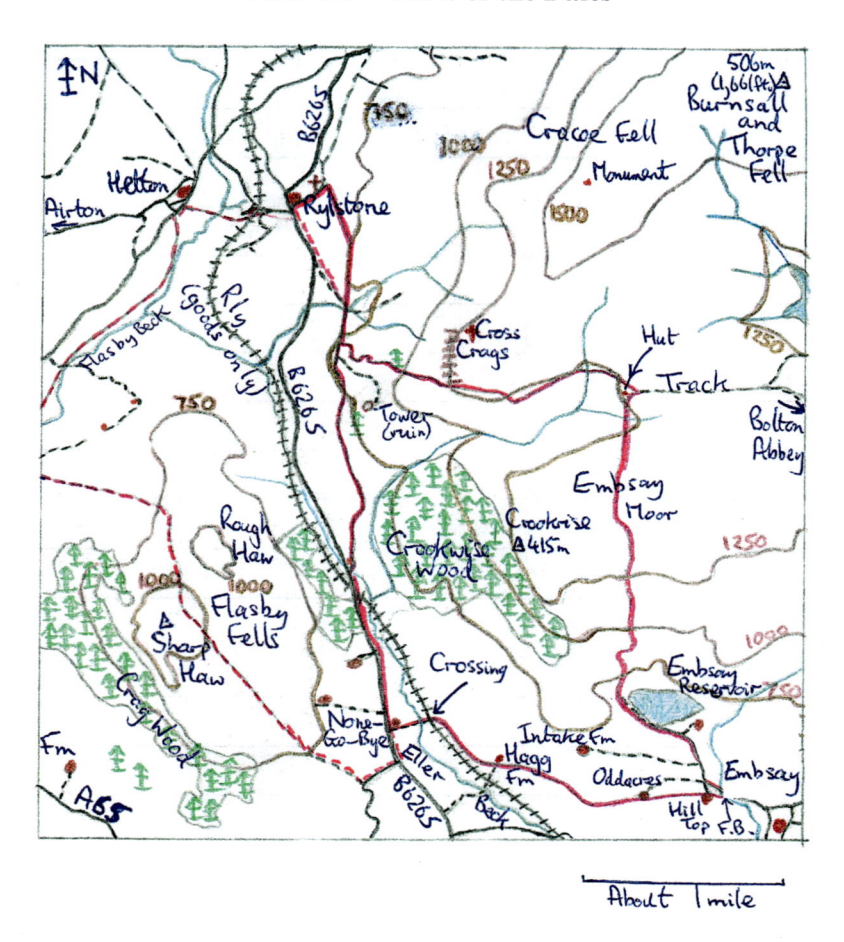

ridge. Before striking uphill, you may admire the graceful and rather unusual shapes of the Flasby Fells, nearby to the SW, another area well worth exploration.

In fact, the bridleway is initially a little indistinct! Swing right, then left through a little dip, and where you start to climb again up a bank the path becomes clearer. Now follow the clear vehicular track, climbing steeply, circling round the left-hand side of a small plantation ahead up the steepening slope. This is a stiff climb for a while, and good reason for a pause - in which case you may look for the bulky mass of Great Whernside seen just E of N: for height, it comes in the Three Peaks category. Nearer at hand, the craggy outcrops on the summit ridge are extensive, and the cross at (982576) is very obvious. Above the plantation, continue along the track (the general direction is ESE): follow it to a gate, pass through and keep straight on. A gully comes in from the left, then following a right-left kink in the track - now very clear - you are nearly at the top of the rise. Spare a moment for retrospection: on a clear day, the view in the Western arc is wonderful! Your eye may scan round, clockwise, from Boulsworth and the South Pennine heights to Pendle, Longridge Fell, the Parlick-Fair Snape-Totridge group, White Hill with other Bowland heights and (by now NW) Ingleborough's summit, with Simon Fell. It could almost call for photo-montage. Pendle, fifteen miles distant, looks its grandest, a tent-shaped profile.

The summit of the path, around the 1200ft. contour, then affords a pleasant promenade on a good track, with extensive plantations (Crookwise) partly seen on the right. Go on through an open gateway in a fence, after which the route is not quite so palpable but still a definite ginnel track. Following a gap in a wall, the route turns to North of East, with waymarker posts: still easy going, and generally firm underfoot. One must again question whether the boards used at one point for footpath repairs were strictly necessary. There are plenty of grouse butts hereabouts, though on my visits - admittedly, generally out of season - I have seen few of the birds. In Spring, however, you might find these heathery moors alive with their sight and sound.

After crossing the second of two small stream courses, your direction has changed to SE: then comes a parish boundary, still marked by two massive stone posts. Watch carefully now for your turning point, about 200yds. further on, where you reach a much clearer, vehicular track. Turn sharp right here (viz. through about 135 degrees), where the straight on track would take you to Barden Tower and other Wharfedale destinations. This part of the route is not actually a right of way, though it appears a well-walked track; a sign says "No Cycling" - well, suffice it to say there are certainly mountain bikers to be seen on the through bridleway. Here is another controversial topic, I know. In some areas, notably Snowdonia, mountain bikes have been officially banned for some time. While I accept that they cause more surface damage than walkers, I still feel the problem has been exaggerated: ask yourself, how much more damage (and permanent!) is caused by laying just one mile of new motorway? Don't keep slating those who come to the countryside for recreation: the real threat to the environment comes from other quarters. There is also a matter of definition: are the National Parks truly for national recreation, or are we going to start qualifying the invitation in all kinds of ways?

But enough of this, let's just enjoy the walk for now. Soon you pass an elaborate shooting butt on your right, then turn more left with the track, crossing a little stream and doubling back. Climb gently to the summit of East Harts Hill, still with good views to the West but restricted at first to the East. Once you start to lose height, the path steadily becomes quite faint: an impressive (bird's eye) view of Skipton opens up to the South, with another rash of windmills intrusively obvious in the SE. A faint tread remains visible, but in thick weather a bearing just W of S (190 degrees) could be advisable. When you reach two well-built stone cairns, keep the same line, ignoring a more obvious track turning away to the left.

Soon, in clear weather, Embsay reservoir becomes visible below, with dinghy sails possibly adding a splash of colour. Descend more steeply, aiming for the right-hand edge: quarries are now in view to the East. Continue the steep descent through bracken, cross a little gully, and meet a definite E-W track at the bottom by a wall. It's too late to do much about it now, but - the retrospective sign says, forbiddingly, "No Dogs Allowed". Turn right, go over a stile, then turn left and go past the reservoir. Another board here gives access information, and a sign says "Bridleway-Embsay Kirk and Crag Access Area". You might be more interested in watching the boats for a few minutes.

Beyond the reservoir dam the lane becomes a rough road, bending left then right. Pass two lanes leading away right, to Intake Farm and Oddacres, then (and this may deceive, as we want to turn right eventually) turn *left* at the crossroads ahead, now joining a metalled road. Just before reaching a millpond, turn right at a footpath sign saying "None Go Bye" - the intriguing name of a farm on the Skipton-Grassington road which we shall pass later. Squeeze through a stone stoop, then cross a stile, soon turning half right over a stile and footbridge where I remember seeing a spotted flycatcher.

Go up to and through a gate, then pass round the back of the farm buildings and over a stile ("Footpath" board). The path has recently been diverted here, but clear signs leave no doubt of the route. Keep on past some outbuildings and go through a small gate in a wall, with a shed adjacent on the right. Squeeze through here, and keep roughly the same line - just S of W - through the fields ahead, climbing two stiles, the first being waymarked. These are pleasant green pastures, still commanding good views, notably of Sharp Haw seen ahead hereabouts.

Wayfinding remains, pro tem, beguilingly simple. Pass through an open gateway, and ahead keep left (South) of Oddacres Farm and Clark House, then pass through a further gate (which shut). Keep on the same line, through another gate (footpath sign) in the next wall, then a simple stone stile in the wall following.

The next field is a considerably longer one, allowing you to admire once again an excellent view of Pendle in the SW. Cross the next wall using stone steps, then turn a little right. Intake Farm is clearly seen now, away on the right below the steep wooded slopes of Crookrise Crag. Keep your wits about you now: there may be an electric fence to bypass hereabouts. Cross a simple wall-corner stile, and keep close to the wall on the right in the next field. After a gap in the fence, you pass a ruined outbuilding, and there is a pond on your left not given by the OS.

Go over a plain wooden stile, then over stone steps in the next wall as you approach Hagg Farm. Pass between the new and old outbuildings, then drop left a little and go through a gate below the house. After going through an open gap in a wall, you approach the Skipton-Grassington railway on your left, now used only to service the quarries up around Cracoe.

Go through a gate bearing a yellow marker "C27C", a legend which will appear on many subsequent markers. Here old 1:25,000 OS maps may be out of date: formerly the path crossed the railway, but since December 1990 it has been diverted (a sign explains all this). Hence keep on to the right of the railway, over a stile, with the B6265 road now close on your left beyond the permanent way.

Trend slightly right, passing through a gateway in a wall (signs point both ways). Ahead, cross a little stream on a slab footbridge, then go over stone steps in a wall by a gate (signs). Now we really do go down to the railway, over a stile and an official pedestrian level crossing. Continue along the rough track to the road at None-Go-Bye farm, bending left before the farm itself: a footpath sign at the end says "Embsay". Here we turn right and go along the Skipton-Grassington road for about three-quarters of a mile. This is not an attractive prospect in high summer, but there is no sensible alternative: a sign up the road reminds walkers that the Crookwise woods are out of bounds. As a much longer alternative, you might consider turning *left* along the road to point (978542), thence joining the bridleway to the Flasby fells: they are, I repeat, well worth exploring in their own right.

Still, it's not too far along the road! Cross the railway again, then very shortly leave the road by a shady lane on the right: a sign, almost lost in the hedgerow, gives "Rylstone 1¾m". Cross Sandy Beck, then pass the attractive cottage of the same name, proceeding along the lane through a gate into more open surroundings. A clear track ensues, mercifully quiet after the road, in a park-like setting; the summit of Rough Haw cuts a shapely figure on your left, beyond the road. When you reach a wall with stone steps, ignore them, keeping to the right with the track. Rock formations on the skyline ahead will again be seen: the OS also indicates prehistoric sites hereabouts ('Pillow Mounds'). Turn more to the left.

Soon the track becomes faint, but simply keep by the wall on the left. After passing through a gate, trend right, now climbing slightly, soon going up by the wall on the right. The wall bends left, then drops to a combined large-and-small gate with a Yorkshire Dales National Park sign. Passing through, you are suddenly on a very clear vehicular track again, and the outward route is rejoined in about 200yds. by the access area board. Just down the lane you reach the stile crossed earlier.

Here you may simply retrace your outward route exactly, returning *via* Rylstone church and manor house, or turn left with the lane. This reaches the 'B' road again in a quarter-mile, with bridleway and footpath signs to Halton Height and Sandy Beck Bar. Pass through the gate (Rylstone's neighbouring village of Hetton is well seen from here) and turn right down the road, reaching Rylstone in a further quarter-mile. A simple but enjoyable circuit with good views on offer, and an interesting contrast to the other routes in this book.

If you have become quite converted to the Dales as a result, you may soon be getting immersed in the Malham area, upper Wharfedale or the Three Peaks! None of them is too far away from here. But do give the remainder of this book a try first, won't you?

12. PENDLE BYWAYS

Downham, Ravens Holme, Twiston Moor, Clough Head, Ings End, Rimington, Ings Beck, Downham. 8 miles. Maps: OS 1:50,000 Landranger no.103; OS 1:25,000 Explorer OL 41 (Forest of Bowland); "Paths Around Pendle" (see Walk 3).

Alternatives: A whole network of paths may be explored in this area. One pleasant short circuit based on our main route is outlined: from Hecklin Farm (804435), drop downhill and follow the circling path which crosses Ings Beck, then rises to Hill Foot Cottages, Twiston. Go downhill again, emerging onto Twiston Lane adjacent to the dam at Twiston Mill. Turn right along the road, reach the mill and again take a path near the stream (Twiston Beck). This path presently reaches the confluence of Twiston and Ings Beck at (803449); turn down the main stream, shortly rejoining the main route. About four miles.

* * * * * * * * *

Background

Getting a bit overwhelmed by these lengthening walks? Take heart, here is an easier circuit, with a built-in alternative that would make an ideal summer evening stroll. We remain very definitely in the province of Pendle, whose influence spreads far and wide hereabouts, but the views are extensive, even from this shorter and lower route. From Twiston Moor and the vicinity of Clough Head, there are superb vistas of the Yorkshire Dales and Three Peaks area on a clear day. The villages, too, each having its own character (strictly Twiston is the name of the area of a parish, not of a village), add much to the interest of the walk.

Those who are not yet familiar with Downham, and may have omitted the opportunity to visit it during the Pendle expedition (Walk 3) can rectify the omission now. Downham is a real gem, unspoilt and carefully kept, as befits an estate village. As ever, one or two little changes have crept in over the years, but it is precisely the unchanging feel of the village which gives it its special charm, now rightly recognised well beyond the borders of Lancashire. I cannot imagine walking into the village without seeing children feeding the ducks by the bridge at the bottom of the main village street. Rimington makes an interesting contrast: much less well known, but attractive too in its own way, the long and open village street giving it a noticeably spacious feeling. A hymn tune takes its name after the village, the composer having lived nearby.* Those whose taste in clothing lies towards the exclusive will surely have visited Cosgroves, in the village centre, already. I should keep the two things separate, though. A walk-round of the shop by a horde of mud-bespattered walkers would hardly be welcomed.

Geographically, the walk explores the northern fringes of the ridge leading away NE from Pendle which terminates in Weets Hill, together with some of the charming stream-courses that have their origins there. Although it is of no great length, the walk should not be underestimated! These Pendle byways include a good deal of up and down, with minor ridges, many subsidiary hills, hidden hollows and steep-sided cloughs - adding greatly to the interest of the walk, but testing for the leg muscles. Perhaps the shorter circuit should be undertaken first!

The Walk
The obvious starting point is the car park in Downham village, just off the Worston road (West Lane). Do allow yourself time for a leisurely exploration of the village, including the church, either before or after the walk. To begin the latter, cross the bridge over Downham Brook at the lower end of the main street and walk up the narrow lane running roughly parallel to Pendle Road, keeping to the right of the brook. The village, incidentally, is curiously deficient in footpath signs - a conscious policy? At the end of the lane, pass through a narrow stone stoop into the field beyond and keep the stream close on your left initially, but trend more to the right where the stream bends more definitely left. You soon reach a hedge/fence where a branch of the stream crosses it (a fair tread is visible now). Cross a stile here, then go up with the stream on your left and climb a more demanding stile.

(Actually, Francis Duckworth lived at Stopper Lane.)

Walk 12: Pendle Byways

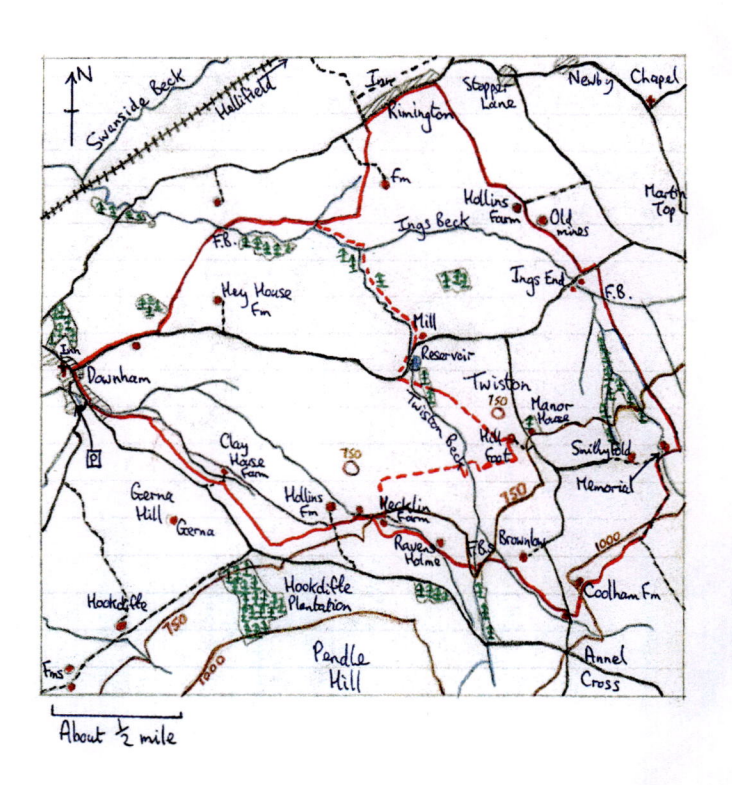

Downham from the Barley Road

Ahead, the stream runs through a pleasant shallow dell, but the route has significantly altered. Actually the new path is easier to follow, with good new stiles and clear waymarkers. We stay to the right of the stream, and well to the right of the farm ahead (Clay House), presently crossing the farm road which leads back to the Downham - Barley road to your right. Ahead the Hookcliffe plantation can be seen, across a bend of the road, with the slopes of Pendle soaring up massively behind, terminating in the summit plateau. Parties of fieldfares may be seen in these upland pastures in winter.

Eventually you cross stone steps in a wall, then turn sharp left in front of a barn, reaching a junction of paths in a little dip with the road still near on your right. Go straight on, climbing slightly, still roughly parallel to the road, and rejoining the old path.

Presently locate stone steps (not obvious from afar) in a wall crossing your route and climb over, then cross the lane to Hollins farm, keeping the same line subsequently. Contour with a fence on your left at first, and enjoy the longer prospects into parts of Bowland now opening up in the Northern arc. Dip slightly, crossing a wall by stone steps, and keep left in the next field with a little copse adjacent. Once past an outbuilding, trend more to the right, then approach Hecklin farm with a striking view of Weets Hill ahead. Hecklin, like Ravens Holme beyond, is an interesting historic building as evinced by the stone mullions.

Turn right here, then circle round the farm buildings (again the path has been altered here) shortly reaching a line of trees behind the farm. Here turn right and resume your earlier W-E line. Keep the ditch (later, fence) on your left, turning steadily to the right, eventually passing in front of Ravens Holme, then turning left through a gate. Ahead, a unique footpath sign on a tyre directs you to turn right up the farm lane: after passing a few trees, leave the lane, turning left by a wall. The 'Big End' of Pendle is about a mile distant here, not so much close as positively threatening.

Drop steeply to a footbridge in a beautiful little wooded valley (Pendle Hill Brook). Beyond there is a visible tread, initially left up the rather muddy bank, then turning right through a gap. Once atop the bank, keep left initially, then turn right by a line of trees and a pronounced dyke. A further stream valley is soon reached: go upstream past a fine little waterfall, then between outbuildings, and drop left to cross a footbridge. Go slightly up the bank (for easier progress), then turn right, upstream.

The "Paths Around Pendle" map indicates the remains of an old mill hereabouts - it is easy to see the probable location, on a little plateau near the stream (Red Syke). Beyond another waterfall, get atop the bank and cross a wall by stone steps, going along a faint tread through a gap in the next wall. From here you may observe a curious knobble on the generally smooth slopes of Pendle, which will surprise many who thought they knew the hill well.

Keep to the left of the buildings ahead - also of appreciable age - and climb stone steps onto the road. Turn right, towards the crossroads on the wide open spaces of Annel Cross Moor.

The original cross no longer exists, but a guide stone at the very intersection of routes may be part of the shaft. Our route, however, turns left off the road well before the crossroads, just by the buildings on the right. Take the left hand gate of the two and go up a rough farm lane, turning left: on reaching Coolham, turn right into a field, going up with a wall on your left. When you reach a wall junction, turn left over a stone stile at the summit of the walk.

This is a good point for a break (there should be shelter, one side or other!), and for appreciation of the far-flung views from this upland spot. The aspect of the views has changed as we turn away from Pendle, and there are long vistas into Bowland and the Dales, as well as miles of pleasing Ribble Valley greenery closer at hand. To proceed, keep the wall well on your right and proceed in a general NE direction through thick, reedy pasture, quite rough underfoot. You should reach a lane exactly at a sharp turn: cross stone steps (awkward) and go left, down the lane.

Turn left again with the lane, downhill by another pleasantly wooded, steep valley. At the T-junction, turn right down a narrow metalled lane, reaching Clough Head over a bridge. Note the imposing memorial on the left to the family of Thomas Bulcock, transposed from Downham churchyard. By-pass the very neat, well-kept house, going through the yard and a gate following, then crossing a field to a high wall. Cross stone steps in the latter, then turn sharp left and go straight down the field. The next section is perfectly simple but perhaps the most enjoyable of the whole walk, strolling down the easy pasture with a glorious prospect of the Three Peaks area and a wide sweep of the Dales ahead when clear.

Keep the wall (or hedge) close on your left, going over a stone stile in a wall and, further down, a simple wooden stile. Locate and cross a footbridge in the dip below, then trend slightly left in the next field. Cross a stile and aim for a short walled section seen in the hedge ahead and cross it by stone steps, a Public Footpath sign adjacent. Turn briefly left down the road (Skeleron Lane), but when you reach a building on the left turn right over a simple wooden stile (no sign here). Proceed along an obvious grooved track, passing a quarry on the right with the early stages of the Ings Beck valley, already attractive, on the left. Go over a stile by an old mineworking* and descend towards Hollins Farm, crossing a stile opposite the building on the extreme right. Cross the farm lane and another stile, then go through a little enclosure and over a stile onto a leafy 'green lane'.

Ahead, an outbuilding has been turned into a most attractive conversion. Turn left through a field before the house (signed), cross a rough lane coming from the house and go straight across over a stile. You reach a clear tread beyond: go straight on (left) at an apparent fork, past a reedy pond and over a stile.

*(William Pudsay, a 16th century lord of Bolton Hall (see Walk 13) is believed to have used metal mined here in minting his own currency).

The easy-going pastoral feel continues as we follow a clear tread through the meadow towards Rimington, passing scattered trees then turning left and emerging at a gate onto the main street (a sign gives "Public Footpath Twiston") - there is also a Forest of Bowland waymarker here, always incongruous to my eyes in this Pendle province.

Turn left and walk up the pleasant main village street, but make a mental note to visit Stopper Lane, Newby and Martin Top in the other direction when you return to these parts: all delightful settlements in their own right. You pass the Black Bull and the aforementioned Cosgroves, receiving quizzical glances, no doubt, if the conditions have made your appearance dishevelled. Opposite Station Road, a right turn at the end of the village, turn left over a waymarked stile. The station at Rimington is long disused, but the Clitheroe-Hellifield line on which it stands still provides an important back-up week-end route to the West Coast main line, as well as a route for Dales Rail.

Take a diagonal tread through the field ahead, cross the lane once reached and go over a stile to the left of the gate opposite. This is noted as a courtesy footpath to Twiston Mill and Downham, and we must be grateful to local ramblers for their efforts here. Turn half right and go slightly uphill, then over another waymarked stile. Ahead, climb and cross the field diagonally to a top corner stile; cross this and turn right. The Twiston Mill path diverges here. You approach Ings Beck, but keep to the right of it, dropping down a bank and then keeping a fence on your left before crossing a wooden stile (quite tricky) over a side stream.

The maps suggest the path runs some distance from the stream, but the tread on the ground obviously follows it closely. Certainly it's a lovely secluded valley, one which I have often walked in the gloaming as things have worked out. A sizeable fir wood on the far bank is passed: after crossing a flat area, with a house visible atop the bank on your side (right), look out for a footbridge and cross it. We are actually less than a mile from

Downham now, and on most days the temptation to linger at this spot will be great.

Once over, climb the bank, aiming half right: a fence converges from your left, then pass through a primitive gate ahead. Turn left now, uphill but keeping away from the fence on your left. Ahead you encounter new field divisions and a slight re-routing of the path, but with waymarkers and new stiles the route-finding is actually easier than before. Turn right, crossing a fence by a stile, then go uphill and locate the next stile in a crossing fence. Keep climbing in roughly the same direction, aiming for an isolated tree to the right in the crossing fence above. On reaching the fence, turn along it to the right (and recover your breath), then turn left with the fence. In a few yards you cross the line of a Roman road emanating from Bremetennacum (Ribchester).

Ahead, there has been restoration of an apparently disused old footpath. Ignore a gate and then stone steps on your left; simply turn half right, observing a new waymarker and following a hedge. Keep the hedge on your left now and go down the field, as per "Paths Around Pendle", presently emerging over a firm, new, waymarked stile onto the Downham-Twiston road. Turn right here; a few more minutes of road-walking will return you to Downham, entering between the old vicarage and the post-office, the latter offering both welcome refreshment and accommodation.

Turn down the main village street, left, to return to the car park. Time now, perhaps, to complete your exploration of the village with the silent monolith of Pendle watching your every move. To be honest, I have known a few people who were unimpressed by Downham, but I suspect the vast majority will, like me, drive away at the end of each visit with more than a twinge of regret.

13. HOUSES IN THE COUNTRY

Sawley, Bolton-by-Bowland, Forest Becks, Anna Lane Head, Lane Ends, Harrop Fold, Beacon Hill, Sawley. 12 miles. Maps: OS 1:50,000 Landranger no. 103; OS 1:25,000 Explorer OL no.41

<u>Alternative</u>: The section of the Ribble up-river from Sawley is a particularly attractive stretch of the Ribble Way, including the so-called 'Pudsay's Leap'. Unfortunately this is, at the time of writing, out of bounds to the walker. Should it re-open . . . You may follow the path to Gisburn (about 4 miles), returning either by arranged transport - noting that there are buses from Gisburn - or on foot, using the easy back lanes and paths.

* * * * * * * * * *

<u>Background</u>

Most of us, I suspect, have had daydreams about our 'ideal home'. Quite likely it would be in some idyllic country location, away from the hustle and bustle, with views of hill and dale, wood and river. Indeed, one of the fringe benefits of walking is that you are likely to come across many places and buildings on your travels, which can fuel such speculations. Here's a deserted farm, or maybe an old wayside house, or even a large barn . . . seen with imaginative eyes, they can easily become your cosy retirement home. Certainly there are a large number of most attractive conversions on view these days, and the Ribble Valley and Pendle country boast their fair share. Why not join them? After all, it only calls for planning permission, determination - oh yes, and the money.

To add that the reality is not quite so simple is probably superfluous. Living miles from anywhere brings its own logistic problems, such as the village shop for that extra loaf you need being miles away, with the nearest school and doctor's surgery being further still. Then again, in times of heavy snowfall, who's going to clear your vital country lane, the only link to the outside world? Still, a little dreaming does no harm.

On today's walk, ranging from the Ribble Valley into sparsely populated tracts of the Forest of Bowland, a whole range of houses will be passed, from fine hotels and restaurants to lonely farms, charming old roadside houses and stone cottages in quiet, unspoilt villages. Giving another dimension to the idea of a House, we shall also be treading ground formerly trodden by the House of Lancaster, in the shape of the unfortunate King Henry VI. As to the walk, it is quite a long and varied one, including a fair pull up to Beacon Hill over roughish terrain, though much of the way runs along straightforward field paths and quiet lanes, with some pleasant riverside strolling thrown in. Beacon Hill is in fact a fine and neglected viewpoint. We stay within the Ribble catchment area, including that of Tosside Beck, a major tributary, though in the lonely uplands above Lane Ends the Hodder catchment is near. Quite a demanding walk, but a satisfying one. The alternative (I write now in the hope of its reopening one day) is a very different character of walk, including delightful river scenery, but though I can certainly recommend it too, I would feel guilty of plagiarism if I described it in detail!

The Walk

Begin in Sawley, by a long graceful bend of the Ribble. Here, you may say, is our first house of the day, namely the Spread Eagle Hotel. While, in the famous phrase, it is not my business to advertise any particular establishment, I have to admit a great fondness for this place: the English Tourist Board's four-star rating is well deserved, and the lovely riverside situation gives the place a special character. Incidentally, there is a dramatic view of Penyghent from here on clear days, looking right up the Ribble valley. Do not abuse the Hotel's kindness by using their reserved parking area (unless of course you intend to remove your muddy boots later and sample the cuisine): there is normally adequate parking along the railings by the river, *away* from the main road, where the lane is wide and lightly used. You may well like to explore the abbey ruins, back along the village street. Sawley (Salley) Abbey was a Cistercian community, founded in 1148.

Walk 13: Houses in The Country

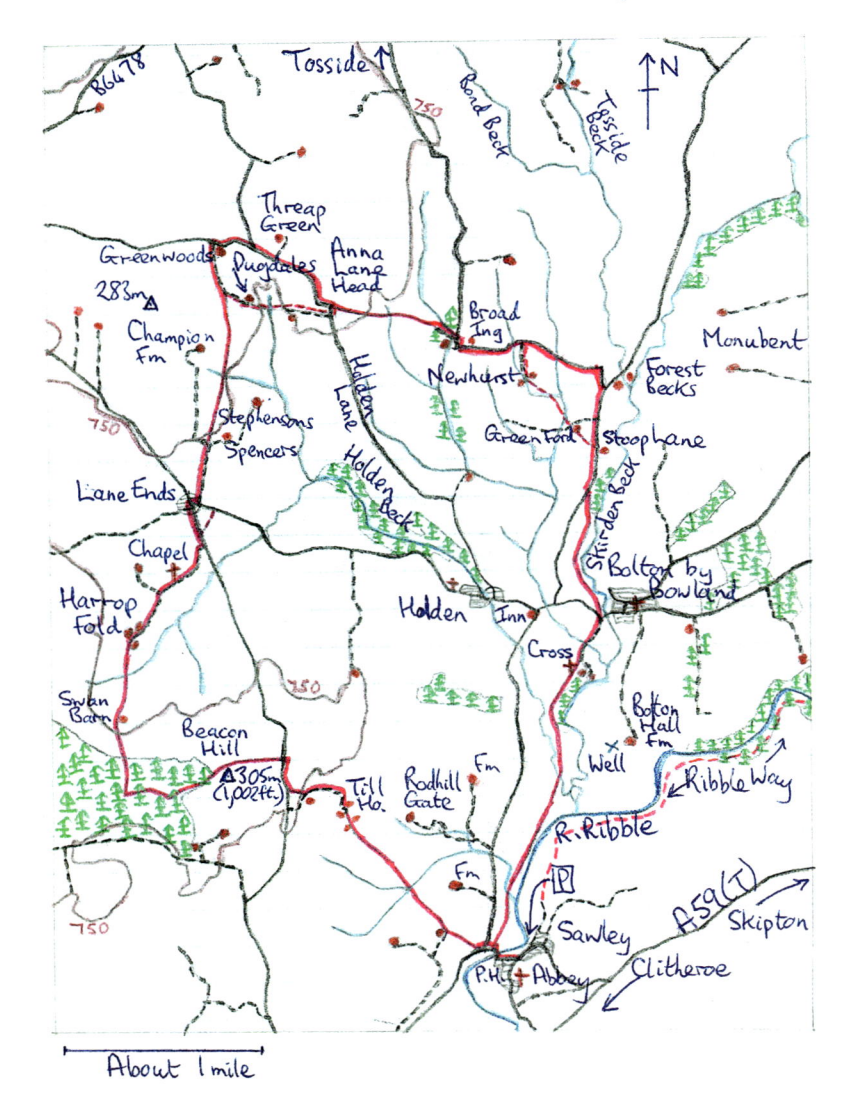

Ribble at Sawley

Walk down the Grindleton road alongside the Ribble and then cross the bridge before entering the field on your right, where the footpath to Bolton-by-Bowland is clearly signed. You may have already seen interesting wild life by this time, for in addition to the more usual water birds I have seen common sandpiper here, and there may be redshank on passage in the adjacent meadows. Keep close to the hedge on your left initially as you cross the river's extensive flood plain. To the East, the wooded hillside behind the village makes a most attractive backdrop. Cross a stile adjacent to a gate, noting a barn to your left by the roadside, and initially keep the same line in the next field. A sign says "Follow White Stones": initially this looks mysterious, but the first one is encountered in about 50 yards.

Cross a footbridge over a little runnel: the white stones then come into their own, guiding you on a half right line over the pasture until you meet the Ribble at a long right bend. Note that this meadow is prone to water-logging in wet spells - in which case keep left and circle round. This is a most impressive stretch of the river, much frequented by anglers who may have to compete with herons. A fine view downstream leads the eye to Pendle, and upstream lies the 'Pudsay's Leap' section. Some of the banks here have been used by sand martin colonies for nesting sites. Yes, there is good reason to linger at this spot! But on we go, the walk still very much in its early stages. Cross a stile and keep near the river initially, then trend left over another stile, leaving the river and keeping the same line in the field ahead. Locate a stile in a fence among isolated trees, with a house on the left, then continue over some wet ground, again turning left and circling if need be, crossing a much improved footbridge over Holden Beck. Go over a stile immediately, then turn sharp left along the fence.

The feel of the environs changes markedly here as we enter the grounds of the old Bolton Hall, demolished around the turn of the 19th century, with a spacious park-like feel and many stately old trees. A branching path, now closed, formerly went off right here, fording Skirden Beck and aiming for Bolton Hall Farm, on the site of the old hall which was the seat of the Pudsays for centuries. It was here that the fugitive King Henry VI was sheltered after the Lancastrians' defeat at the battle of Hexham in 1464, one obvious sign on the map being the legend "King Henry's Well" applied to a spring in the grounds. The tragic King, who succeeded in 1421 as an infant, a man of courtesy and belief, but afflicted by mental illness and quite lacking in the steel required of a monarch in such turbulent days - stayed in these parts for about a year until his apprehension by the Yorkists. Direct royal associations with this area are few, and the story is an intriguing one: you can read more in Ron Freethy's book "The River Ribble".

On this particular walk we pass straight on, over a waymarked stile, with a glimpse of Bolton-by-Bowland church visible through a gap in the trees on the right. Continue on a clear tread, go through an iron kissing gate and trend towards the wood on the right, possibly through heavy going. Turn more to the right, then cross a corner-stile (waymarked in reverse). Keep the same line in the following field, next crossing a stile in a fence away from the field edge. Go slightly uphill, aming for what appears to be a stone trough by an isolated oak, but when reached proves to be the base of an old cross, as noted on the map: in these parts wayside crosses are fairly common. The wooded cliff seen on the right is an impressive feature. Proceed downhill now, turning slightly left, and cross a stone stile (signed) onto a lane, following it to the left.

In about a quarter-mile you reach a road, with Bolton-by-Bowland immediately to your right, over Skirden Bridge. If you are not yet acquainted with Bolton, you should certainly take time out to become so: it's a lovely unspoilt village, with a number of interesting old buildings, and the church has its own strong associations with that Henry VI story and the Pudsays. This walk continues straight across, however, over a stile (new Public Footpath sign here) and goes up with the beck on your right. Climb the low bank to your left, then return to the beck, over a corner stile and continuing initially atop the first level of a double bank. Skirden Beck is a typical stream of these parts, brisk and clear, and has its own stream birds such as heron and wagtail.

Climb to the upper level and cross a stile, with now a fine high level prospect of the beck. After the next corner stile, turn more inland: the beck turns away to the right here, but the path stays close to the hedge on the right, above what is now a steep bank. Drop slightly and cross a stile, with a small spring on the right: in the next field, keep the same line at first, then trend slightly left over a stile. Ahead, you pass through an overgrown area, then over a stile onto a road by a reassuring new footpath sign with Oaktrees Nurseries adjacent.

Turn right up the road, which is usually fairly quiet but once formed the route of the Clitheroe-Settle bus service. After a few minutes' stroll past pleasant hedgerows you reach Stoop Lane, a handsome and attractively renovated property (dating from 1703) set in a beautiful garden. From here I have usually proceeded by road, but you may like to try a path leaving on the left, opposite the house. This is a signed path, but appears to have gone to seed: it passes through two outlying farms, Green Ford and Newhurst, before rejoining the road route. See the supplementary notes at the end.

The road is certainly not unpleasant here, however, and on a longish day it will provide easier going. Beyond Stoop Lane, continue N for about a quarter-mile to a junction (Clitheroe 7, Settle 9) just before the pleasant hamlet of Forest Becks. Turn left along a very quiet, unsigned, narrow road headed ultimately for Tosside. The junction, with a raised concrete platform (once for milk churns?) offers a reasonable stopping-place. The lane itself is leafy and peaceful, seemingly a long way from the usual walkers' country. Pendle is still dominant in the South, and as height is gradually gained Wheathead and Weets Hill also show well. The field path from Stoop Lane (now signed) is passed in half a mile from the junction, then we continue to climb past the very remote cottage at Broad Ing, recently treated to major restoration. Soon the road turns sharp right in a wooded section; in a further fifty yards, turn left off the road down a shady track through the trees - a bridlepath, now signed. I once surprised a fox along here.

The way here is generally rather muddy, but perfectly clear. In a few hundred yards you pass through a gate and emerge from the wood, then keep by a fence-cum-hedge on the right, continuing to climb. The reward for gaining altitude soon comes, with a sudden prospect of Penyghent, Fountains Fell and the Cracoe fells in the N to NE arc. Indeed the character of the walk has quite changed, as we have entered breezy, open high pastures. Bend left with the track, crossing a runnel (Bleara Syke) in a dip, then go very slightly left through a gate not indicated on the OS. Keep the hedge on your right: the Waddington Fells now bulk large in the view to your left. Ahead, pass through a gate onto a rough lane, soon reaching the road at the lonely Anna Lane Head.

Here again, you could investigate the field path via Veepings and Dugdales, reached by first turning left along the road (Holden Lane). There is little or no evidence of current use, however: as I said earlier, these parts have been generally by-passed by the walker. (Again, see the supplementary notes if interested.) Take heart, though, the main route is cast-iron! Turn right from Anna Lane Head: the road offers a fine high-level route, with a view of the Bowland Fells ahead and a sense of spacious remoteness. The detached house at Threap Green, passed on the right, offers self-catering accommodation! Truly an away-from-it-all spot for relaxation. Turn left at a crossroads just beyond, signed "Slaidburn 3, Trough of Bowland 8". Pass Greenwoods Farm on your left at the apogee of the walk, then take a bridleway - signed at last! - immediately after the buildings.

Proceed along a clear track initially, past the farm and through two gateways. Though not the highest point of the walk, this is a haunting spot, with far-flung vistas and true solitude. Here I was once entertained by several late summer swallows skimming over the adjacent pastures. Where the obvious track bends left for Dugdales, keep straight on by the side of a fence (right) and go on through a gate. Only a faint tread shows now in the lush pasture. After another gate, our later objective, Beacon Hill, becomes prominent ahead, Pendle to its left. Begin to lose height now, and after one more gate watch carefully. Ignore steps on the right (a branching path): descend instead to the N-S flowing stream, then go up through a little gate, keeping the same direction ahead ("Past Lane" on the OS). After a sequence of two metal gates, keep to the right of the wall ahead; Harrop Fold can be seen now, ahead and below. At the end of this field, pass through a small metal gate in the left corner where in winter the field is often waterlogged, then go down with a row of hawthorns on the right.

You soon join the farm lane from Spencers, which should be followed, easily, South to the road, where there is another bridleway sign. Turn right, entering the hamlet of Lane Ends almost immediately. On your right is the local community centre, once the village school which boasted its own bus service from Bolton by Bowland. At the junction, turn left (signed Harrop Fold 1) down another quiet, tree-lined road. No-one seems to be about in these parts. Here I was once joined by a party of long-tailed tits, foraging in the roadside greenery.

Very soon, turn right off the road down what is initially a metalled surface (signed Harrop Fold ¾), though also a walkers' right of way. Pass on through Harrop Gate farmyard on a zig-zag course, then past the remarkably situated Harrop Chapel, an independent chapel, still used for divine worship. The long anticipated Harrop Fold proper is next: for many years this was a guest house with an English Tourist Board four-star rating, and developed a reputation far beyond the local district. Now it is again a private house, and for tranquillity both it and the nearby properties could hardly be better placed. Observe the route through the grounds carefully: pass through a waymarked wooden gate adjoining the Manor House, then follow a clear track, turning off left through a metal gate (also marked). Keep close to the wall on your right in the pasture ahead. The distant views are still good down here, particularly NE to the Dales. Further on, pass through a gateway on the right, aiming for the isolated landmark of Swan Barn: go through a waymarked gate to its right.

A stiffish pull ensues up the rough, reedy pasture ahead: quite cruel, coming late in the day! Aim diagonally for the wall on the left, on a faint intermittent tread, nearing the plantation above. At the top, ignore the high wall stile on the left, but you will be glad to admire the splendid retrospect, particularly in the N to ENE sector with Ingleborough, Penyghent and Fountains Fell standing out nobly. Go through a gap in the wall at the top (waymarked), near the left corner. With the plantation now straight ahead, turn sharp left and cross a stile at (745482): the 1:25,000 OS misleads here, probably a result of forestry operations. Go up on a clear tread by the side of the forest, with a wall on your left, then turn right when you see a waymarker, going through a rough felled area with the plantation still on your right. Cross two stiles in fences, both marked, then turn sharp left alongside another afforested area. Climb up a clear track between walls, given the splendid name of Shivering Ginnel by the OS.

In about 300 yards cross a stile and take the left fork at a path division. Route-finding becomes easier now as you near the summit of the walk. Climb steadily, turning slightly left between walls, first crossing a stile then going through a wall-gap. The trig.point on Beacon Hill is now a very short detour on your right, and though not strictly legal perhaps, it does offer an excellent panorama, with many places visited in these pages on view. Pendle looms large and detailed in the SE, and you may get a glimpse of the sea in the far west.

Continue in a roughly NE line, keeping the wall on your left and losing a little height now. Bend right a little over rough ground, proceeding with a fence now on your right. Here I was once fortunate enough to see a sizeable charm of goldfinches, two dozen perhaps, no doubt attracted by the thistles and other weeds hereabouts: an outburst of tinkling high song and a brilliant splash of yellow and white, lighting up a dull autumn afternoon. Cross a stile, the fence still on your right, passing a covered reservoir just before reaching a gate onto the Lane Ends - Grindleton road (wooden public footpath sign). Turn right and proceed downhill for about 300 yards.

At point (758479), turn left off the road through a gate adjoining a sign, "Public Footpath Sawley". Go down the field with a hedge on your left, reach the bottom left corner and cross a simple wooden stile onto a metalled lane opposite a house. Turn initially left, then sharp right down the lane, keeping on over a cattle grid. Follow the lane as it bends right then down through Till House, ignoring branching paths. After a left-right zig-zag, keep on below Till House and over another cattle grid (waymarker here), approaching the last house in the lane. Follow waymarkers to the left of the buildings, over a stile into a garden annexe, then turn right, passing the house and keep on over a stile. Once beyond the house turn further left into a paddock area - you may well meet a horse here! You will welcome the sight of journey's end now, namely the valley greenery and graceful curve of the Ribble below you.

Cross the paddock diagonally to the opposite corner and over another stile, waymarked on the far side, after which route-finding becomes much simpler. Go straight down the long field ahead, adjacent to a fence-cum-hedge on your right initially, then turn slightly left over another waymarked stile. Keep the same line at first, then trend slightly right, crossing a footbridge over a pleasant small stream in the dip. Once across, turn left over a stile in a hedge almost at once (white disc here) and go uphill - courage, it's the last climb of the day! - through a green pasture. Aim for two isolated trees at the top of the rise: here is a clear double sign ("Rodhill-Sawley") and a board. At certain times of year - particularly when the cattle are grazing - your ingenuity and nerves may be taxed by having to negotiate one or two single-strand electric wire fences here. Beyond the Ribble is in view once more.

The way is now downhill again, gently at first to a right angle of fences, then down with the fence on your right. A white disc again confirms the way here. Cross a corner stile at the bottom of this field, with Sawley and the Ribble palpably close, below and left. Keep the same line past Acreland on your right, noting another disc and remaining atop a little bank. A new fence (clearly signed) has appeared here, with a stile, keeping the walker close to the stream on the right. Go through a rapidly-growing copse, among dense vegetation and possibly heavy going underfoot. On reaching a gate, pass through onto a clear track with houses left and right below. Instinctively one feels a little nervous about (as it appears) walking through someone's back garden, as happened earlier near Till House, but be assured this is correct.

You quickly emerge onto a lane, passing a Friends' Meeting House (right), and in about a hundred yards this joins the Sawley-Grindleton road by a modest Public Footpath sign. Turn left, then right at the road junction and rejoin the outward route at Sawley Bridge in a few yards, ending your long walk in tranquility by the Ribble once more.

Yes, quite a patchwork of a walk! Again, there are a number of variations and off-route places to explore on other days. The theme of country houses, though, does give a unity to this walk, for although remote in one sense these parts are all lived in: here there is not the isolation of the heart of Bowland, we are on the fringe. It will have its own considerable attraction for town dwellers, though, and on returning you may already have that ideal home lined up.

Alternatives to roadwalking sections

As noted in the text, there are two possibilities, commencing at Stoop Lane and Anna Lane Head. Both are apparently little used and will be found more enjoyable during dry weather.

1. From the house at Stoop Lane, take the footpath sign opposite, going through a gate, then turning half right through the field ahead. Beyond a slight rise, you approach Green Ford farm (this meadow may be very wet) and presently pass through a small wooden gate in a wall. Pass between outbuildings, through the farmyard, emerging half right through a metal gate. Cross a concrete bridge over a stream, then keep roughly the same line, leaving the stream and locate a simple wooden stile in the hedge ahead. You reach a little stream: turn briefly left up it, then ford it and cross another stile.

Turn half right in the next field, crest a rise and approach Newhurst farm. Here an attractive new building has been added on the far right. Dip towards a track by the stream, pass through a metal gate and swing right through the farmyard. Join the farm lane to the right of the main building and go up this rough track to join the road in about 300 yards at a double footpath sign. The stream makes an agreeable companion latterly, and in retrospect Pendle now cuts a fine figure.

2. On reaching the road at Anna Lane Head (762518), turn briefly left down the road, but in less than 100 yards turn right along a rough track: this is a footpath but unsigned, bearing only the legend "Veepings" (of the building ahead). Go over a cattle grid and keep on the track to the right of all buildings ahead. Pass through an open gateway to the right of the second house, possibly extremely muddy in season. Drop slightly left onto a wet track and cross a footbridge over a stream. Go up a little bank opposite and soon turn half right, approaching Dugdales. Pass through a metal gate on the right and join the farm lane, turning left through another gate and uphill. Where the lane bends right you may keep rising on the same line over grass to rejoin the main North-South route from Greenwoods at a gate in the field corner. Views are good along this high, open stretch.

14. THE LUPINE ROCKS

Cowling, Wainman's Pinnacle, The New Allotment, Keighley Moor, Worth Valley, Wolf Stones, Lumb, Cowling. 12½ miles. Maps: OS 1:50,000 Landranger nos. 103, 104; OS 1:25,000 Explorer OL 21 (South Pennines).

Alternative: It is not necessary to descend from the track at (996382), near Highfield House, to the Worth Valley road. Simply turn right along the track and follow it for about a mile, WNW and then W, until the Pennine Way and the main route are joined at (982386). This is shorter, but scenically inferior as the fine views of Ponden and the upper Worth Valley are largely lost.

* * * * * * * * * *

Background

Today we complete our trilogy of walks incorporating sections of the Pennine Way with the most northerly of the three, linking the Worth Valley with the Colne-Keighley A6033 road. To complete the circuit, routes over the heather moors to the East of Cowling have been employed, very little used by walkers apparently, but quite practicable with careful wayfinding, as the author found after some frustrating sallies on possible alternatives. Indeed, one criticism of the Pennine Way which can be made, it seems to me, is that in many areas it has drawn in an excessive amount of foot traffic to the neglect of other local paths. The positive counter to that argument, naturally, is that when the other routes are found they frequently offer very pleasant, quiet walking.

Wolf Stones is itself the summit of a large wedge of open Pennine moorland tapering between the two above-mentioned roads and finally cut off at Laneshaw Bridge. Though of no great height (at about 1,450ft. it is substantially below Black Hameldon and Boulsworth Hill to the South), it is quite isolated and just lies on the main Northern England watershed, factors making it a very good viewpoint. The stones themselves are no more extensive than many other millstone grit outcrops in the South Pennines, but their situation makes them fairly conspicuous from afar. North of Wolf Stones, the Pennines continue to decline steadily towards the Aire Gap: there is no higher ground along the Pennine Way in that direction until Fountains Fell is reached. One therefore has a pronounced feeling of completing a well-defined section of the Pennine Way at this point, with apologies to the succeeding lesser height of Pinhaw (1,273ft.), coming appropriately at the Northern edge of the OS "South Pennines" map.

Open heather moor is the keynote of this walk, and on a dry bright day your hours will pass very pleasantly, with some extensive vistas and generally good going underfoot, though some careful attention to wayfinding will be needed during the outward half. The mile or so to the north of Wolf Stones, however (Ickornshaw Moor) is peaty and may be wet or very wet in season. It is also quite clear hereabouts that the commonly used route of the Pennine Way does *not* correspond to the right of way given on the 1:25,000 OS, nor to the route suggested in Wainwright. I shall clarify this point in due course. Although a fairly long walk, there are only a couple of steepish climbs to negotiate: gradients are not excessive in this part of the Pennines. Some 1,300ft. of climbing are called for in toto.

The Walk

From the centre of Cowling, where there should be no difficulties with parking, the easiest beginning is to go west to the crossroads at (970431), where the solid tower of Cowling parish church is very commanding below, and turn up Oakworth Old Road as signposted. On the 1:25,000 OS this is "Old Lane". Climb past a pleasing mix of properties, old, new and conversions: soon the obelisk of Wainman's Pinnacle becomes very obvious, atop a craggy height on the left. Quite soon we are into the high pastures: in about half a mile turn sharp left with the road (a signpost gives "Oakworth 5½"). You could investigate paths given on the OS leaving on the left as alternatives to this opening stretch, but they betray little evidence of use.

The road, at any rate, is generally quiet and the views steadily improve as we climb and the outskirts of the town are left behind. On your right are the rounded, extensive moorland

Walk 14: The Lupine Rocks

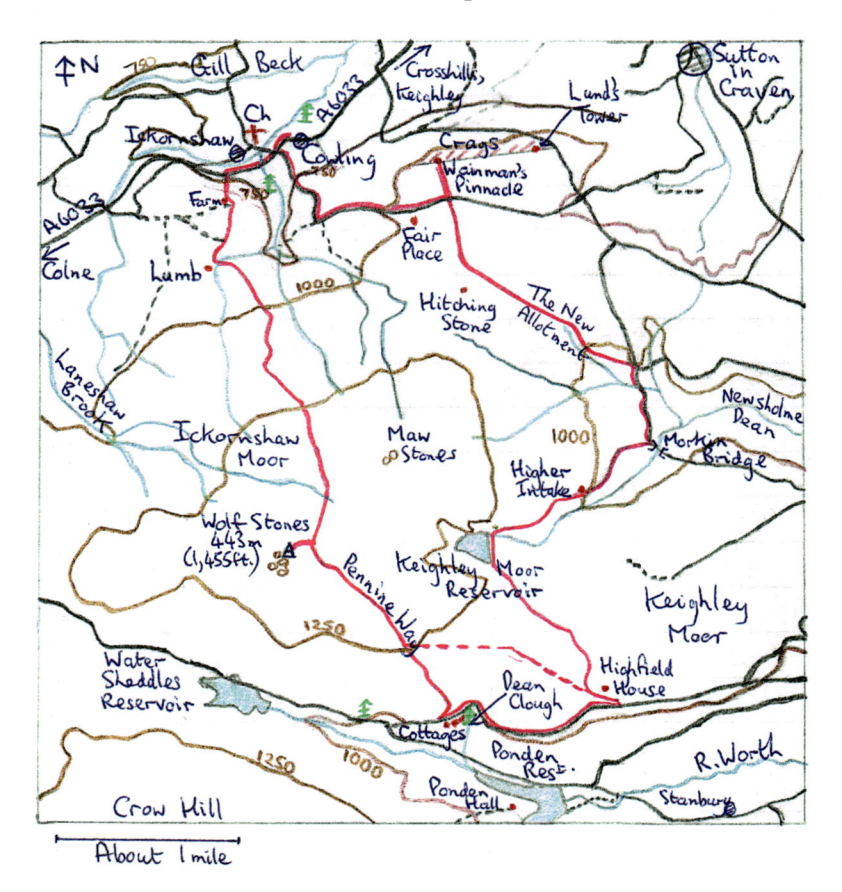

slopes culminating in the summits of Maw Stones and Wolf Stones. Pass a recently restored farm on the left (a stone above the first-floor level door gives a date of 1699), and as you continue up the road a remarkable object comes into view on the right, the huge isolated boulder given as "Hitching Stone" on the map. We shall pass close by this imposing bulk soon, but before turning south it's worth making a short detour to Wainman's Pinnacle.

The simplest way is to turn left off the road by a wall very near the summit of the road on Stake Hill. A beeline of some 300yds., passing through a gate, leads to the strategically placed obelisk which lies on a typical gritstone edge falling steeply to the north. Naturally this makes a popular short stroll for locals, with families keeping wary eyes on children climbing on the many large boulders. Further along the edge, half a mile ENE, is Lund's Tower: to the NE you look down the valley to Glusburn and Silsden in Airedale.

You may of course decide to do Lund's Tower also, time permitting - it is arguably the better viewpoint - but, in any case, retrace your steps presently to the Oakworth road. Cross a stile on the far side up against a wall (the OS appears erroneous here), then go along close to the wall on a faint tread. The great mass of Hitching Stone, presumably a glacial erratic, is directly ahead here. Note also a shallow gully, away to the SE, which we shall be using later. Pass a wall junction, then cross a wooden stile in a fence, and when you reach the little stream (Hitching Stone Slack), cross a simple stile on your left in what is by then a fence. This is waymarked but again seems somewhat at variance with the OS.

The next half-mile, over rough tussocky moorland in a general ESE direction with no visible tread, will test your route-finding ability. Red grouse are in evidence now, their haunting near-human voices being probably the only sound. Initially it is easiest to go at 90 degrees to the fence, then cross the stream at a suitable point before turning more to the right. Climb a little bank, where the going is drier, bilberry and heather being in evidence. Contour round the bank and look for a faint rough track which has come from the vicinity of the Hitching Stone - the latter should be about a quarter-mile WSW from here. Keep roughly SE with the track thereafter, soon entering the wide shallow gully visible earlier: go down the left side of it. This curious little defile becomes well-defined, with a solitary tree on the right and the Hitching Stone still in view. When you reach a wall, leave the track, going a few paces right and crossing via three through stone steps. Ahead, the gully narrows in a heathery area: keep to the left of, and above, the developing stream, following sketchy treads as well as you can.

When the banks to right and left decline, drop nearer to the stream in the area named as The New Allotment on the map, at around the 1,000ft. contour. The general direction is still SE, trending more S (bearing 160 degrees) as the ground flattens out. In retrospect, the defile passed through is a striking feature. Keep left of the stream, and when you reach a wall look carefully for a narrow wall stile situated at a gap in the barbed wire. Once over, resume the SE line: still no visible path, I'm afraid! Keep to a line between the wall (left) and stream (right), the ground wet in places. Partridges have replaced the grouse hereabouts, a confirmation of the lower altitude.

Here we briefly leave our home 1:50,000 map, going directly onto the South Pennines Outdoor Leisure 1:25,000 if you have it, also for a short distance onto Landranger no 104. Another small stream develops on your left: ford it near a right-angled wall corner and follow the latter to the left, now on a vehicular track. You re-emerge onto the Oakworth road at a gate, the rocky summit tors of Grey Stones Hill visible ahead. Turn right and go easily down the road past outlying farms for about three-eighths of a mile to Morkin Bridge. Here the vigorous little stream tumbles over a waterfall - look for this, on the left. Our route is across the bridge, then turning right through a gate up a metalled lane, where I recall an autumn party of mistle thrushes passing over, betrayed by their rather harsh call. Pass the farm of Higher Intake in about a half-mile, going straight on through two gates, still climbing on a metalled surface. Another big 'erratic' boulder is shortly passed as we enter heather moor again.

Presently the dam wall of Keighley Moor Reservoir is reached, at about the 1,200ft. contour. The surface becomes unmetalled, and as usual the reservoir environs make an inviting stopping-place. On turning left along the wall, White Hill (above Hebden Bridge) becomes quite prominent in the south. Beyond the reservoir, the main route keeps to the vehicular track going SE: there is a branch going right here (not given on the OS), which constitutes an ultra-short cut to join the Pennine Way. Under the new access situation (see opening notice) this path, signed 'Millennium Way', is now a recognised route. The track we follow becomes a bit sketchy, though always perceptible, and is generally firm and dry underfoot, an agreeable heather moor stroll. Presently, about a half-mile from the reservoir, you meet a wall which should be followed, still SE, through an area of many grouse butts.

Where the wall turns further left, bear slightly right on a faint track, reaching a crossing wall near a grouse butt. Follow the wall right, watching for a wooden stile which should be crossed into the adjacent rough pasture (this avoids the need for a later wall-climb). Go down subsequently with the wall on the right, eventually passing through a gate onto a rough vehicular track. Here you may exercise the choices indicated at the beginning, either turning right to join the Pennine Way in about one and a quarter miles or, at the expense of a little extra effort, turning left to meet the road shortly. In my opinion the prospect of the upper Worth Valley makes the latter a desirable detour.

After turning left, then, pass through a gate, with a wood and an imposing, recently restored house following on the left. About forty yards after the latter, with Highfield House now on your left, drop down by a wall on the right to join the Laneshaw Bridge-Oakworth road. Turn right and follow the road for about three-quarters of a mile with Ponden Reservoir and the valley laid out attractively below, a pleasing mixture of rich greenery, scattered dwellings and rocky outcrops. Look up the slopes beyond, too, for a glimpse of Top Withins and Withins Height as a backdrop. Ponden Hall is also glimpsed by the reservoir, another location with Bronte associations - some considering it to be the Thrushcross Grange of Wuthering Heights.

The road zig-zags through the pleasant rocky defile of Dean Clough, where the Pennine Way joins us from below. Beyond Crag Bottom cottages, watch for the point on the right, clearly signed, where the Way turns off by a right bend of the road. Turn uphill initially on a vehicular track, soon passing a rather unsightly quarry-cum-rubbish tip, which fortunately is greening over now. During the summer months this is a likely place to spot ring ouzels. Follow the zig-zag track up until an acorn (long-distance footpath marker) directs you over a stile on the left, the track petering out to the right.

The walking, on a clear tread with initially a wall on the left, is straightforward up a steady climb; the retrospective valley views remain most attractive. Two stiles are crossed, a brief enclosed section between them, then the route becomes open on the right once more. About 300 yards on, the Way is crossed by a path, the earlier alternative from the environs of Highfield. We keep straight up, with grouse now probably in evidence once more and a good chance of observing golden plover too. Presently the wall on the left also ends, but a clear tread continues, turning more left now (WNW). From here Keighley Moor Reservoir will normally be plainly visible, some half-mile to the NE with the faint track mentioned earlier coming from it.

The gradient eases into the summit plateau of Wolf Stones, the view now dominated by fine prospects of Pendle and Boulsworth in the western arc. Occasional cairns accompany the path, though not at the critical point where you need to turn into the north, unfortunately. This occurs immediately after two small pools, with both the summit outcrops and trig-point in view, less than half a mile away. A beeline to the summit cannot be recommended, however, across rough and heavy ground. The Way itself is well marked on the next section, with minor diversions, returfed sections, and - more recently - large flagstones. Once again (you will by now expect what's coming) I have to ask: is it really necessary? Apart from the ugly artificial appearance, I see no evidence on the ground of the excessive erosion which could justify such walking aids.

Just after a big cairn and a carved Pennine Way sign on a rock, you reach the fence which is effectively the local summit of the path, and the boundary between North and West Yorkshire - the three-way junction with Lancashire occurring at the very summit of Wolf Stones. A detour to the trig-point is strongly recommended, and best achieved by turning SW (225 degrees) a few paces N of the fence, on a faint tread. Five minutes should bring you to the column, then the big outcrop from which the summit derives its name.

Your impressions of this summit will, even more than usual, depend on the day and the hour. In mist, wind and rain you will doubtless query your sanity, but be assured that the view from here may be one of rare beauty. I was fortunate enough to be here once on an early Autumn evening, with the whole moor seemingly steeped in beautiful, soft light, the mist beginning to gather in the valleys and all thoughts of squelchy bog and peat banished. On another visit in Spring, while taking a few minutes' break by the outcrop, I was fascinated by the sight of a short-eared owl, quartering the ground in broad sweeps with meticulous care and consummate skill, doubtless searching for small rodents. Its wings almost brushed the tussocky moor grass on occasion.

The view is extensive, as befits such a watershed point: Boulsworth and Pendle striking noble poses from SW to W, some Bowland fells - up to 25 miles distant from here! - the Three Peaks area, the Flasby and Cracoe fells and long prospects down into West Yorkshire, again beginning from the impressive Worth Valley. Yes, it can be difficult to leave! But leave we must, Cowling being still well over an hour's tramp away.

Return to the Pennine Way near the fence and follow it, initially N over another path-diverted area. The next section was formerly wet and peaty for perhaps half a mile, though the peat groughs were pale imitations of those on the High Peak. Now a clear line of stone flags renders the going trivial. Here we meet the divergence of the official Pennine Way with the more obvious used tread mentioned earlier. In a nutshell, the Pennine Way is given (on both the 1:25,000 OS and in Wainwright's "Pennine Way Companion") as continuing fairly directly N, or a few degrees W of N. In my view it is not worth seeking out. The main track, marked with a thin grey dashed line on the 1:25,000 map, diverges initially WNW from the Pennine Way, then turns more parallel to it. The tread is clear on the ground and fairly well cairned: indeed the 1:50,000 map implies - though not clearly - that this is the recognised Pennine Way route. Gradually, as height is lost, the surrounding moor becomes firmer and the stone flags are discontinued.

Civilisation is back in view, Cowling parish church tower providing a welcome directional fix, with other scattered valley dwellings - plus lights if the hour is getting late. Watch for the point where, after turning more into the W again (ca.280 degrees, briefly), the path leaves a developing track and turns into the N once more. In any sort of decent visibility you should see an isolated hut, about a quarter-mile ahead, and the tread is still clear. Go downhill, fording a little stream, soon reaching the solidly-built shooting hut by another stream valley. A Pennine Way sign on a rock follows: proceed downhill by a stone wall on your left. The difficult routefinding is behind you now, the scene becoming quite parochial. You pass three little chalets, keeping by the wall on your left. After another chalet, bend right then left with the wall; Wainman's Pinnacle is now very obvious in the NE, and the official Pennine Way rejoins our route beyond the stream of Andrew Gutter, after we have crossed a rudimentary stile (Pennine Way carved) and passed some outbuildings, then turned left by a Pennine Way sign.

Proceed downhill, cross a wall stile and immediately turn sharp left by another Pennine Way sign, the church now less than a mile distant below you. Pass a ruin and cross a broken wall, then descend sharply to cross a little footbridge, subsequently going up to the right; a waymarker then indicates the point to turn left, on a reasonably clear tread. After a little ford, cross some stone steps, then pass through a wall gap, onto a clear green lane going uphill, reaching another PW sign by a wall. Turn right here, and go on round the hairpin bend at Lumb Beck Waterfall, a striking little force familiar to Pennine Wayfarers, rather spoilt by occasional dumping of rubbish. You are now on a clear vehicular track: go through a waymarked gate, turning left, up a lane. Pass straight on through another gate (the main track turns left here, shortly becoming a road). Go down the walled lane ahead, crossing stone steps in a wall (signposted) to the right of Lower Summer House.

Go briefly down the farm lane, but where it turns left go over a stone stile in a wall on the right (Pennine Way sign). Proceed downhill through the rather heavy pasture ahead, trending towards the wall on the left but keeping atop a little bank further down. After passing some trees, drop down and more left to reach stone steps and a gate onto the road by a double Pennine Way signpost. Cowling is about half a mile along the road, right, and it will seem a welcome haven after your long walk.

A sustained cross-country trek, then, certainly "o'er moor and fen" if not "o'er crag and torrent". Gradually I have warmed to these South Pennine journeys over the years, and I hope your experience will be the same. The small towns, villages and outlying farms seem to have become an integral part of the scenery with time, just as much as the surrounding windswept moors, and they add a definite warmth and humanity to the walking. The contrast with the earlier section of the Pennine Way, from the High Peak to Stoodley Pike say, is striking: there the feeling is of a grander but bleaker environment. In truth, this subtle ever-changing quality is one of the Way's great strengths, as we weave the thread from Edale to Kirk Yetholm, unfolding a clearer picture of Northern England as we go - and, in an indefinable way, discovering something of ourselves too.

ON THE WAY: A REFLECTION

We were eager explorers then! Day by day in the August of that scorching summer we set off resolutely each morning on our quest from Edale to Kirk Yetholm. What a contrast to our later journeys to the Highlands, with provisions enough and to spare, and home comforts most nights. Fair enough: they are holidays, to be enjoyed, not endurance tests. But on the Pennine Way our rucksacks held perhaps twenty-five pounds' weight, less when our water bottles were drained at the day's end, all our worldly goods for some two weeks and more. Travelling light, indeed, and in retrospect there seems a most appealing quality about that simplicity.

We were pretty naive as walkers too! In truth it was like an apprenticeship, building on what we had learnt the hard way the year before. Basic points about map and compass work, reading the lie of the land, time and distance, the nature of the terrain underfoot. What was learnt then truly remained with us.

How vivid many of the experiences of the Way still seem! Nowadays it is easy to be quite blase about walking: we seem to be pre-programmed, tuning ourselves to a familiar routine as it were, and often only something exceptional registers with us. It was not so then. Fuelled by that sense of quest, and the determination which it generated, every day and every hour seemed to count.

We cannot be so foolish, even with the deception of hindsight, as to claim all parts of the Pennine Way are equally enjoyable. To be honest, many sections of the Way are plain hard work, long hours of toil over undistinguished moorland or pasture without recompense in terms of surroundings or view. Yet the highlights are there, the visions of beauty in remote places, the hard-earned and eagerly accepted rewards. After the peat bogs, endless reservoirs, then miles of low-lying Craven pastures, come the excitement of Malham and the limestone Dales; after the weary traverses of Tan Hill and Sleightholme come the beauty of Teesdale, the majestic High Force, Cauldron Snout and High Cup.

Were those of prime importance, though? No, I think not: the achievement was the thing, and the fact that thousands of others had done it before us and thousands more would do it after us mattered not a jot. *We* had done it, and the sense of satisfaction on reaching Kirk Yetholm was no less real for being intensely personal. Truly, after a few days the outside world had vanished from sight, and only that distant finishing post counted. A childish sort of satisfaction, do some say? Maybe so; I do not defend it. I only know it was positive for us, and that the apprenticeship was a crucial step on the way to a fuller and deeper appreciation of walking and of the British countryside, so that we can now say the walk's the thing, the finishing post matters less, indeed it is never reached.

We had our introduction to Wainwright, too - for surely the man is unmistakably seen through the transparent medium of his books - in "Pennine Way Companion". It was a good title, above all because the book really was a companion, a welcome breath of humanity - even earthiness sometimes - to amuse on the treadmill sections, to find simple but fitting epithets on the memorable ones. You came to forgive his irritating mannerisms, his pedantry, his pronounced pro-Lakeland, anti-Pennine bias, on account of the sheer integrity. The Pennine Way is a rigorous challenge, even a weary tramp at times, and here was one author who was not trying to convince you it was really a rose garden.

Indeed, on reflection, is it not remarkable that the "Companion" is one of his best-known books, despite his barely concealed dislike of the walk? We accept without question, of course, that after Lakeland the rest of the English outdoors is second best, but I think there was more to it than that. The weather was surely a factor, for his fieldwork was done in the mid-1960s, spanning some particularly wet, unsettled years. Then, of course, his decision to work on the Way piecemeal, rather than as a single journey or set of single journeys. While that probably led to a vastly better book for those who came after, I cannot believe that it gives the same degree of satisfaction. The different impression given by his early book "A Pennine Journey", a genuine single expedition, speaks for itself, and it is more than just the difference in years. With his Lakeland books, you felt the satisfaction in writing was equal to the satisfaction in doing the walks: with the "Companion", he himself admitted it was the production of the book, not the walking, which provided the enjoyment. It is a tribute to his sheer professionalism and pride of performance that the "Companion" was such a success; surely no-one believes the 'free pint offer' was anything more than peripheral!

I have digressed, for the Pennine Way is not Wainwright, Binns, Oldham or any other of its authors, it is supremely your own experience of it. Self-discovery, yes, sometimes of a sharp and painful kind, weaknesses in our physical and mental make-up we had barely been conscious of. How maddening those foot blisters or raw spots could be, how seemingly impossible to get them out of mind. How frighteningly easy, when tired, to quarrel over minor points, giving way to pride, or to noble submission. How easy to lose temper and patience over mistakes in preparation or route finding, especially when what lay before your eyes seemed to bear no relation to map or guidebook. The way of the walker never runs smooth: it was good that we learnt the lesson then, and were disillusioned!

Yet those were the negative points, and they were outweighed. To make that great watershed crossing from Teesdale to the Eden valley, to conquer Cross Fell, finally to stride down that last gentle slope into Kirk Yetholm - these and a score of other satisfactions somehow tasted sweeter for being tasted together. We had forged a partnership, and somehow, despite all the problems, it had worked: that same driving urge to complete the Pennine Way had taken hold of us both, and in a mysterious way had helped us to accept each other as we were. With the triviality of most of our difficulties shown up, the true companionship and support were expressed all the more strongly.

Then those characters and companions we met along the Way, how they enriched the miles! Not least Michael and John, for their actual companionship over the early miles, then their encouragement, and good wishes for the rest of the journey. A host of others, of course. The old boy in the pub at Colden, who recognised Pennine Wayfarers at a glance, and was proud to have done some of the Pennine Way himself . . . the few yards near the end of his garden. That surly RSM of a warden at Hawes youth hostel, a throwback to National Service and the 1950s, thankfully only a minor cloud passing over the sun. Then those two grand Geordie lads we met in the later stages, and their contempt for the local ale, immortalised in a hostel book somewhere: "The watter in the Wear's better than the beer down 'ere!" I could go on.

It was a stage for us, seemingly an insignificant part of life's pilgrimage, yet perhaps of far deeper moment than we suspected at the time. Yet it was a means to an end, not an end in itself. At the time, I was quite convinced I should one day do the Pennine Way again, perhaps quite soon. Now I think it most unlikely, as I think you do too. We have moved on.

We were free then, unfettered! Cares, responsibilities, the professional demands of our jobs, were still for the future. No need, then, to rely on walking as a kind of safety valve, an invaluable means of unwinding at the end of another demanding week, such that nowadays the tension seems palpably to drain out as we tread the miles. When you were young, you girded yourself and walked where you would, as He said - not of course in the sense that the route was our own, but that we expressed ourselves by doing it. Yet if it be true - in a sense - that now we sometimes feel almost as if we have to walk, I believe that ceases to be important once the walk has begun. Time and again moments of realisation come to us, as when we watch the sun and shadow driven across the distant fell-slopes in a lively breeze, linger on some remote summit to take in each sector of an extensive panorama, or stand transfixed as we watch a rare bird of prey. However often we have seen these things before matters not: we contemplate them as new, flashing upon that inner eye, and in that re-creation we may know His presence. Then we may feel free again, as we were then, yet more profoundly so.

We shall forget many other events of the 1970s, and would prefer to forget others, but those sixteen days will remain deeply etched in the memory. The very names of White Moss and Featherbed Moss have not ceased to terrify, for all that they were tamed in '76; the soulful, near-human cries of a thousand grouse passed en route still haunt us; the near-dehydration as we entered Hawes on that baking day still stands as a warning. Somehow those experiences and others seem far more vivid, even now, than any number of routine days passed in classroom or laboratory. For in truth, is it not most refreshing to be thrown on our own resources, to be compelled to take speedy decisions and respond to sudden crises? Society seems to be moving in the opposite direction: everything gets handed to us on a plate, we believe everything the media tells us (woe betide the weather forecaster who gets it wrong!), and above all we believe the implicit myth of self-sufficiency. Of course the Pennine Way is small beer compared to some of the challenges that present themselves to the walker worldwide, but the principle is the same. You have to do it for yourselves.

It was good that we did it! Whether it be true that we became better men through walking the Pennine Way, I know not: perhaps after all that was tongue in cheek from Wainwright, as you once said. The Coast to Coast walk is certainly more attractive and varied, the Offa's Dyke Path of more historic interest and greener, but the Pennine Way beats them - not only in the satisfaction of its completion, but in its rugged strength and character. Entirely unpretentious, the Pennine Way displays itself openly, withough apology. In its raw bleakness, its straightforwardness, but also in the genuine warmth of the communities along its length, it is a true statement of much about Northern England. Perhaps those are what we responded to, qualities that in some measure compensated for lack of attractiveness along much of its course: qualities which we admired and perhaps aspired to. Therein, I suggest, is the basis for our self-discovery.

No, I would not have missed it for anything. Thank you for being there.

THE FOREST OF BOWLAND

When the Forest of Bowland was designated an Area of Outstanding Natural Beauty (AONB) by the Countryside Commission in 1964, a substantial tract of Northern England, previously little known or appreciated, was justly brought to greater prominence. Often when I mention Bowland to friends I get the reaction, "Yes, I know it, I've driven over the Trough Road". That makes about as much sense as saying that you know Manchester after driving down Deansgate, indeed probably less. As a first taste of the area, offering a few enigmatic clues, the Trough Road may indeed serve as an introduction: sadly, for most people it is never followed up, and the delightful river scenery, remote hidden valleys and sense of vast space and solitude on the high fells of Bowland remain undiscovered.

In the last few walks of this book the walking, to my mind, reaches a climax as we essay increasingly ambitious forays into the heart of this still mysterious region. Over the years I have developed a great affection for Bowland, and I felt that a general preamble on the natural features of the area would enhance the reader's appreciation. Some of the material is based on an article published in the magazine "Country Walking" in June 1992.

As originally described, the AONB includes both the Forest of Bowland and Pendle Hill, but though there are undoubtedly good administrative reasons for this definition it makes little sense geographically. Although the two areas are separated only by a narrow strip of land around the Ribble, they differ greatly. That difference lies not so much in the lie of the land or the underlying rock, but in character. Pendle is open to the four winds, bold and uncompromising, with very little in the way of hidden corners or recessses to explore: indeed, as I wrote earlier, this is - paradoxically - its strength. The true Forest of Bowland has an elusive, arcane quality: here are hidden valleys quite invisible from any road, extensive wild plateaux unseen from the valleys, secluded villages and other settlements rich in history. Only slowly does Bowland reveal its secrets to the explorer, but the search is worthwhile many times over, for here there is scenery unique in Northern England. I have dealt at some length with Pendle in Walk 3, and in what follows I confine myself to its larger, shyer and lesser-known neighbour.

Attempts have been made, and I believe are continuing, to convert Bowland into a full National Park. That would undoubtedly have consequences for the walker, but for now it remains an AONB, and no-one can justly deny its claim to beauty. You will not find the area marked on Ordnance Survey maps, though - they mark only National Parks, not AONBs. Other maps which show the delineation include the North-West Tourist Board's official map of NW England, and the Countryside Commission produce a useful map of the whole area at 1 inch to a mile with a clear border showing the AONB.

On the ground, the situation is not always so clear! You may encounter numerous "Forest of Bowland" signs in unexpected places, while others are missing, and to see them in the environs of Pendle always strikes me as a curious faux-pas - though as noted earlier, this is the letter of the AONB definition.

The heart of the Forest of Bowland, in the sense of the high fells, is in effect that area bounded by the Hodder valley and the country lanes flanking the M6, from East to West, and by the Lune-Wenning valley and the Bleasdale and Chipping pastures from North to South. This constitutes, as Wainwright observes in "A Bowland Sketchbook", "a compact, well-defined mass of some 150 square miles", roughly half of the total AONB area. Much of this interior consists of open moorland above the 1,000ft. contour, a significant part exceeding 1,500ft. and reaching its summit at Ward's Stone (561m, 1,839ft.) seven miles ESE of Lancaster. This heart of Bowland is virtually innocent of A and even of B roads except at the very periphery, wholly unspoilt and untouristy in a most refreshing way.

The general character of the moorland is in many ways similar to other high moorland areas of Northern England, gritstone and peat being the order of the day, but there are differences and significant local variations. The whole area lies well to the west of the main watershed of Northern England, and consequently takes more of a battering from the prevailing

The Forest of Bowland

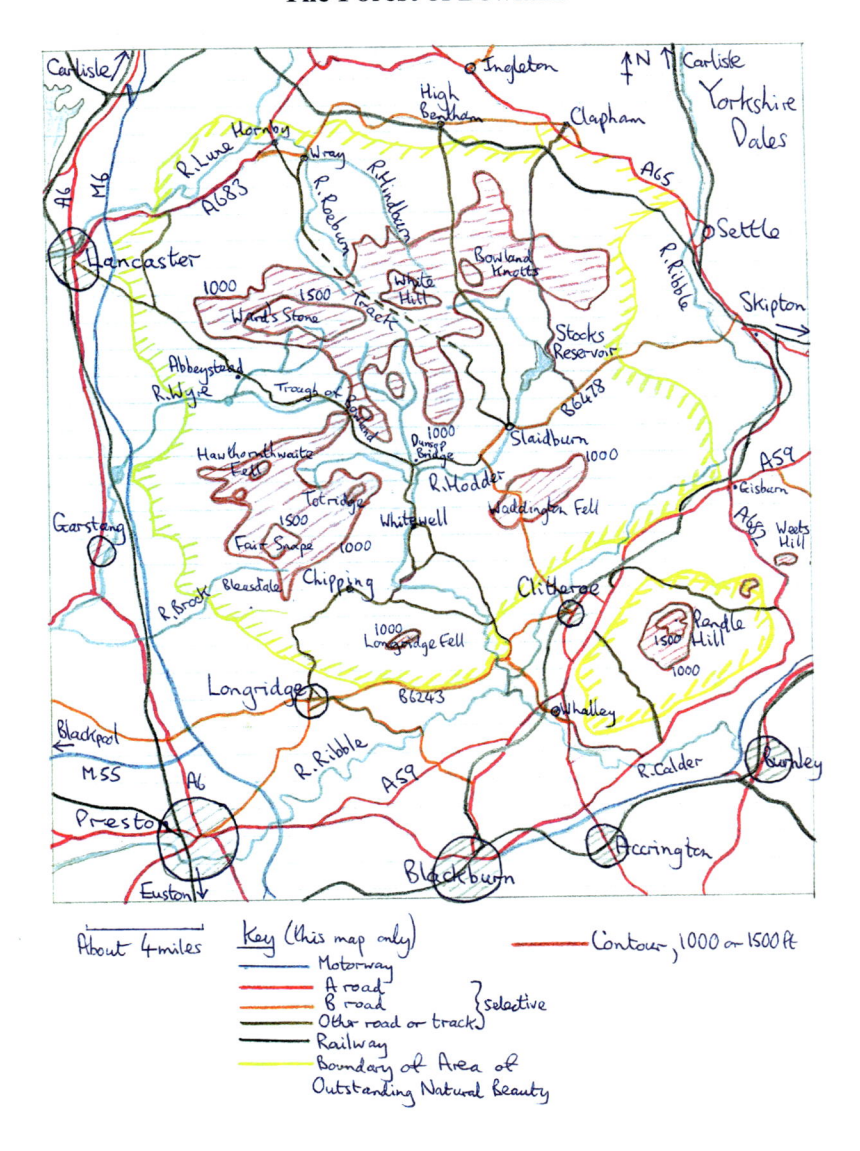

Forest of Bowland, looking N from Whin Fell

Forest of Bowland, Brennand Valley

westerly winds and rain than relatively sheltered parts of East Lancashire or the Dales. I have often seen Bowland fells looking dark and storm-lashed when the Ribble Valley and even Pendle were innocently bright.

Notable differences occur, too, between those parts of the region drained by the different river systems: Hodder, Lune and Wyre. Although the roadside section of the Marshaw Wyre West of the Trough is undoubtedly beautiful and deservedly popular with passing motorists, I would dispute Wainwright's claim that the Wyre is the most important of Bowland's rivers. Certainly the Hodder Valley and surrounds enclose the finest scenery, and to my mind they also epitomise the secretive nature of much of Bowland. From outside you may only glimpse major sections of the Hodder Valley: it is hidden by intervening heights such as Longridge and Waddington Fells. To discover the hidden side valleys, even to see some parts of the main Hodder valley like that between Whitewell and Dunsop Bridge, you must go within: the reward is real beauty by any standards of English scenery. By contrast, the North and West - flowing streams, though passing through fine countryside, hold fewer secrets.

Probably the best known aspect of Bowland, however, is the western one, as glimpsed by travellers on the M6 and main-line railway between Preston and Lancaster. Parlick and Fair Snape, Hawthornthwaite Fell and the Clougha-Grit Fell-Ward's Stone ridge are all visible at intervals, smooth-looking sweeping fell lines above the cultivated land and forests nearer at hand. A fine tract of open country, and summits blessed with splendid coastal views, but perhaps a little bland and unexciting compared to the heart of the district.

The northern flank, centred on the Hindburn and Roeburn valleys, is probably much less known, and certainly far quieter in terms of the routes of communication. It is delightful nevertheless, and from the B6480 road or the Lancaster-Skipton railway you may gaze south over miles of charming, unspoilt pastoral scenery, the fells seeming quite distant. A whole series of interesting villages lie along here, from Hornby, Wray and

Wennington to the Benthams, all worth exploration and full of character.

We return to the eastern aspect, though, and while as I indicated above it is here that the secretive character of Bowland is most pronounced, travellers along the A59 Whalley-Clitheroe by-pass may glimpse a fair arc of the fells on the far side of the Hodder, especially the Parlick-Fair Snape-Totridge ridge, with the indentation of the Trough further north. As noted earlier in the book (Walk 2) a splendid prospect of this side of the fells may be had for the small expense of climbing Longridge Fell. Another good aspect results from crossing to the north side of Waddington Fell. Above all it is the finely-etched contrasts which make the Hodder valley and its surrounds so impressive: from the remote windswept fells around Cross of Greet at the river's birth to the tranquil pastures downriver where grey, shadowed lines of moorland still sweep above, the river itself alternating between briskly flowing sections, dazzling in sunlight, and still pools.

It will have been apparent for some time that I derive great interest from the wildlife, particularly birds, which I spot during my outings, and Bowland has a rich variety of birds. During one traverse of the Hornby Road on a balmy June day I counted two dozen species without difficulty even after discounting common birds like finches, thrushes and tits. Various waders, game birds, the gull colony on Tarnbrook fell, birds of prey, unusual passerines . . . truly a fascinating area for all who love birds and are prepared to watch and wait patiently. Here we encounter controversy, though, of which the hen harrier displayed on the Forest of Bowland road signs is an unfortunate symbol. Harriers have undoubtedly been seen in Bowland - part of their notable extension of range since 1945 - but as long as the high fells are carefully-guarded grouse moors they will inevitably be unwelcome to some. Indeed there is little doubt that some systematic persecution of birds of prey does go on, including the spoiling of nest sites. On the other side of the coin are accusations about the methods used by the RSPB, some of which were expressed by the BBC programme "Country File" some years ago. The sadness is that the birds, caught in the middle, are the ones who lose out. Turning to animals, both roe and sika deer may be encountered in the afforested areas and have given many embarrassing close encounters to motorists.

Anyone who loves moorland walking will be attracted by the high, sweeping skylines of the Bowland fells, and here awareness of the new access situation is particularly important – see the introductory notice in this book. Much of this high ground is still highly-prized grouse moor, and despite the great increase in accessible areas for the walker, the owners retain the right to restrict that access at times. Even before the recent changes, however, a number of rights of way existed as clearly delineated on the OS maps. Refer also to the earlier Walkers' Notes.

Bowland, it must be said, excels in mysterious and romantic place names and how inviting they look! I remember poring over my first OS 7th series map, entranced by names such as Wolfhole Crag, Good Greave and Bloe Greet. At the time many of these were out of bounds.

The steady opening up of Bowland Fells began in the 1990s, when, for instance, the permitted access areas and paths on Fair Snape Fell and Ward's Stone (Walks 18 and 17) were created. National bodies, especially the water authorities and Forestry Commission, played their part. When I was writing this book I commented on the changing situation and speculated on possible further changes (see Walk 17), and largely out of historical interest I have retained those comments. Previously there were regular trespasses on White Hill, part of a wider protest against 'Forbidden Britain'. Quiet, behind the scenes negotiations were taking place simultaneously and probably had a much greater effect: all walkers who visit the district may now enjoy the results. Yet even now many would say the former restrictions contributed to the special Bowland ethos, notably in helping to preserve the distinctive wildlife referred to above.

Nor should it be assumed that even rights of way on Bowland fells will be easy to follow: good map and compass ability are important here. A lack of natural features makes navigation in mist tricky, and I have heard stories from my

Slaidburn friends of quite experienced walkers getting embarrassingly lost. It can be a long way back to civilisation.

Bowland possesses very little in the way of public transport, but what there is, is of value and should be known. It may help you, for instance, to turn an A to B walk into a circular by eliminating some relatively tedious road walking. Probably the most useful is the bus service from Clitheroe to Slaidburn, either via Bashall Eaves, Whitewell and Dunsop Bridge or direct over Waddington Fell. Formerly privately run from Leedham's Garage at Dunsop Bridge, this is now run as a community bus service by Lancashire County Council: some buses, moreover, continue beyond Slaidburn to Settle. There is a limited Sunday service. In the last few years, a minibus service has been run from the East Lancashire towns over the Trough to Lancaster on Sundays and Bank Holidays in the summer months, and though more limited in scope this may also help the walker (see, e.g. under Walk 17). Further details on both these buses may be had from the Tourist Information Centre, Castle Street, Clitheroe (01200-442226). Moving on to trains, an important recent development has been the reinstatement of passenger services between Blackburn and Clitheroe, at first on Saturdays only, later (May 1994) on weekdays too. It is intended that these trains should connect with the Clitheroe-Slaidburn bus, and I have used this facility on a number of occasions. Further north, the railway line from Lancaster to Skipton skirts the district, and as I note in Walk 20 this provides a possible long way home from the Hornby Road via Wennington.

A word or two on accommodation also seems relevant here. While all my walks are conceived as day walks, and traditionally it was through day trips that Lancastrians got to know Bowland, the situation is changing, and visitors are coming to Bowland from further afield. Certainly it is quite feasible to use one of the towns on the perimeter - Clitheroe, Longridge or Lancaster - or one of the northern villages as a base. But there is an increasing amount of bed-and-breakfast available in the heart of the district, and to savour the true Bowland atmosphere a stay in Chipping or Slaidburn (also YHA here) can be recommended -

or you may be able to spot some bed-and-breakfast for yourself while on the road. An interesting alternative for the more intrepid is provided by the camping barns recently introduced by the YHA, though not exclusive to their members. These are situated at Greengore (near Hurst Green), Chipping, Downham and Quernmore.

Three significant roads, or tracks, cross the heart of the district (with a further minor road a little further east) and they make an interesting study for anyone wishing to discover Bowland. Proceeding clockwise, first comes the Trough of Bowland road itself, in particular the section between Dunsop Bridge and Lancaster. Two generations ago it was an extremely popular walk: nowadays the volume of traffic is such that it can only be recommended, as a walk that is, out of season - or midweek. Still, it remains as spectacular as ever, and though the road feels rather hemmed in for much of its length, with restricted views, there is real satisfaction on crossing the watershed and eventually looking out over Morecambe Bay. Want to try? It's about 25 miles from Clitheroe to Lancaster.

Moving round, the next road is the Hornby Road, actually a track for much of its length and something very special for the walker: I describe it in Walk 20. Next comes the minor road from Slaidburn to Bentham via Cross of Greet, mostly very quiet for road traffic, indeed only a through road since about 1950: quite an acceptable route for the less ambitious walker, with good views. Finally comes the little-known, but increasingly used, minor road leaving the B6478 at (748543) and heading for Clapham. This skirts the eastern side of Stocks Reservoir (picnic sites) and crosses the skyline at the so-called Bowland Knotts, interesting rocky outcrops forming the extremity of the high fells in the NE sector. Under the new access arrangements (see Introduction), it is now permissible to explore the Knotts and enjoy their splendid all-round views. A path from the summit of the road, linking with Whelpstone Crag, had been commonly used previously. In addition the path – and right of way – from Cross of Greet Bridge via Catlow Farm, meeting the ridge line at the road, offers a fine walk.

Among the most attractive and certainly most characteristic features of Bowland are its dramatic hidden valleys, unseen from any road, tiny green oases hemmed in by great expanses of sombre fell. In particular the Langden, Brennand and Whitendale valleys should not be missed by the walker, and as I have not included Brennand in any of the twenty walks (for Langden see Walk 18, for Whitendale see Walk 19) I can certainly recommend the short walk up the Dunsop valley and on to Brennand from Dunsop Bridge as a preliminary introduction to the secrets of inner Bowland. In particular the view looking NW towards Brennand from the confluence of the Brennand and Whitendale rivers can be hauntingly beautiful in certain lights. To vary the return, rather than directly retracing your steps from Brennand, you may either take the bridlepath round the north side of Middle Knoll and return via the Whitendale valley or take the bridlepath over Whin Fell (Ouster Rake) which emerges onto the Trough road about a half-mile west of Sykes farm and about two and three-quarter miles from Dunsop Bridge.

In conclusion, I extend a special invitation to those whose walking haunts do not normally extend to the high fells to make an exception here in Bowland. Certainly explore them with friends or a guide, if you will, but be assured that a special atmosphere can be tasted here, definite but elusive of expression. Bowland's high fells are truly different from the Dales or the South Pennines, having a primitive quality which calls the walker back, away from cosy fireside or driver's seat, to tread again the lonely open spaces of an unspoilt landscape that seems little changed from the time when Man's chief business was survival. Let's go, then, to seek that atmosphere for ourselves, with an even greater resolve than usual to leave no trace of our visits.

15. THE SQUIRE'S ESTATES

Slaidburn, Dunnow Hall, Newton, Farrowfield, Waddington Fell road, Smelfthwaites, Easington, Slaidburn. 7 miles. *Maps:* OS 1:50,000 Landranger no. 103; OS 1:25,000 Explorer OL 41 (Forest of Bowland).

Alternative: The upland section of the walk may be omitted completely, leaving an ideal short stroll for a light evening, by going directly from Newton Bridge or the bridge below Dunnow Hall to Easington. Both these routes converge at (706505) after which a diagonal traverse across the field, ENE, leads to the road just below Easington.

* * * * * * * * * *

Background

Without a doubt the village of Slaidburn is one of the most interesting settlements anywhere on our map, in many ways the true Bowland counterpart of Pendle's Downham. Its origins can be traced back at least as far as Saxon times (Slaidburn = 'sheep pasture by the stream', or from 'slad', meaning stone, which itself may have marked a battle site). Not the least of Slaidburn's charms is its elusiveness: it lies tucked away, out of sight from any road until the last minute. Although other walks in this volume will start from Slaidburn, they will be lengthier affairs, probably leaving you little time for exploration of the village. Here, then, is a shorter walk allowing a more leisurely exploration of Slaidburn and environs. I have developed a great affection for the village over the years, and above all I hope the locals are successful in their resolute determination to keep it unspoilt.

To this day Slaidburn remains an estate village, a state of affairs stretching back over the centuries and currently maintained through the King-Wilkinson family. This has certainly contributed to the maintenance of a strong and unique village character, highlighted by a 1993 article in "Lancashire Life". The present Mr. King-Wilkinson has been in charge since 1979, and the family connection with the village goes back to the early 17th century. It is a common complaint today that villages in the Dales or other parts of rural England have lost their old character through outsiders moving in, pushing up property prices way out of the locals' reach, frequently reducing village properties to second or holiday homes. Not in Slaidburn! Here the vast majority of properties are rented through the estate and only rarely do outsiders get a look in: the very different atmosphere which results in the village is clear even on a brief visit.

Nor is it just residential properties which are affected. The village boasts a thriving primary school - how many village schools have died in the last generation! - which again has a long history, from an 18th century endowment, originally as a boys' grammar school. Until 1937, part of the "Hark to Bounty" inn was used as a courtroom: recently a TV company requested permission to film a courtroom scene here, but this was refused. How nice to find someone who refuses to bow down and worship the Great God of Television.

Above all, a few hours in Slaidburn and environs can be recommended as a delightful step back in time, far removed from bypasses, motorway cones and nose-to-tail snarl-ups - and thronging crowds. Atavistic, Slaidburn might be, but in no way is it artificial, and that is its great charm. The village is this way because it has chosen to be so, not through any pressure from outside. Here, about twenty miles equidistant from Blackburn, Skipton and Lancaster is an unassuming haven, quiet and friendly. Come and make its acquaintance: you will not be disappointed.

The Walk

Now for the walk! From the main car park in Slaidburn near the bridge over the Hodder, turn briefly right along the road - noting the cafe on your right, recommended for visiting now or later - but turn off to the left before the now disused Wesleyan chapel (waymarker), towards the river. Go along a developing path by an embankment, then up the wooded riverbank. A new footpath sign at this charming spot gives you the choice of following a riverside path or turning up the main path to St.

Walk 15: The Squire's Estates

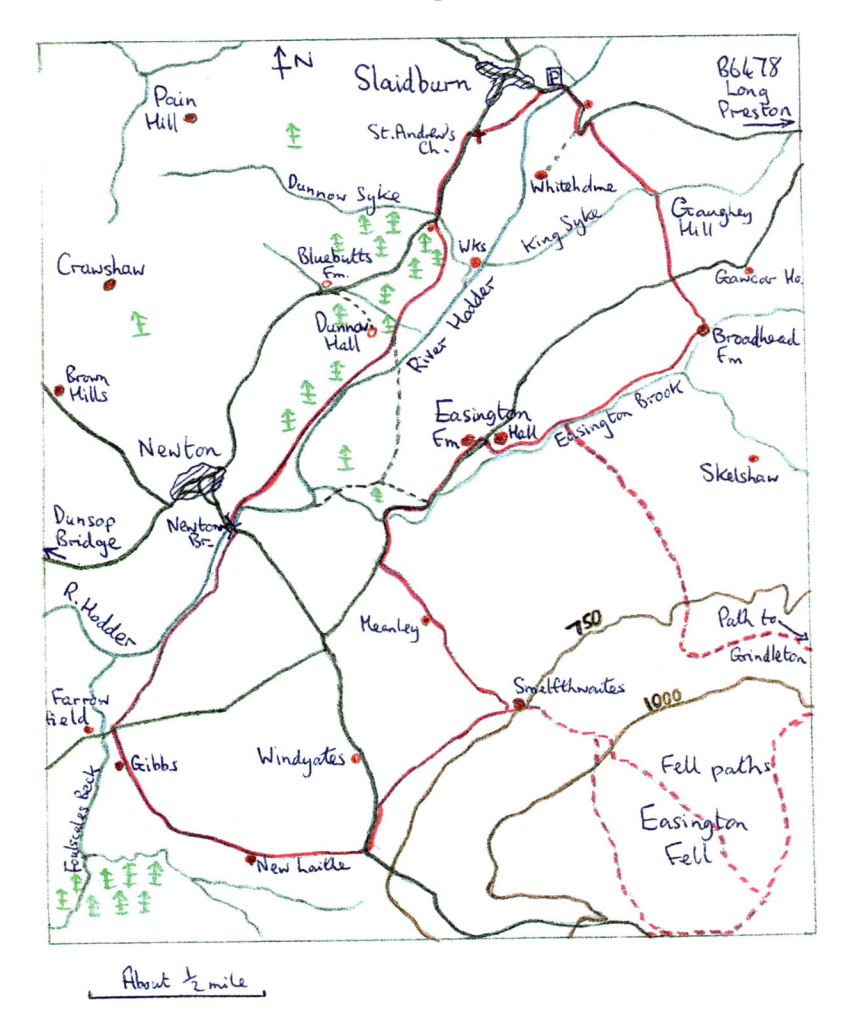

Village Green, Slaidburn

Andrew's church. For the latter, pass through a waymarked gate then keep to the left of two field corners jutting across the meadow; after the second, go down by the fence and through a kissing gate into the churchyard.

Here an apologetic notice by the AA corrects a mistake made in one of their books, recommending a route where no right of way exists! We go through a wooden gate and pass to the left of the church. It's a sure right of way, but it is difficult to cross a churchyard at any time without a more reflective mood overtaking us, a cloud briefly flitting across the sun. Here are the histories of generations of local families, resting in peace, making our visit seem an intrusion. Still, the passing sober note will do the pilgrim no harm: *memento mori*.

Beyond the side door of the church, which should certainly be inspected if you have time, go left over grass to an iron kissing gate by a sundial and onto the road. Turn left down the road for about a quarter-mile. To the left, over the fields, lie the imposing buildings of Whiteholme, long disused but now occupied once more and intended to be made available for holiday lets. Where the road turns right and uphill, go through an iron gate adjoining a house, presumably once the Dunnow lodge, and proceed down the driveway. A small sewage works is soon passed on the left, and here the earlier alternative by the river rejoins our route. Go straight on through a kissing gate, with dramatic rocky outcrops now adjacent on the steep wooded slopes to your right.

Soon the driveway emerging from Dunnow Hall is reached - it crosses a bridge over the Hodder to the left, one way to enter on the short alternative route to Easington. The hall itself has lain disused since the second world war, when it was used as a special school: it still cuts an impressive figure, more so when seen from across the river. We continue downstream on the right bank, the steep cliff still soaring above, through a meadow liable to waterlogging in winter and on through a kissing gate. Go along the obvious path, soon dropping slightly left through a wooden gate (ignore the metal one). Keep by the fence, briefly leaving the river, and Newton soon comes into view.

Before reaching the wall, turn right over a stile, then sharp left over a stone footbridge. Go along with a wall on your left, through a gate and over a wooden footbridge (clear signboard here) then downriver. Very soon climb steps to a gateway and reach the 'B' road at a gate just ahead: a sign say "Public Footpath Slaidburn". Turn left over Newton Bridge: you may well spot sand martins hereabouts in the summer months. Where a track on the left may be used as another short-cut to Easington, we take a gate on the right, "Public Footpath Farrowfield". A sternly-worded notice says, "It is requested that walkers keep strictly to the footpath" - which is all very well, but as usual in lush meadows the tread is practically invisible. However, we must assume the spirit and not the letter of the law is called for.

Certainly the river continues to make a fine companion, and on this stretch we gradually exchange the earlier park-like surroundings for a more open, rural aspect. Totridge Fell looks impressive ahead, appearing as an isolated summit with the plateau behind not seen. Keep fairly close to the Hodder initially, then trend left towards a wall, up stone steps and over a stile. Continue pleasantly downriver, then through a dip and presently over a stile. When the river bends away right, go slightly left and upfield, over a wooden stile by a gate and keep the same line in the next field, on a faint tread, through a gap in the next fence. Proceeding slightly uphill, you presently pass a metal gate onto the road, the official exit being a stile in the hedge just further on (Public Footpath sign), immediately before Farrowfield.

The road reached is a quiet minor one linking the Waddington Fell 'B' road to the hamlet of Cow Ark. Cross it and go up the rough lane serving Gibbs, keeping left of the buildings and through a wooden gate onto a green lane, fenced on both sides. Numerous pheasants can usually be seen hereabouts, with the expected winter parties of fieldfares and redwings. More interestingly, passing this way once I heard a sharp exchange of calls and, looking up, witnessed a fierce altercation between a crow and a kestrel, which fortunately for both parties ended in separation.

Go through a second gate and climb steadily, trending left with the fence. Even from this modest elevation the retrospective view soon opens up nicely, and Penyghent can be seen, NNE. Much nearer in the south are the interesting rocky outcrops of Crag Stones, recently opened up through a permissive path: a possible traverse from the environs of Browsholme towards the fell road would now make a good walk. Still, the present one isn't bad either. About a quarter-mile beyond Gibbs, go through a gate on the left, then through another onto a rough lane, which follow left. It's easy going now: you go through two gateways and pass the outlying farm at New Laithe to reach the fell road in a further half mile, the extensive heathery fell-slopes ever closer on your right. The more distant view has expanded by now to include Parlick Pike, White Hill and Ingleborough when clear.

Turn left briefly along the road, past a little copse, but in about 200yds. take the rough lane on the right, serving Smelfthwaites. This is another easy stroll of about half a mile: you pass two thin copses, one either side, then turn left through a gate just before the splendidly situated farm (dating from 1688). Go down by a stream, with a wall on your right, and enjoy a splendid panorama stretched out before you: Newton, Dunnow and Slaidburn below, with lonely Croasdale and White Hill supplying the backdrop.

Aim to the right of the lately restored buildings at Meanley below and pass through a gate, the earlier stream course now well on the right, and deep. Go on through a wooden gate and join the farm lane, descending steadily to the minor road. Turn right, cross the bridge over Easington Brook and reach Easington in about half a mile: this is an ancient and independent settlement in its own right, mentioned in the Domesday Book. Once past the first building on the right, turn right down a lane and through a gateway below, turning left onto another rough lane. This seems to be the way used now, rather than the footpath marked on the 1:25,000 OS leaving the road a little further on.

Pass the Manor House on your left, and go up the most agreeable valley of Easington Brook, where in season you may expect to see a variety of water birds. Ignore the bridge ahead, keeping up the left bank (true right) of the brook by leaving the lane and turning left through a waymarked gate. The brook is usually clear and vigorous, with a fair volume of water even in summer. Go on through another waymarked gate, then turn slightly left, away from the stream, through a marshy spot where I once disturbed a snipe. You climb a low bank, and soon Broadhead Farm appears ahead: make straight for it, and pass through a gate with an arrow waymarker.

Very much on the last lap now, about a mile to Slaidburn as the crow flies, and visions of a welcome cup of tea in the offing! After the gate, turn half right into the farmyard and come to a crossroads of tracks. You could extend the walk here by continuing up the valley to Harrop Hall, another fine and ancient residence, but our route turns left and follows the farm lane back to the road. Gawcar House, a roadside building on the right, also cuts an impressive figure. Go straight across the road, where a sign says "Public Footpath Slaidburn"; the retrospective sign gives "Public Footpath Skelshaw". Cross a stile and go up by a wall on your left, the slight eminence of Gaughey Hill on your right. Pass through a gate (left), then turn sharp right and go down by a wall adjoining a wooded area. Pass through a little dip, crossing a stream, then go up over stone steps in the wall ahead. Here turn half left, crossing another shallow depression; when you near a copse on the left, turn more to the right over a slight rise, soon dropping to a gate onto the Slaidburn - Long Preston road.

That elusive Slaidburn is at last clearly in view again! Simply follow the road to the left, through a sharp hairpin bend, and the bridge over the Hodder is soon regained: note its confluence with Croasdale Brook, just to the right. The main car park is then down the road on the right, and if you are desperate for that cup of tea you should arrange to be back before 5.00 p.m.

In truth, we passed through quite a few estates on the walk, so I must apologise for the frivolity of the title. Echoes of the past accompanied us all the way through a remarkable variety of residences, old and relatively new, inhabited and deserted. Slaidburn itself remains the centrepiece, however, a delightful throwback, always welcoming at any hour or season: long may it remain so! As to the walk itself, it was included for enjoyment rather than exertion, but if you feel it was a bit short, stay on this channel. We shall soon be taxing those leg muscles more strenuously.

16. BOWLAND - GETTING TO KNOW YOU

Dunsop Bridge, Hareden Brook, Whitmore, Burholme Bridge, Thorneyholme, Dunsop Bridge. 7½ miles. Maps: OS 1:50,000 Landranger no. 103; OS 1:25,000 Explorer OL 41 (Forest of Bowland)

* * * * * * * * * *

Background

Perhaps some of you will cast a quizzical eye at the title of this walk. Surely we have been walking in Bowland, earlier in the book? The pedant has outfoxed himself, this time!

It is, of course, a question of definition. Certainly, if we accept the authorities' definition of the Area of Outstanding Natural Beauty as delineating Bowland, then earlier walks in this volume have truly been 'in Bowland'. But I am not wholly satisfied by such a definition. After all, a line on a map is one thing, but the character or feel of an area is quite another. For myself, and I suspect others who know these parts will agree with me, a distinct change seems to come on crossing the Hodder, whether at Burholme Bridge or on entering Newton or Slaidburn. To the west and north lies the heart of the Forest of Bowland, the soaring fells and mysterious hidden valleys; to the other side of the river lie the foothills, encompassing plenty of fine walking - as witness our Whitewell circular - but the hors d'oeuvre rather than the main course. Old Ordnance Survey maps gave some tacit support to this view, using the name "Bowland Forest Low" in the Bashall Eaves - Whitewell area but implying that the true Forest of Bowland began beyond the Hodder. For myself, I know that a special keen anticipation comes on starting a walk at Langden, Dunsop Bridge or Slaidburn. It may also be apposite that Wainwright, in his book "A Bowland Sketchbook", restricted his drawings in this sector to that same area north and west of the Hodder.

This walk, then, will introduce you to what I regard as the true heart of Bowland, as we enter the final and most demanding set of walks in this book. Today, though, there will be no excessive demands, just a satisfying walk of moderate length which will, I trust, open the curtain to give you a glimpse into the heart of Bowland and leave you with a thirst to return for more. The walk lies between around 300ft. above sea level at Burholme and around 1,000ft. at the Totridge Fell-Mellor Knoll col, with no particularly steep climbs, and on a pleasant day I can promise you a thoroughly enjoyable time.

The Walk

You could begin at Burholme, where there is a little off-road parking, but Dunsop Bridge is the natural starting-point, there being a sizeable car park on the opposite side of the road to the River Dunsop. Here, if you get your timing right, you may enjoy an ice-cream or other refreshments from the post office-cum-cafe before beginning the walk. Go down the road towards the bridge, but instead of crossing its high arch, take a signposted bridlepath on the right adjoining the river. This is initially a metalled road, though no public road for cars, serving only the houses upstream. The Dunsop is a fine, vigorous stream, quite tumultuous in spate (as witnessed by the disastrous flood of 1967 in Whitendale further upstream) and you will enjoy its company. Dippers are frequently to be seen on the stream hereabouts: the fells surrounding the valley are Staple Oak and Whin Fells (L) and Beatrix Fell (R). Cross two fields, then beyond the cottages, passed on their left, keep close to the river and cross a waymarked stile. Proceed upstream briefly on a clear track, then cross the river by a good new footbridge and turn left down the lane, metalled once more. In the opposite direction there is a fine view up the Dunsop valley.

Before reaching the house ahead (Closes Barn on the OS), turn right off the lane and cross a stile. This is marked as a clear bridlepath on the map, but is obviously little used now. Pass by an area of allotments, then through a tall iron gate into a rather wet featureless pasture: uninspiring going, I must admit, hereabouts but it does cut out some road-walking. I would advise you to keep fairly close to the wall on your left - there is no obvious path anywhere. You may admire swallows skimming through the pasture, considerably enhancing the surroundings.

Walk 16: Bowland – Getting to Know You

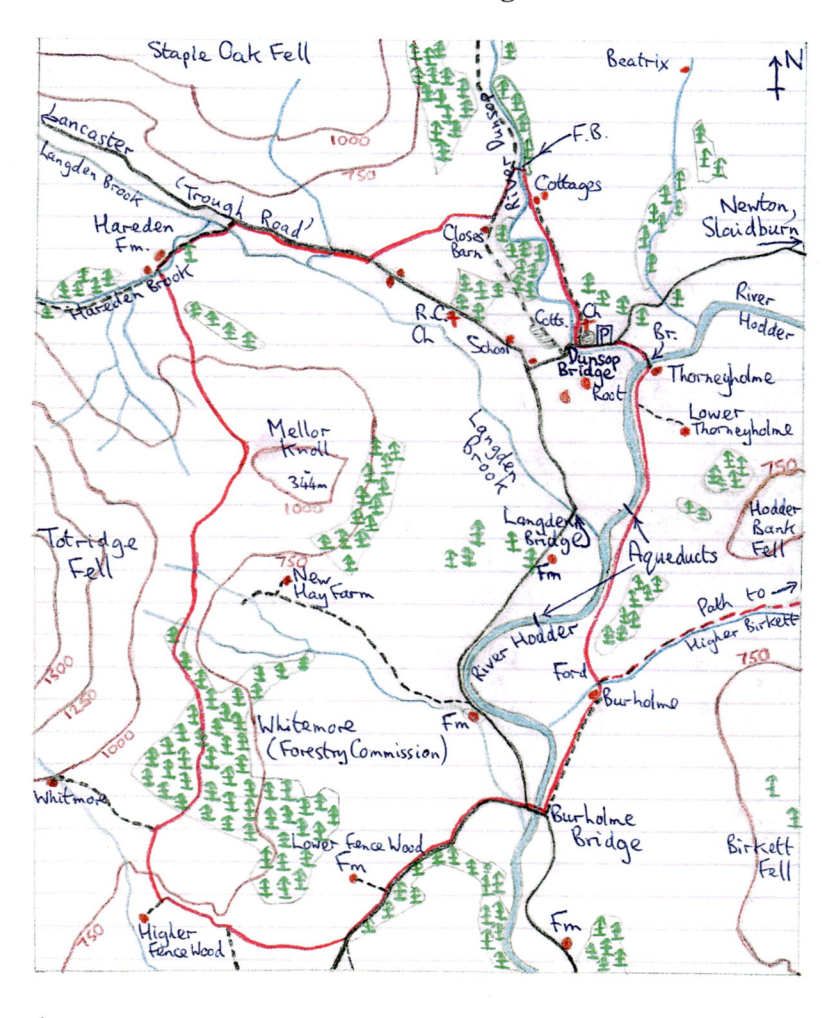

Dunsop Valley, N of Dunsop Bridge

When the wall does a right-angled turn left, keep straight on with roadside buildings on your left, and presently converge onto the Trough Road by a gate with a bridlepath sign. Turn right and go down the road for nearly half a mile, then cross the road and a bridge over Langden Brook before starting to climb up the valley of Hareden. Views up the road are excellent, especially of Hareden Nab and valley. Rather mysteriously, the OS marks a bridlepath as crossing the fine broad stream *above* the bridge, but there seems no authorisation or necessity for this. Go up the pleasant lane ahead, ignoring a branch to the left, crossing the stream to the right then re-crossing it left beyond the kennels. The oldest building of Hareden dates from the 17th century. Here, back on the left (true right*) of the stream, take the clearly signed path over a stile and up the steepish hillside beyond. Note that the main track up Hareden Brook is not at present a right of way but may be explored under the new access situation.

Trend left up the hillside, soon meeting a wall: follow this up, with a clear vehicular track developing on its other side. Cross the wall at a waymarked stile. You will naturally take in the retrospective view towards the Trough of Bowland from here: be patient, it gets even better further on. Beyond the stile, ignore the track adjoining the wood, striking instead diagonally half right, uphill, across the field. Ahead is the curious knobbly summit of Mellor Knoll; behind, the interlocking spurs of the Bowland fells, with (delightfully!) very little road in view. Keep above and to the right of a little gully, aiming for an isolated tree, then pass right again. Cross another stretch of vehicular track and keep climbing, with the bank on your left now quite steep. Trend towards the wall now approached on your right.

After the preceding ill-defined stretch of path, things become much easier for a time. Follow the more definite track seen by the wall and continue uphill, aiming right of Mellor Knoll's summit seen ahead. Pass through a gate and keep on the track. The steep ridges and gullies soaring up to Totridge Fell's

*'*True right*' means the right of the stream looking downstream*

summit on the right look most impressive: I recall watching a glider drifting over the fell here on a bright, breezy day. Within the last decade a new permissive path to Totridge's summit has been opened: a vigorous climb of about 200m from the gate, roughly one mile in lateral distance, rewarded by excellent views.

On the main walk, you reach a track junction, within a few hundred yards of Mellor Knoll's summit. Ignore the left branch: keep right, noting a green and yellow marker post ahead - there is only a faint tread on this section. The line is roughly SSW, and you are on a level promenade at the summit of the walk, the Mellor-Totridge col. Soon an interesting view appears ahead, of the limestone knots to the W of Whitewell with Longridge Fell beyond: in retrospect, the cleft of the Trough of Bowland proper can now be seen. You pass a second, later a third, marker post, then aim for a gateway - possibly open - in the wall ahead. Beyond, keep fairly close to the wall on the left, but *above* it (cf. the OS, which suggests the main right of way path is *below* the wall: this looks disused now). When you reach the wooded area, get close to the wall and follow it, over a small ford. Ahead you soon reach a stile with a small gate adjacent (Forest of Bowland markers). The far side of the gate makes a good stopping-place, among mature beech trees in a park-like area, with pleasing views down to the Hodder valley below.

The farm at New Hey, finely situated, is prominent below with its smart white exterior. Go along the track, losing a little height, in a slight groove, turning right when you observe a waymarker. You quickly merge with another track (again, cf. the OS) and soon bend left. Ford a little stream and continue along the fairly clear track through scattered trees on a delightful terrace. It is an unusual type of walk for these parts, but a beautiful section, contouring through the woodland with Totridge Fell still soaring up on the right and a lovely prospect down to the Hodder on the left. I recall hearing, and catching a fleeting glimpse of, a cuckoo hereabouts during a Spring visit. The more distant views from here extend far into the Dales on a clear day.

The track remains clear as you continue by a fence on your left and pass a gate on the right. Soon you leave the terrace, entering a conifer plantation by a gate at the old Lancashire - Yorkshire boundary (pre-1974). At the time of writing these trees are quite mature, and after the way of these places the next section seems rather gloomy, though the track is broad and obvious, and lately much improved underfoot. One hopes that any changes in the status of the Forestry Commission will not lead to the closure of this and similar paths.

In about three-eighths of a mile the path emerges into daylight again. Pass through a gate and follow an obvious track ahead, with a little brook on your left. When you reach the farm lane coming down from Whitmore by some hen coops, you will surely admire the view up to the superbly situated farm, right - nestling beautifully in a deep 'cwm' or hollow below the fell, quite unseen from the main valley road below. Turn left along the lane, nearing the limestone knolls or knots seen earlier. According to Alan Lawson, calamine (or zinc carbonate) was once mined near here: the 1:25,000 OS notes old quarries, one near Lickhirst Farm, under a mile away, and another just off our route, ahead. The latter is passed when, after taking the left branch at a division of lanes, we soon zig-zag past a little gully on the left.

Shortly after the zig-zag, the main path bends to the right: we keep straight on, following a fainter track, soon passing through a gate. Continue downhill on much the same line in the long field ahead, gradually merging with the fence on the right, keeping alongside it after passing a little hut. The view ahead of the Hodder valley between Whitewell and Dunsop Bridge is beautiful, with Hodder Bank and Birkett Fells making an agreeable backdrop. Lower down, leave the field by a gate, passing onto a road (that coming from Doeford Bridge and Chipping) by a public footpath sign, with a wood on the opposite side.

Simply follow the road left, downhill, for about three-quarters of a mile. Beyond the end of the wood, the countryside has a much more open feel, and the Whitewell-Dunsop Bridge road comes into view. In retrospect you will easily pick out the Totridge-Mellor col traversed earlier, now perched high above.

On reaching the road junction, turn right over the stately arch of Burholme Bridge. Just seventeen miles to Lancaster, the signpost notes! - via the Trough of Bowland, of course. At one time, 'over the Trough to Lancaster' was very much a recognised walkers' route, but the volume of traffic today is such that it can only be recommended out of season. Still, it remains a splendid journey, with kaleidoscopic changes of mood and dramatic scenery.

Immediately after the bridge, turn sharp left along Burholme Farm lane, keeping close by the Hodder initially. The sharp V-shaped cleft of the Dunsop valley to the north is very effectively seen hereabouts, and the Hodder runs swiftly close at hand, with a rich variety of bird life often on show - particularly during migratory seasons. Pied and grey wagtails, dippers, gulls, waders including oystercatcher, common sandpiper, redshank and herons, to name just some, may be seen. On reaching the farmyard at Burholme, trend a little right at first between the buildings, then left: the farm has been smartly repainted recently. Go over a little footbridge, then pass through a gate. An alternative longer route, worth investigating sometime, turns off to the right here, climbing Fielding Clough to the Birkett-Hodder Bank *col* (and on to the Newton - Dunsop Bridge road).

We keep straight on after the gate, well to the left of Burholme Wood seen ahead, home of many rabbits and noisy pheasants. Pass through an open gateway, then turn half right along a faint track. After the next gate, we are soon back by the Hodder, another lovely stretch. Beyond another gate (large and small ones adjacent; pass through the latter), the confluence of the Hodder with Langden Brook is passed at a gravelly stretch. An obvious and rather garish metal bridge (actually a pipeline aqueduct) is now immediately ahead, seeming incongruous among so much easy-going pastoral scenery. Do *not* cross this, but keep close by the riverside, briefly negotiating a wet area. Here I was once intrigued to watch what appeared to be a territorial dispute between two dippers, each bird doubtless patrolling its own stretch of river as a rule. Sparrowhawks may also be seen hereabouts, benefitting from nearby tree cover.

Ahead, cross a simple wooden stile, and go on upriver. A strand of fine trees on the far bank adds to the attraction of the riverside here. When the river begins to bend right, we merge with a vehicular track and go on through a gate. Here is another confluence, of Dunsop and Hodder: don't be distracted, but note a footpath sign on a wall directing you to the left (still close by the river) whereas the gate straight on leads into the private grounds of Thorneyholme. This was once an hotel, and later a health farm but is currently a private house once more. Go through a metal gate and turn left over a bridge, passing down a driveway of fine Scots pines. Where the road is joined there is a small footpath sign opposite (easily missed): the car park is now clearly just ahead, across from the Dunsop.

Not as long or demanding as a number of our walks, but a very satisfying circuit with some really beautiful views. Today we have only explored the fringes of the high fells, where the true majesty and mystery of Bowland are to be found, but scenically this Dunsop-Whitmore-Burholme triangle ranks with the best. I hope your appetite will be sufficiently whetted to move on to those high fells, which we shall explore in the final set of walks as the book, to my mind, reaches its climax.

17. ONLY BY PERMISSION

Tower Lodge, Tarnbrook, Tarnbrook Fell, Ward's Stone, Grit Fell, Jubilee Tower. 10 miles. Maps: OS 1:50,000 Landranger nos. 102, 103; OS 1:25,000 Explorer OL 41 (Forest of Bowland).

* * * * * * * * * *

Notice
This walk, and the surrounding area of Bowland, have benefited more than any other in this book, from the walker's point of view, from the Countryside and rights of way act (2000). See the notice at the beginning of the book. I have kept largely to my original text to avoid major rewriting but it will remind my readers how much less restrictive the situation is now!

Background
In some respects we are stretching our limits by including this walk in the collection. To begin with, the walk barely qualifies on the map criterion: only a part of it lies on no. 103, and the actual summit of Ward's Stone lies off it by a mile or so. Of more significance, possibly, is that very little of the route lies on open rights of way, namely only the first section from Tower Lodge. Once you reach the Tarnbrook Wyre, you are on a defined access strip which stretches from Tarnbrook over the summit of Ward's Stone to Quernmore. The landowners are at liberty to close the access when they wish to do so; this happened for instance in the summer of 1992, when I was doing my fieldwork, and as I found then to my cost, it can be the dickens of a job to find when the route will be opened again. When, as on that occasion, the reason for closure appears tenuous – 'drought conditions' which were more apparent in some dusty office than on the ground - the frustration to the walker is heightened.

What is your attitude towards permissive paths, concessionary routes, access strips and the like? Some walkers, I know, react to such as a bull to a red rag. They will point to the long tradition of organised trespass in this country, as for instance that on Kinder Scout in the 1930s which was an important link in the establishment of the Pennine Way. Consequently they have no hesitation in turning a blind eye to the authorities, indeed openly defying them. At the other end of the spectrum, there are walkers who will avoid those areas altogether. If the walker isn't welcome, they say, we would rather go elsewhere, eschew access strips and the like, and keep to the known rights of way.

My position is somewhere between those two extremes. Half a loaf, as they say, is better than no bread; and remember that the situation in the Bowland fells has improved markedly for the walker, as the courtesy paths on both Ward's Stone and Fair Snape Fell (see Walk 18) are fairly new. Naturally, in common with many other walkers, I keenly anticipate further developments. Concessionary paths, I believe, need not be regarded as inferior to open access areas or rights of way. Regulation of pedestrian traffic to defined bands helps the maintenance of distinctive local environments and minimises the disruption of wildlife - factors which should positively enhance one's enjoyment of the walk. In this particular case, moreover, Ward's Stone is a natural objective for the walker: it is, after all, the summit of Bowland. A remote and fairly bleak summit, true, described by Wainwright as a lunar landscape, but excelling in its views over Morecambe Bay to the southern Lake District. That alone should convince the waverers that this walk is worth the effort: and, far from having suspicious eyes watching your every step lest you stray outside that access strip, you are more likely to walk in near-isolation, in my experience.

A little digression: where should the next new footpaths or access areas be established in Bowland? Let me indulge in some kite-flying by making three suggestions.

1. A path linking the Hornby Road with the Bentham road near Cross of Greet Bridge, taking in the summit of White Hill and Bloe Greet. This, apart from its intrinsic worth - White Hill is the second highest summit in Bowland - would open up some very appealing new circular routes.

2. A path continuing up the Brennand River beyond the farm (where a non-access track already exists) continuing to the summit of the interesting Wolfhole Crag, thence either joining the Ward's Stone route or again linking with the Hornby Road.

3. Opening of the track up Hareden Brook to the public, thence linking with Saddle Fell and on to Fair Snape, or to Bleadale Water and Langden.

Just a little gentle dreaming, yes, but what splendid prospects those three routes would offer the walker! It would be nice to think they had a chance of becoming reality by the next century.*

Returning to the subject in hand, Ward's Stone, as I said earlier, may only be tackled via the access strip. To turn the walk into a circular is possible, but a very long walk and/or considerable road-walking would be required; the alternatives are either to retrace your steps - always a less than satisfying business - or arrange some transport at both ends. A two-car walk is one obvious solution, but there is an interesting alternative, if you get the details of time and distance correct. During the summer, minibuses run along the Trough Road regularly on Sundays and Bank Holidays between Jubilee Tower and Tower Lodge. Clitheroe Tourist Information Centre willl have details. In this way, you may park at Tower Lodge by the Marshaw Wyre at (604539), finish your walk by the Jubilee Tower at (542573) and take the coach back to the start - or vice versa. In fact, the access strip continues beyond the summit of Grit Fell as an access area to the attractive Clougha Pike, thence descending to the village of Quernmore. But I think it is much more satisfying to explore Clougha from the Quernmore side, an ideal short stroll - and there I really would have strayed far beyond my map remit.

Geographically, it will be clear enough even to those with the most cursory interest in such matters that we have strayed far from our usual stamping-grounds here. The walk as described is

* *These suggestions were made when the original MS. for this book was prepared in the 1990's. For a progress report, see the end of this section (p188)*

entirely within the Wyre catchment area, though on the highest section over Ward's Stone and Grit Fell you are treading the Wyre-Lune watershed. But make the most of your excursion away from the Hodder-Ribble province: the views en route are different, but inspiringly so, and on a clear day you will gaze admiringly over Morecambe Bay and across to the Lake District, as well as recognising more familiar mountain shapes in the Yorkshire Dales. The walk is a tough one, calling for about 2000ft. of climbing, and with some heavy going underfoot: in mist, moreover, navigational skill with map and compass will be needed. Despite the relative proximity of the Three Peaks and the peaks of Lakeland, the walk has nothing in common with those areas: it has its own definite Bowland character, elusive and secretive.

The Walk

Parking space is available in limited measure at Tower Lodge by the roadside (unfenced); this attractive tree-lined fringe of the Marshaw Wyre is a justly popular spot. Alternatively, you may begin the walk in Tarnbrook, avoiding some extra climbing involved on the main route (but also missing some fine views): the routes converge half a mile E of the hamlet. Note, however, if relying on the coach to return, that you will then also have to walk back from Lee to Tarnbrook. Tarnbrook is in fact a charming, peaceful hamlet of neat stone cottages, well worth a visit in its own right but patently unsuited to much traffic.

A rather apologetic "Public Footpath" sign marks the start of the walk by Tower Lodge, where you climb a stile and follow a clear track uphill leading N. Pass through another gate, adjoining a thin strip of woodland, and initially bend left with the track, but leave it where it turns back sharp right, following instead a waymarker post. The 1:25,000 OS maps are a great help here, as there is no discernible tread initially. Turn half right, cross a ruined wall near what seem to be the remains of some old outbuildings, and maintain the same line till you locate a waymarked stile in a fence running N-S. Things become easier now, with a visible tread: keep roughly the same line over another two stiles, the first in an E-W wall, the next in a N-S one.

Walk 17: Only By Permission

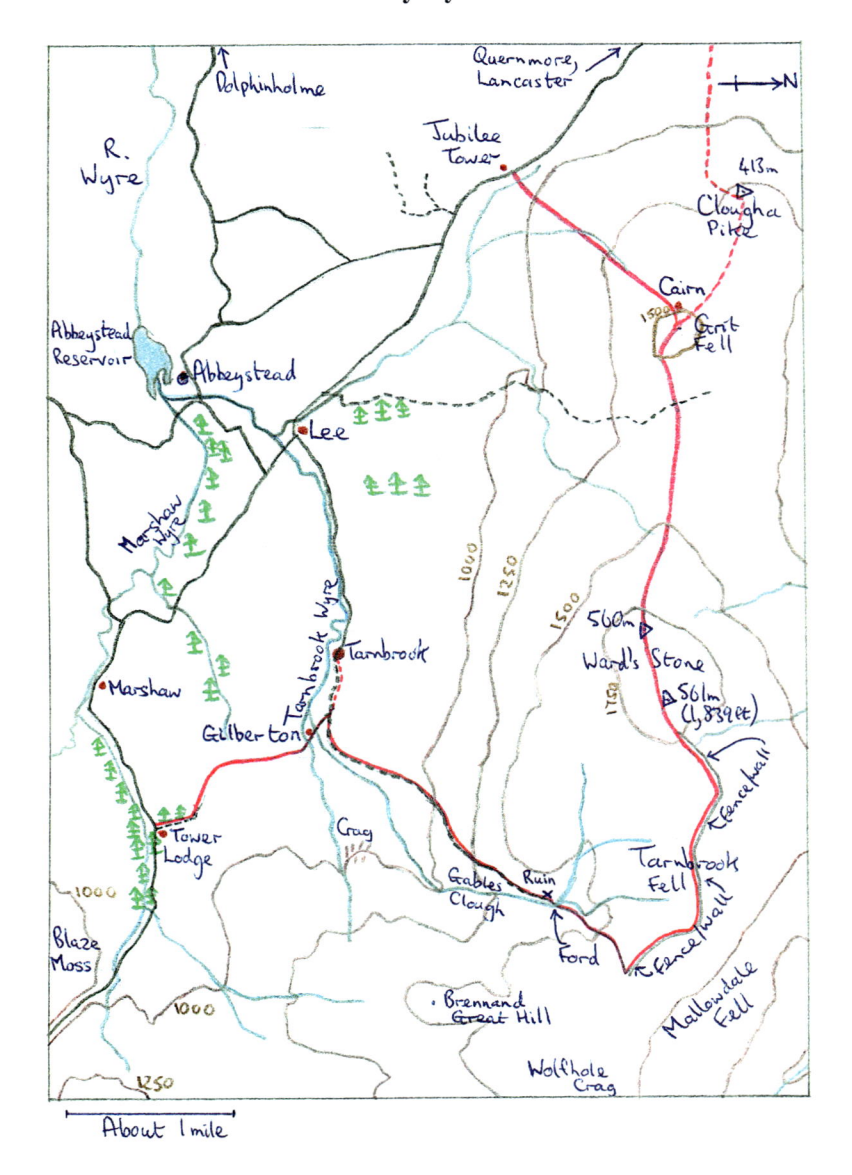

Turn sharp right down the wallside here, with a striking and bluntly powerful view of your objective ahead, rising across the Tarnbrook Wyre valley.

Pass through an open gateway and keep on downhill. Always irksome, this! All the lost height must be regained later - and more. But it's worth the effort. Negotiate the next wall via stone steps in the corner, then pass through a gully with a deep little ravine visible over the wall on your right. Further downhill, trend slightly left through a waymarked gate, then turn right, passing between farm outbuildings (Speight Clough) onto a clear track. Turn left with this, but before reaching the main farm (Gilberton) go half right to cross a footbridge over a most attractive stretch of the Tarnbrook Wyre - I have seen common sandpiper here. Turn left, and almost at once you join another clear track: follow it (right) over a cattle grid to a junction, where there is an informative sign concerning the route and the access strip.

Tarnbrook hamlet lies about a third of a mile to the left here, but we turn right along the well-defined vehicular track, which was clearly visible during the earlier descent, rising across the slopes of Tarnbrook Fell. Follow this track into the growing solitude ahead, the Tarnbrook Wyre valley always down on your right. It's a well-graded climb initially, but steepens about one-and-a half miles beyond the access sign as the river comes nearer again. You enter the attractive, narrowing ravine of Gables Clough, the track now levelling out again. Beyond the second of what appear to be turning circles, the track downgrades to a path, with a stone hut (excellent shelter!) on your left and the stream negotiating small waterfalls on your right.

A little further on, the path fords the stream (care in spate!) and continues over open moorland, initially close to a branch of the main stream, then turning away NE. A new, made track has greatly eased the next section: it is easily followed and aims for our next objective, the border fence. Be careful in thick mist, nevertheless, and keep the general NE bearing in mind. After about half a mile you will reach a fence, to be crossed by a stile with two large peat tors just to its right. This is a significant point in the journey, where the Wyre-Lune watershed is attained. Much of the walking up to now has been of a hidden, secretive character, truest Bowland: now quite suddenly you encounter - on clear days - a fine and dramatic view of the Three Peaks area, the northern flanks of the Ward's Stone massif being steeper than the slopes you have just crossed. Ingleborough, with its cut-off summit, looks particularly grand from here. You will be making the acquaintance of a large number of seagulls, Tarnbrook Fell housing a major colony: lesser black-backs appear to be especially abundant.

From this point, route-finding is greatly eased by a fence and/or wall which continues in a wandering fashion to a few hundred yards from Ward's Stone summit. You should resist any temptation to make a beeline for the summit: as well as being harder to follow, this would make for purgatorial progress over much rougher ground. On the watershed (followed by the fence/wall) there are some boggy patches, but nothing too severe - and you can't get lost.

Keep initially on the NE side of the fence, then, through a peaty area, and after around a quarter of a mile recross the fence by a stile. Just a little way ahead is a section of substantial wall, behind which I was once glad to shelter on a day of strong easterly winds and enjoy my tea. Looking round from south to west the scene is primeval indeed: open moorland, exposed peat and craggy outcrops of the prevalent millstone grit, which become ever more extensive and weathered as we near Ward's Stone summit.

In another quarter of a mile, turn sharp left with the wall, then continue just S of W onto an extensive plateau, now over the 1700ft. contour. Keep following the fence/wall, first with a pronounced bend to the right, later encountering a stile by a junction, less than a mile from the summit. It seems natural to cross the stile, though in fact the going is then more taxing, with a steep little gorge and an extensive squelchy area to negotiate. Whichever you decide on, turn left - but before going on you will be transfixed by the view ahead, if clear, a superb prospect of Lakeland (Coniston fells prominent) across Morecambe Bay.

In half a mile we finally say goodbye to the fence at a sharp re-entrant; if on the N side you will have to cross it, using a strategic boulder. Watch your step from here on, in mist! There is a long stretch ahead with no guiding fence or wall, but many rocky outcrops which may confuse. From the fence terminus, a bearing of 260 degrees will bring you to the East (true) summit of Ward's Stone in 200yds., with a triangulation pillar: 561m (1,839ft.). Look around you, if you can, and take it all in: this is the highest ground for many miles, and the panorama is extensive, with distant glimpses of other places visited in these pages - and much more. Pendle stands some 17m to the SE: still that distinctive, proud outline, though overtopped by a few feet by our present summit. I remember my intense feeling of childish disappointment, long ago, when discovering that my 'local hero' Pendle was just worsted for height by what I then regarded as a dull, sprawling mass. Strange anthropomorphism! Unspectacular, Ward's Stone may be, but it has its own very pronounced, strong character. The weathering of the gritstone here has produced some remarkable shapes, reminiscent in miniature of the High Peak area: Queen's Chair, Grey Mare and Foal, Cat and Kittens, the 1:25,000 map calls some of them - names of poetic licence, true, but also 'echt' Bowland in their way.

 We press on towards the more popular, though marginally lower, western summit. In clear weather this is visible from the true summit, and a faint tread with a cairn or two will also help. In mist, the bearing between the two summits is 250 degrees. This is arguably the finer viewpoint, not in the sense of being more extensive, but in that the relatively sharp fall of land between NW and SW gives more depth and prospect to the view in that arc. Here again there are numerous rocky outcrops, including the dominant specimen which gave the hill its name, large enough to provide a fair measure of shelter. In characteristic Bowland fashion, though, the name seems ambiguous. Is it a reference to a particular person? - or ward' meaning protection, custody?

 Easy going, now, mostly downhill to the finish. En route to Grit Fell, the first few yards through the rocky outcrops are a little indistinct, but soon a discernible tread begins, waymarked by a few posts, and significantly easier going than the Tarnbrook side. In mist, the bearing is marginally N of W (280 degrees), keeping to the height of the land on a moderately well-defined ridge; on a fine day, particularly if the time draws on, it may become a very pleasant walk into a golden sunset, Morecambe Bay dominating the skyline ahead. An unusual type of walk for East Lancashire landlubbers, but a most refreshing change. Just at the Grit Fell - Ward's Stone col, an estate road or track cuts the access strip at right angles (the 1:50,000 OS is in error here; the track exists on both sides of the path, as on the 1:25,000 map). Notices here warn the walker severely not to stray from his permitted band, but I understand there are no plans to install searchlights or border patrols - as yet.

The path, at any rate, remains cairned and easy to follow, with a gentle rise of about 120ft. then required to attain Grit Fell's summit. From here, proceed NW for a very short distance, then cross a fence by a stile (more access area information signs here) and turn left along the fence. Soon this turns more sharply left, marking the start of the last lap as we now head quite smartly downhill SW, aiming for the Jubilee Tower, which is quickly spotted. You pass a huge and rather professionally constructed cairn, the Shooters Pile, deemed worthy of a drawing by A.W. in his sketchbook. Very simple going now, but the views over the Bay and of the western fringe of Bowland to the south remain extensive, one definite bonus of doing the walk this way round. Keep close to the fence on your left and evade the more boggy patches as well as you can.

In fact it is easy to slip into autopilot here, and perhaps miss something interesting. This happened to me once when I was slow to pick up a clear, whistling call that should have been distinctive. Yes, golden plover - and, looking up, then right, I saw a pair some fifty yards away. But in the instant of looking up, there was something else altogether: about the size of a mistle thrush or a little more, brownish above, flying swiftly, pointed angular wings, banded tail. Female merlin? Quite possibly. I have seen merlin in Scotland, unmistakably, and the habitat hereabouts is eminently suitable. Never heed those who scornfully dismiss 'dull moorlands': they merely show their own dullness. For those with eyes to see, there are many prizes to be had up here.

Soon you will be down at the Jubilee Tower, enjoying the view from the parapet if you will, and hoping your minibus will be on time! Always check beforehand - the exact times vary from year to year - but remember we are talking about Sundays. The Clitheroe Tourist Information Centre should have details. You may also have time to read the fascinating story of the Quernmore Burial, given on a plaque in the adjacent car park. Dark Age antiquities, this one from the seventh century, are not common in these parts. The journey once begun is short, traffic permitting: about twelve minutes, barely time in which to begin recollecting the day's walk. But your eyes will be drawn to the left as you pull away, to the boulder-strewn slopes of Ward's Stone, and in the mind's eye, out of sight, the mysterious hidden recesses of Bowland resting silently once more.

<u>Footnote</u> to suggestions 2 and 3 (p181)

Recently, routes close to both 2 and 3 have been granted. A new concessionary path now continues to the E from Saddle Fell, then turning NE to the summit of Totridge Fell before dropping to join the Hareden bridleway (Walk 16) near the Totridge-Mellor Knoll col. The section between Totridge summit and the bridleway was noted in Walk 16. Finally, a new section of concessionary path now links Tarnbrook Fell and the Hornby Road, taking in Wolfhole Crag.

18. PRIMEVAL VISIONS

Langden Brook, Langden Castle, Fiendsdale, Border Fence, Fair Snape Fell, Saddle Fell, Bleadale Water, Langden Castle, Langden Brook. 12 miles. Maps: OS 1:50,000 Landranger nos 103, 102; OS 1:25,000 Explorer OL 41 (Forest of Bowland)

"I will give you the treasures of darkness, and the hoards in secret places". Isaiah 45.3.

Alternatives: Two excellent through walks spring very naturally from this circular. From the gate in the old county boundary fence at (587484), a path goes directly across (SW), sketchily at first, becoming clearer on the slopes of Holme House Fell, then heading for its terminus at Bleasdale. Or from the summit (either) of Fair Snape Fell you may pick up the excellent ridge to Parlick Pike, thence dropping to Fell Foot and on to Chipping via paths and quiet lanes. For more detail on the ascents of Parlick and Fair Snape from the south, see Gillham (op.cit).

* * * * * * * * * *

Background

I well remember how profoundly this walk impressed me on my first visit - and I should not consider myself, normally, as a first impressions person. Certainly I was moved sufficiently to record those impressions in writing, with all the accepted inadequacy of prose, soon afterwards. Although memory is a factor, there is unquestionably much to be said for writing down one's feelings quickly in such a case, and I was glad to have done so. This is another walk which breaches the boundaries of map no. 103, but I make no apology for that.

If there is a quintessential Bowland walk, this is it. A matter of taste? Well, yes, inevitably there must be that caveat. I do not say it is the most beautiful or satisfying walk in the book, even for me; perhaps the Whitendale - Croasdale circular (Walk 19) is that, perhaps my feelings change on that subject with time. But to see the true nature of Bowland, to feel the pulse of the Forest - yes, this walk will show you Bowland's inner secrets in a special way. It seems a journey back in time, moreover, away from the feverish pace and insidious noise of our age to an uncomplicated - but still disturbing - solitude; a solitude stretching back over the centuries. These inner secrets are not easily yielded: indeed, this is probably, in a technical sense, the most demanding walk in the book. About 1500ft. of climbing are called for, but more significantly the going is heavy on the fell-tops: those with no experience of walking in peaty moorland will undoubtedly find it laborious. However, those who have knowledge of the first twenty-five miles of the Pennine Way, Bleaklow, Black Hill, White Moss and related horrors, will consider our walk quite a stroll. Before you lace your boots up, I must emphasise that a compass - and the ability to use it - are *de rigueur* here.

The walk as described is a true circular from Langden Castle, but note that the section along Bleadale Water is *not* a right of way, though a long recognised footpath runs up here. The land here is owned by North West Water, part of the Bowland Estate, and the current status of the Bleadale Water path is that of a concessionary footpath: this applies up to the link with the border fence on Saddle Fell. In practical terms, this means the route is subject to closure at certain times of year, notably nesting time and the grouse-shooting season.* You may then be requested to use an alternative route, possibly involving the retracing of your steps to the gate in the fence at (587484) and back down Fiendsdale to Langden. Still a fine walk, of course, though not as satisfying as the circular.

Concerning the actual walking, note too that the Bleadale valley is narrow and steep in its higher section, and the path could be hazardous after heavy rain or when icy, with possible landslips. To link up with the fence on Saddle Fell, moreover, above the head of Bleadale, you will need to negotiate half a mile of featureless heather moor, very tricky in mist, and tough going.

* See, again, the introductory notice to this book. Even under the new extended access situation, the possibility of closure remains.

Walk 18: Primeval Visions

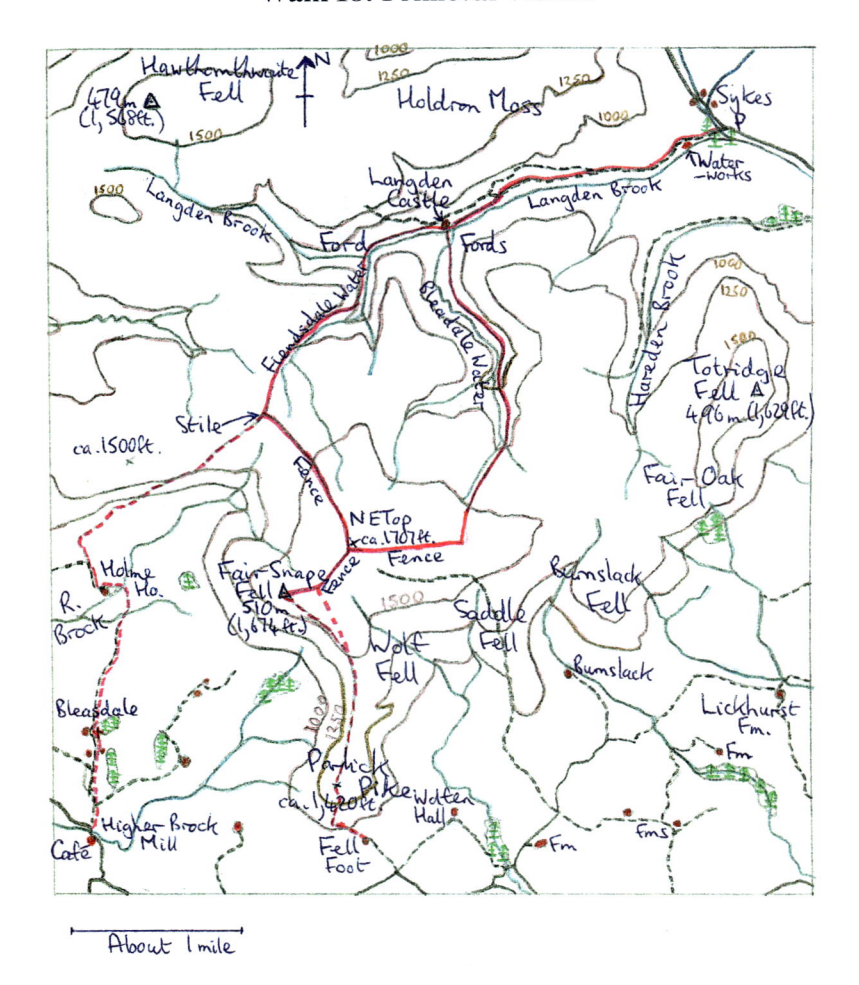

Finally, this section involves two stream crossings which may be impossible when they are in spate. You have been warned! Now let the walk commence.

The Walk

Begin on the famous Trough Road, the traditional way from Clitheroe to Lancaster, at (633513). Here you will find a good amount of parking space, a refreshment van which will seem even more welcome on your return, and a clear footpath sign indicating the through route to Bleasdale. The first section is actually quite out of keeping with the main part of the walk: a shady, tree-lined metalled lane on the right of Langden Brook, leading past the well-maintained water bailiff's house. Indeed, many who had parked will prove simply to be enjoying this short, pleasant stroll. A notice formerly affixed at this point, explaining that the house was not Langden Castle (Gillham, Wainwright) no longer exists. On passing through the gate following, and leaving most of the tourists behind, the real walk begins as we enter the narrow and deepening confines of the impressive Langden valley. Initially the path is a broad vehicular track, quite an ugly scar, with the afforested slopes of the quaintly named Miry Ellis beyond the stream on your left. The width of the boulder-strewn watercourse hereabouts testifies to the brook's power in flood. Beyond a small neat hut (also waterworks property) the track becomes tidier, and further on, nearly a mile from the start, take the left-hand path, clearly signed, at a division (an estate track goes uphill here). The scenery has rapidly improved, and would not in any way disgrace a Scottish glen, albeit in miniature: a narrow thoroughfare accompanied by the fine stream, closed in by steep flanking slopes. The view ahead is opening up, too, of the high fells terminating the Langden and Fiendsdale valleys.

Further ahead, where the main track turns uphill, a narrow avoiding footpath can be used to cut out a little climb and re-descent; if you keep to the main track you encounter a division, again clearly signed, where the previous loop of estate road rejoins our track. Either way, Langden Castle soon comes into view in all its glory - not of architecture, but of setting. It is certainly a fitting place, about two miles out, to make a first halt and take in this memorable scene by the confluence of the main Langden Brook and Bleadale Water: a little flat oasis quite hemmed in by the soaring fells. I have often stopped here for a bite to eat, sometimes waiting for the elements to relent before continuing. Only a tin-roofed shepherds' hut, perhaps (possibly a hut for shooting parties once), but I know few more welcome ports in a storm, and in addition one of those hidden, secret locations so characteristic of Bowland.

Beyond the castle, keep up the *main* Langden valley, crossing a side-stream from Holdron Moss, Black Clough, then again take the left fork at a clearly-marked path division. Here the vehicular track is definitely left, the path to follow being indicated by a succession of tipped poles, cairns and waymarker discs. Cross Langden Brook finally beyond Bleadale Nab, at the next side valley branching off to the left, fording the stream alongside a cairn. This may need care should the stream be in spate. Keep well above the deep bed of Fiendsdale Water on your left, climbing rapidly at first up the steep bank of this superb narrow valley. The path, a little indistinct at first, becomes much clearer as height is gained: a stiff pull for a time as height is gained, then swinging round to the right at an easing gradient, with excellent retrospective views opening up over Fiendsdale. As Gillham rightly says, it seems quite remote from any human interference here: you are more likely to make the acquaintance of growing numbers of grouse as you climb.

Eventually you emerge onto the plateau at about 1400ft., and on a clear day you will already be appreciating the extensive views. Ward's Stone, the summit of Bowland (see Walk 17) lies almost exactly north from here, six miles distant, with White Hill, the second highest point, some miles to its east, lying above the prominent nick in which the Hornby Road (Walk 20) runs. Towering above these intermediate heights, still in the N to NE arc, but more distant, you may pick out the characteristic shapes of Ingleborough, Penyghent and Fountains Fell.

Don't get too carried away by the scenery, though, as route-finding becomes quite tricky hereabouts - though a few cairns are placed to help. In really thick weather, take a SSW

(200 degrees) bearing, which will bring you to the old boundary fence in under half a mile, a particularly boggy stretch just before it. Here you may opt for the through route to Bleasdale, with the comforting knowledge that the hardest work is behind you. Our main route, however, turns SE along the fence - after crossing it. This fence, an invaluable help in hill fog, formed the Lancashire - Yorkshire border until 1974. Though the 1:25,000 OS appears to suggest that the path crossed the fence twice (Gillham, too, implies this as the recommended route), it seems simpler to me to keep on the W side of the fence: you will have enough work to do evading the worst of the peat bog, and you are in a defined access area. After a mile and a quarter's tough going, your direction having turned round to SSE, you reach a fence junction, with the true summit of Fair Snape Fell (1707ft.) immediately on your left, marked by a cairn.

Only hardened 'summit baggers' are likely to linger here, for the views from Fair Snape's lower (SW) summit are more attractive, particularly in the coastal arc. Reaching it is trivial in clear weather. A reasonably distinct tread, with one or two cairns, is now developing between the two summits of Fair Snape and actually affords easier going underfoot than the route adjacent to the fence. A new fence here cuts across your route, crossed by a simple stile. In mist, follow the fence SW until it turns sharply left, then strike out for about a quarter of a mile on a WSW (250 degrees) bearing. This more popular summit has a range of items on show: a triangulation column (1675ft.), a substantial and effective wall shelter and a large cairn which may bear a pole (Paddy's Pole) - if not broken or vandalised. A superb viewpoint, but it has always been a rather lonely windswept summit for me, more truly in the Bowland character perhaps, as I have sat here enjoying alfresco snacks.

On a clear day, you will gaze long at the view in the western sector, stretching from the Ribble estuary (indeed, from well south of it) round to Blackpool, with the tower clearly visible, Fleetwood, then Heysham - the power station being bluntly obvious - Lancaster, Morecambe Bay and the southern Lake District. I recall with amusement Wainwright's scorn vented on those who, from the summit of Coniston Old Man, sighted . . . "Calder Hall . . . Blackpool Tower . . . Millom and sundry other man-made monstrosities. This book" (with almost audible disdain) "does not deign to cater for such tastes".* Well, I make no such judgements, but if you *do* wish to admire fells rather than coastal scenery, the main (NE) summit is certainly a better point whence to view the remainder of Bowland, the Yorkshire Dales, Pendle and environs and the South Pennines.

Continuing the walk, there is another choice to make. If you intend to complete the through walk to Chipping, it is simplest - particularly in mist - to regain the boundary fence by the sharp turn, then follow it, SSE at first, over the splendid ridge onto Parlick Pike. In fact, a more direct, cairned route from the summit leads SE to the fence further along the ridge at (597464). To complete the Langden circular, however, regain the fence junction by Fair Snape's NE summit, cross by a stile and this time follow the fence E above the spurs of Wolf Fell and Saddle Fell. After about three-quarters of a mile of hard, boggy going from the fence junction (a steady fifteen minutes: Naismith! - for use in mist) another junction is reached with a fence dropping SSE. On a clear day, the view remains excellent during this promenade, the bulk of Totridge Fell now looming ahead. From the junction, at (608474), cross a rudimentary stile at a boggy patch and take a NNE bearing, following it closely - not easy over rough ground and thick heather. In ten minutes at the most you should pick up one of the streams feeding Bleadale Water, just where it begins to cut more deeply into the plateau. Get down close to the stream - there is a lone sheltered tree by its side - and follow it as it curves round left, picking up other small streams in the process. A few very helpful waymarker posts now assist on this section. Soon a sketchy but serviceable path develops on the right of the stream, and this can be carefully followed into the deepening valley, with impressive scenery now opening up.

From "The Southern Fells" A.Wainwright (Westmorland Gazette)

Does anyone, incidentally, know the origin of the curious - not to say sinister - name 'David's Tomb', applied to a nearby part of the moorland?

Bleadale Water, down which you are now proceeding, is a real gem, just as spectacular as Fiendsdale, though arguably even more attractive, being dotted with trees and becoming of generous width. You pass a small waterfall on a left-hand branch of the main stream, and later a small ruinous hut at another confluence by which time the going is easier. Though the path remains sketchy, it is always easy to follow, on the right bank of the stream, allowing you to enjoy this beautiful secluded stretch of Bowland at leisure, the hardest walking now behind you. A number of sheep are usually met on this section, on the grassy areas near the broadening stream. Some new fencing has appeared on this stretch, but gates allow a straightforward passage.

The valley, too, broadens considerably, and after a pronounced swing to the right you will see Langden Castle in front of you once more. But there may be a sting in the tail, as Bleadale Water must first be forded, and this may necessitate some searching for a suitable spot if the stream is high. Once over, the second ford - of Langden Brook itself - is actually easier; then, after negotiating a boggy patch, you arrive by the Castle with the comforting knowledge that a brisk half-hour's walk down the track will return you to the car park at Langden intake.

I usually reach this spot somewhere near dusk, with not another soul in sight, and time ahead to meditate the day's walk. One question I have often asked myself is: what do you mean by a beautiful walk? By conventional judgement, this one would hardly be considered so. But I would contend there are different sorts of natural beauty. There is beauty of immediate surroundings - a stroll in Borrowdale on a bright Autumn day, say, with the trees turning. Then again, there is beauty of grandeur, as one might feel on contemplating Malham Cove or Scafell Crag. Yet again, there is the beauty of an extensive panorama, as one might see from Bowfell's summit. Our present walk, admittedly, has nothing like those, but it does have - in substantial measure - the beauty of solitude: the sense of a primeval, unspoilt landscape and a pervading stillness are strongly felt. Please don't come this way in large numbers! To me, it would seem almost a desecration of places like Fiendsdale and Bleadale Water.

Such considerations may pass through your mind as you return, a little tired perhaps, but somehow enriched, past the waterworks house and down the tree-lined avenue. A cup of tea, perhaps, at the refreshment van? Yes, probably very welcome. For me, though, at that moment of return, civilisation seems less attractive, at least initially. Eliot's Magi were disillusioned with "the old dispensation" on returning from the Christ-child's manger, and would be "glad of another death". Once back at that Langden car park, I know surely enough that before long I shall be glad of a return to hidden Bowland.

19. DEEP IN THE FOREST

Slaidburn, Burn Fell, Dunsop Fell, Whitendale, Salter Fell, Croasdale Quarry, Croasdale House, Slaidburn. 13 miles. Maps: OS 1:50,000 Landranger no. 103; OS 1:25,000 Explorer OL 41 (Forest of Bowland).

Short Alternative: From the junction of bridlepaths on Dunsop Fell at (675544), follow the track ENE down to the end of Wood House Lane. Return to Slaidburn via the road or the very attractive path from Wood House along Croasdale Brook; 6.5 miles.

* * * * * * * * * *

Background

Oh, no! Not *that* sort of a forest. The forest of Bowland, I mean - today we shall truly be in the heart of it, enjoying some of the best scenery it has to offer: the superb hidden valleys, remote high fells and fine streams. But yes, 'forest' does seem a curious term to use for this part of the country, and since I have glossed over the word previously this seems a good place to mention that it appears to derive from the old French 'foris', meaning land - of an open sort - that was fit only for hunting. The concise OD moreover, gives a derivation of 'forest' from the Latin 'forestis silva', meaning a wood outside the walls of a park.

The walk itself is a grand one, and if undertaken on the right day it will linger long in your memory. It has that sense of spaciousness which belongs to Bowland in a characteristic way, combined with a feeling of remoteness. The short alternative, while being a pleasant stroll in itself - and offering fine views - deprives you of the walk through Whitendale, and to miss any of the hidden valleys is to be deprived of one of Bowland's chief glories. It is quite a tough walk, incorporating about 1,500ft. of climbing, but not so demanding as the Langden - Fiendsdale - Fair Snape route (Walk 18); here, the going underfoot is generally pretty good, apart from some boggy patches atop Dunsop Fell. A compass should be taken for the sake of the latter section, which is lacking in natural features. The middle section makes use of the Hornby road, which you will get to know better in the next walk, our finale.

The Walk

From the main car park (and bus terminus) in Slaidburn, opposite the pleasant green alongside the Hodder, enjoy an ice-cream or other titbit if you will from the adjacent cafe, then set yourself resolutely to the walk. Return through the village centre, continuing past the "Hark to Bounty" at the T-junction, and on past the handsome Georgian town house, used as the squire's residence for a time earlier last century. Keep following the road (Back Lane to the locals) through the outskirts of the village, past the health centre and up the steep little hill following, a hint of some strenuous walking ahead. On your right runs Croasdale Brook, which you will get to know better later: here it passes through a delightful wooded gorge, with a steep rocky cliff on the far bank. The fine path to Wood House follows the brook here, as given in the short alternative, but for the main route it would take us too far out of the way. In any case, the road walking is pleasant here, traffic being fairly light. Continue past outlying farms and other houses, one of which used to keep some interesting birds of prey, beyond the turnings to the once noted restaurant at Parrock Head and the lane to Myttons, a craft centre well worth visiting. Shortly the road turns sharp left, and a little further on a public bridlepath sign guides you to a lane on the right (gated) where the real walking begins.

The lane, still metalled initially, serves the remote residence at Burn Side nestling under Burn Fell. Curlews are frequently in evidence on these upland pastures. Pass through one gate, then another to the right of the house, over a little stream, then through an enclosure where there are usually goats eyeing passers-by quizzically. Beyond the environs of the house, you are truly into the open country, and the path is initially sketchy. Drop down sharply to re-cross the stream (there is a waymarker disc here, but more helpful when coming from the opposite direction). Beyond this, the best line involves following the course of a low dyke - unfortunately broken by some boggy patches - through the rough pasture. You remain fairly close to the wall on your right,

Walk19: Deep In the Forest

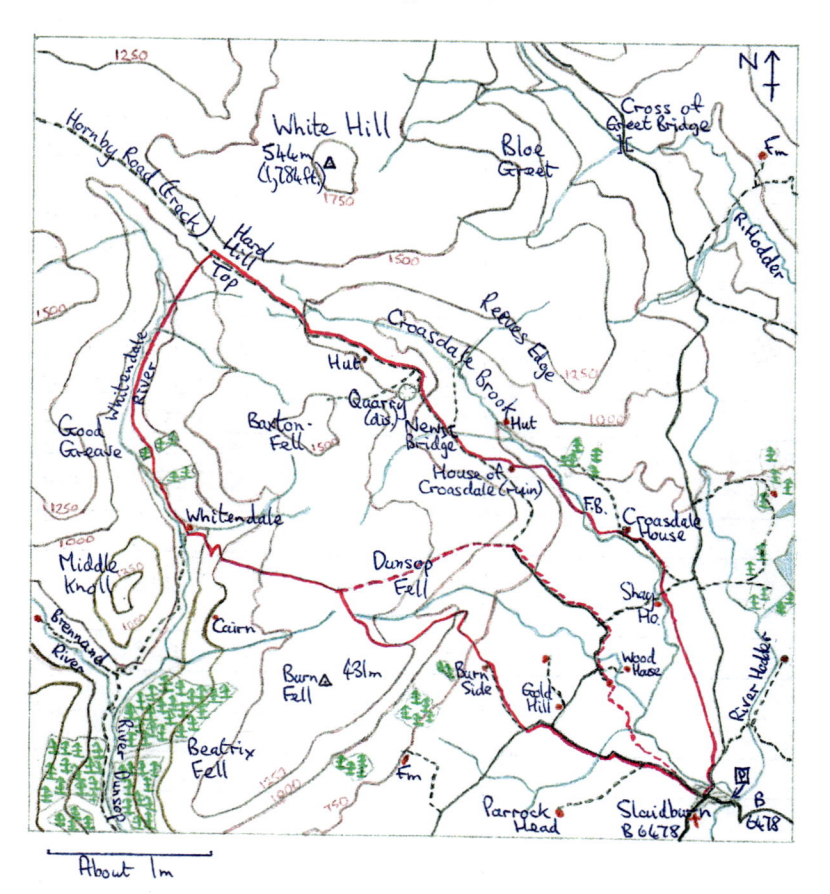

and at the top of the field pass through a gate, turning sharp right ahead onto the open fell.

The going improves here, a parallel dyke and groove providing a clear guide even in thick weather. You pass a few straggling trees, and will be conscious of steadily lengthening views: the normally shy Stocks Reservoir can be seen fairly clearly hereabouts, and views into the Dales are also opening up. Watch carefully for the coming left turn up the path - though there is still a groove, it is initially a little less obvious, turning back on your route but going up the spur of Burn Fell. There is in fact another fainter track further on, keeping lower down in the valley of Dunsop Brook, but this is not recommended as you would have a stiff scramble further on to regain the plateau.

After a fairly stiff climb initially, the gradient slackens higher up the spur, then the path - clearer now - swings round into the W, later NW. This is simple enough in clear weather, but those unfamiliar with moorland in mist should beware. I was surprised, not to say slightly alarmed, to meet some walkers once at this spot, coming in the opposite direction with clearly very little idea of just where they were - despite having a certain guidebook with them. Soon you will circle round the head of Dunsop Brook; the views down this fine little steep-sided valley looking NE are impressive in clear weather, Penyghent and Fountains Fell prominent on the horizon. The going becomes rather boggy for a while on a flat stretch around the 1300ft. contour; the line is NNW in thick weather, and you steadily converge with a wall running on your left, a reassuring landmark. Another well-used track also converges a little further on at pt.(675544); this is the bridlepath over Dunsop Fell, running down to the Hornby Road above Higher Wood House, used in the alternative, and is well waymarked with poles over the higher ground.

Our route goes "further up and further in", in the words of C.S. Lewis. Pass through a gate in the wall at the path junction, with a clear North West Water sign, and follow a WNW line: here again, waymarkers, cairns and a fairly clear tread will help in mist. In addition to the red grouse so familiar on Bowland fells, you have a fair chance of seeing golden plover hereabouts. These attractive birds, far more typical plovers than the commoner lapwing, have a characteristic reedy, whistling call, a haunting cry which is locally familiar in parts of the Pennines. Pick your way carefully through the peaty ground, which in half a mile or so begins to decline in front of you, noticeably by the time you reach a big cairn with a tall marker pole where I have often stopped. To the left you will spot a large, solidly-made cairn, and in front stretch the sweeping lines and deeply indented valleys of the Bowland fells: silent, mysterious, beautiful.

A little further on the path, now very obvious, breaks into zig-zags in descending the steep fellside, with striking views of the oasis of Whitendale Farm below you. A gate is passed through on the 'zag', then a sharp turn down a final stony stretch to Whitendale. What a place! Neat, beautifully kept buildings, the fine stream passing between wooded banks, hemmed in by soaring fells - but supremely, a pervading stillness. It is truly a spot you will return to in your dreams. Up to now, you will probably have met a fair number of walkers doing the circular from Dunsop Bridge: from now on, I wager, you will meet very few.

Pass by the farm buildings, which incidentally offer bed and breakfast these days, then turn right along a track adjacent to the Whitendale River, through two gates and a pleasant wooded stretch. Keep to the main track initially, eschewing branches to the right or left (over a bridge). Where the stream turns away left, and the track trends towards it, some care is necessary. Leave the track and aim across the fairly lush pasture ahead, heading for a gate between two fairly new afforested areas, where there is a welcome waymarker. For once, the 1:50,000 map is somewhat clearer than the "Outdoor Leisure" here: if you have kept close to the stream you will need a little manoeuvring to regain the path.

Go between the afforested areas, and simply follow the tread in front as you gradually ascend the upper Whitendale valley; it is clear enough, with occasional posts and waymarkers, and a stretch for sheer enjoyment. The path soon closes on the stream on your left, at first above a steepish wooded bank, then more or less on a level with it. By now you are above the Whitendale intake at (654559), so the stream runs free and vigorous, compared to its regulated state near the farm. The sense of seclusion is great, the fell slopes long and all-enclosing. Once again, further up and further in! Watch for the point, between Higher Stony Clough and Brim Clough, side streams coming in from the right, where you branch away from the main stream: the path is still waymarked here, but it is sketchy enough for some uncertainty in very thick weather - you are around the 1,000ft. contour. If in doubt, take a bearing of about 040 degrees (anywhere between NNE and NE will do), which will bring you safely to the unmistakable Hornby Road track. After leaving the stream, it is a fairly vigorous pull of 300ft. up to the track, which here is grassy but perfectly clear.

If you have already fallen in love with the area by then, you may decide to turn left and go all the way to Wray or Hornby! You have my blessing. Today's circular, however, turns right along the track, at the summit of this walk (around 1,350ft.), en route for Slaidburn. The extensive slopes of White Hill, whose summit stays out of sight, are on the left, and you will appreciate the easier going. Lately some of the swampier areas have been filled in, facilitating progress. Pass through a gate after about half a mile, then begin the gradual descent through the lonely reaches of upper Croasdale, ignoring branching tracks to the right (one of these serving a neat stone-built hut, for shooting parties). In about a mile and a half, the track swings sharply right and loses height, creating a natural grassy bank: a suitable place to take a break, with more extensive views now opening up. To the right are tracks leading to Croasdale Quarry, long disused but still a striking amphitheatre.

Keep along the track for now, down to and over New Bridge, the setting becoming relatively more pastoral. The whole area is rich in varied and interesting bird life, and on this particular stretch I have seen whinchats in summer. Beyond New Bridge, cross two more side streams, then watch carefully for the spot where you leave the track for the path (now waymarked) which branches off left into lower Croasdale, just where the main route bears slightly right. There's no reason why you should not follow the main track back to Slaidburn, via Wood House Lane, but the path described gives you an intimate view of the fine Croasdale Brook, and the pastures beyond afford a pleasant contrast to the preceding fell and moorland.

Going along the path, which is clear enough initially, ford a small stream and swing right, soon passing through an old gateway adjoining the ruinous House of Croasdale. "Houses in the Country" again - and what a situation! Will anyone be tempted one day to renovate the place and live here? Despite the apparent peace and stillness, however, the area has known tragedy, for in the summer of 1992 a light aircraft crashed on the fells nearby in poor visibility with the loss of four lives. Further upstream you will note a small stone hut, given on the 1:50,000 but not the 1:25,000 OS. Beyond the ruin, head half left downhill on a thin but still waymarked path over rough wet ground, presently fording one stream then another at a ruinous wall. The steepish bluff ahead may be crossed directly or turned on the left, the path becoming a little clearer as it approaches the fine Croasdale Brook which makes a good companion. The OS (both 1:25,000 and 1:50,000) suggest a ford of the main stream here, but this is not recommended, and could be hazardous should the stream be in spate. Instead, keep to the path with the stream not too close on your left.

Much height has been lost by now, and the upland grouse have been replaced by the odd partridge (or pheasant, in the woods further on). Go through a gate, turn downstream for about 200 yds. and cross the brook at a sturdy new bridge. * Climb half right up the steep bank opposite. From the top of this rise there is an excellent retrospect of Croasdale, one of those haunting views that will remain with you.

At the top, keep to the right of the field ahead, soon joining a fence, with a steep drop to the brook beyond. Where the fence

The former bridge, directly by the gate, was destroyed by flood damage some years ago.

goes down the bank, don't lose height, but circle round and descend on a much clearer vehicular track, soon fording a small stream (Moor Syke) and turning right by a footpath sign, then through a gateway and past Croasdale House. Soon there is a branch on your right with a footbridge leading into a wood, an interesting alternative to explore some time, but the main route goes straight along the track. Follow it through left and right bends, past some outbuildings, and on through a small wood over a stream. Beyond the next gateway, watch carefully for the point on the right where the path leaves the track, aiming for a stile near the right-hand end of the wall ahead. Once over, cross the pasture ahead and go over a stile onto the lane serving Shay House (on the right). In the familiar manner, these intricacies of stiles, gates and field paths are much more demanding of description than moorland paths, where the route often speaks for itself.

You may turn left up the Shay House lane and then return to Slaidburn by turning right down the Bentham road. However, it is pleasanter to keep to the field paths, and the route-finding becomes easier. Pass through a gate (or over a stile a few yards to its right) across the lane, and in the large field ahead, keep close to Croasdale Brook initially but, when the stream turns to the right, go straight on, inclining a little left to stone steps and over the crossing wall ahead. Keep close to the fence on your right initially, but when it turns away right, go straight on until, just after you near a bend in the brook, a clearly marked wall stile points the way ahead. Continue essentially in a straight line, uphill at first, over a succession of three stiles, probably with a last lingering retrospect up Croasdale after the first: the memories of the grand places visited earlier already seem distant. After the third stile, aim for the intersection of two walls by the left-hand corner of a copse ahead, where there is a stile, and - at last! - a view of Slaidburn, with the car park on the left, including (we hope) a sight of your own transport waiting. Follow the wall on your left gently downhill until it turns away left at a right angle, then incline slightly left to meet the Bentham road by a stile, clearly signed "Croasdale".

Relax now, the hard work is all over: a few hundred yards of tarmac will return you to the unfailing charm of Slaidburn, and by a left turn at the junction to the car park. Why not enjoy a drink or evening meal at the "Hark to Bounty"? - a welcome, and welcoming, haven after your exertions. But even better will be the memories of one of the finest walks our part of Northern England has to offer. Hidden valleys, superb viewpoints, remote and romantic places and names, many of which will never be seen or suspected by those who automatically speed on to the Lakes or the Dales. Is it asking for trouble, then, to describe them? Possibly, but I cannot see these spots ever becoming overrun or the paths eroded. Go deep into that forest yourselves - in small numbers - taste and see, and be thankful.

20. UP, UP AND AWAY: THE HORNBY ROAD

Slaidburn, Wood House Lane, Croasdale Quarry, Salter Fell, High Salter, Roeburndale and Hornby. 15 miles.
Maps: OS 1:50,000 Landranger nos. 97, 103; OS 1:25,000 Explorer OL 41 (Forest of Bowland)
Alternatives: From Slaidburn to Salter Fell via Croasdale House (Walk 19). Or from Dunsop Bridge to Salter Fell via the Dunsop Valley and Whitendale (introduction to the Forest of Bowland + Walk 19) - thence on to Hornby in both cases.
Alternative finishes at Wray or Wennington (B.R. station).

* * * * * * * * * *

Background
The Hornby Road, or Salter Fell track, is in a different category from the other walks given in this volume. To begin with, and most obviously, it is necessarily a through walk from A to B; secondly, it leads us right off our map, out of our familiar Ribble catchment area into that of the Lune; thirdly, it poses a significant logistical challenge from the point of view of transport. Unless you have car transport at both ends, you will find both Slaidburn and Hornby difficult of access, and - incredible though it may sound in this day and age - the whole outing will become a full-day expedition. Indeed there would be much to be said for arranging overnight accommodation and enjoying the experience in a more leisurely way. Slaidburn has a youth hostel and hotel, and Hornby too has accommodation.

Having said that, don't be dissuaded! It is a magnificent walk, providing great satisfaction in its completion, and offering memorable views, particularly on crossing to the N of the Ribble-Lune watershed. For that reason, it is objectively better to do the walk from south to north. The walking itself is not at all difficult, certainly not if you keep to the main route which is a well-defined track throughout: it is more a question of stamina, and may catch out those who are not used to doing more than 10-12 miles. But the gradients are not severe, and the central part of the walk, in particular, keeps a fairly straight course: this old track knew what it was about. Its origins appear to lie in the transport of salt to Morecambe Bay (hence Salter Fell), and, as Slaidburn is known to be a Saxon settlement, it is likely to go back several centuries.

Above all, my memories of the Hornby Road are of solitude, and I write with the not uncommon, paradoxical feelings of a guidebook writer: please don't follow in large numbers! Long sweeping skylines, briskly driven clouds, remote side valleys, grouse whirring over the moors on either side - and an occasional passing traveller. Those are the characteristics of this memorable tract of Bowland. Wainwright, not a man to be over-lavish with praise, described it as "possibly the finest moorland walk in Northern England" - and his yardstick, remember, was the Lake District. In his book "A Bowland Sketchbook", he outlines the walk from Slaidburn to High Salter. Gillham, too, restricts his description to the section between the road-end above Higher Wood House (692548) and High Salter. But these bowdlerised versions of the walk, to me, reduce its true worth, while still requiring all the transport arrangements. Let's go the whole way, from Slaidburn to Hornby, as the name suggests. You should note, again, the very useful bus service from Clitheroe to Slaidburn. At the far end, there is quite a frequent bus service from Hornby to Lancaster, or if you go on to Wennington there are a few trains on the Lancaster-Skipton line.

The Walk

From the car park and bus terminus by the Hodder in Slaidburn, walk back through the village centre and past the "Hark to Bounty", as for Walk 19. If you have not yet acquainted yourself with the pleasant path from Back Lane to Wood House Lane *via* Croasdale Brook, this would be a natural occasion on which to do so. Or continue up Back Lane to the signposted junction saying "Myttons Farm Crafts", and turn right, reaching the same point by Wood House in a further half mile. Simply follow the metalled lane until, beyond the last farm at Higher Wood House, you reach the terminus of the official road at (692548). Turn right here, through a gate, soon joining the bridlepath descending from Dunsop Fell; the road is still a

Walk 20: Up, Up and Away – The Hornby Road

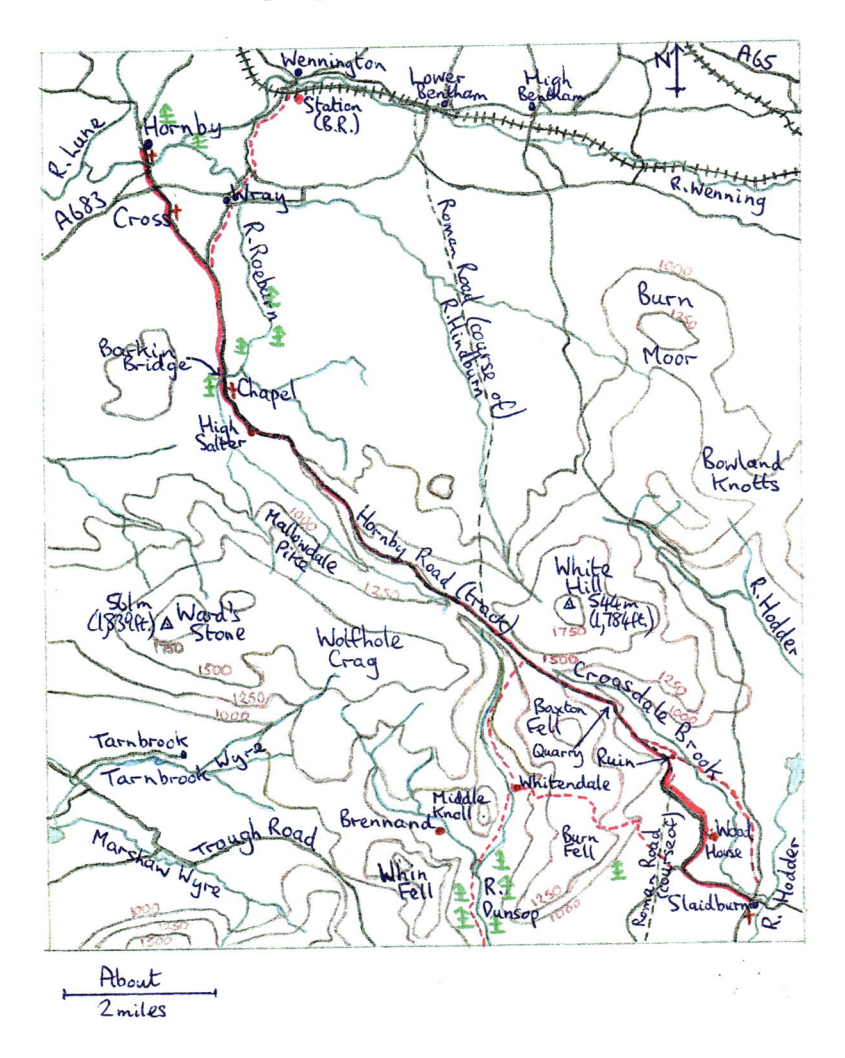

metalled surface at first. In about threequarters of a mile, the path up Croasdale past the ruinous House of Croasdale also converges with the road. Naturally, you could just as well make use of this excellent route (the reverse of the terminal section of Walk 19) to attain this point.

In a real sense, further descriptions - at least for the next eight or nine miles - are superfluous! Simply follow the track, reliable and unlosable, all the way. It is a marvellous walkers' highway, and with no worries about route-finding, you will appreciate your surroundings all the more. Suffice it for me to point out some interesting features visible along the way, and to try to convey the sense of change as the watershed is crossed and the final goal approached.

As well as the ruinous House of Croasdale (not visible from the Hornby Road, but about 300yds. to its east), one or two other huts or outbuildings can be seen in the otherwise desolate reaches of Upper Croasdale, and indeed one wonders whether more settlements formerly existed here. Beyond the New Bridge, at (685561), the old quarry becomes a large and striking feature: in its heyday, would there have been shanty dwellings nearby? It seems a fair speculation: this spot is already several miles from Slaidburn. Nowadays, only animals and birds, especially the latter, are likely to disturb the tranquility around the quarry. Incidentally, if the RSPB are really concerned about local bird life, would they not be well advised to do their observation a bit less obtrusively? I have seen very overt surveillance work going on hereabouts which can only increase the suspicions of passers-by. But have no fear, gentlemen! I shan't give any secrets away in these pages.

Immediately after New Bridge, a track (private) turns off to the right, crossing Croasdale Brook and aiming for the open fell beneath the rocky outcrops of Reeves Edge. I have observed sizeable numbers of gulls here, perhaps an offshoot of the noted colony on nearby Tarnbrook Fell, together with wild geese. Keep your eyes peeled: on a Spring day, the surroundings can seem alive with birds of all kinds. Climb past the quarry, ignoring branch tracks leading to it on the left, the plateau summit of

Baxton Fell behind. You are well over the 1100ft. contour by now, and will remain so for several miles. The legend 'Roman Road' printed on the Outdoor Leisure map hereabouts prompts us to wonder: just how old *is* the Hornby Road?

A difficult question to answer with any confidence. What is certain, however, is that between (694552) and (656585), a distance of about 3.5 miles, the Hornby and Roman roads are coincident: the line of the Roman road, a section of that between Ribchester and Burrow-in-Lonsdale, has been well researched (see "Walking Roman Roads in Bowland", by Philip Graystone, University of Lancaster). This leaves two possibilities: either the Romans inherited and developed an existing trackway, or they planned it themselves - as suggested by the careful contouring of the route. Either way, the implication is that the extant Hornby Road probably pre-dates the earliest known settlement at Slaidburn. Quite likely there is scope for further investigation of this intriguing subject. We should, at any rate, be grateful that the modern major North - South routes in this area, in the shape of the M6 and the main West Coast rail line, run far to the west and leave this old hill track in peace. Note that the point of divergence of the Hornby and Roman roads is indicated on the 1:25,000, according to best available evidence - on Botton Head Fell - but not on the 1:50,000 OS.

Back near the head of Croasdale, the stream diminishes and the fells close in, with further craggy outcrops - the Great and Little Bull Stones - visible beneath White Hill on the right, as we attain the highest stretch of the road. The first fence encountered effectively marks the watershed between Croasdale and Whitendale, only a minor one as we are still in the Hodder-Ribble basin here. Whether you have previously walked up the Whitendale valley or not, you will be impressed by the retrospective view here, looking far back to Middle Knoll, with the slopes of Good Greave closing the view on the right. The striking craggy outline of Wolfhole Crag, effectively the eastern terminus of the Ward's Stone - Tarnbrook massif, is also visible to the west. Beyond the junction with the Whitendale path, less than a mile of track - formerly boggy on this section, now much improved - separates us from the true Hodder-Lune watershed, at the old county boundary fence. Since 1974, all is now Lancashire, of course. As usual in such cases, the change is more apparent on the map than on the ground, but soon the upper Roeburn valley begins to descend on your left.

There is in fact a tantalising glimpse of Morecambe Bay when you reach the boundary fence, to whet your appetite. Hereabouts we part company with the Roman road: the exact point of divergence is in fact disputed, and not too clear on the ground, but best evidence (see Graystone) considers it to cross the fence to the NE, then turning away N before becoming clearer again on Botton Head Fell. Wolfhole Crag still dominates the view left, a noticeable green metallic shelter or hut visible on the very stony slopes below the summit, and usually a fair percentage of the Tarnbrook gull colony visible on that side. The track beyond the fence is a little less attractive, being liberally sprinkled with pale chippings, making a scar visible some distance ahead, in contrast to the green lane of the previous section.

If the Hornby Road were simply a climb to the watershed, than an immediate descent, it would still be a first rate walk. In fact there is an intermediate section, perhaps the most intriguing of all, between the boundary fence and Alderstone Bank, where it seems to linger as if reluctant to leave the high moorland. The distant view is quite lost here, a typical example of hidden Bowland, where you feel you could be almost anywhere with only the bird life for company. You pass a rocky area, Guide Hill on the 1:25,000 OS map, where there are some natural stopping-places - and seats. Soon after the Roeburn valley begins to develop depth and character on the left, and White Hill, with one of its observation towers prominent, shows to advantage in retrospect: it remains out of sight during the area of closest approach.

The long ridge of Mallowdale Fell dominates on the left as Wolfhole Crag recedes. Then comes a dramatic, thrilling moment: just beyond the last ford marked on the 1:25,000 OS as you begin to turn the shoulder of Alderstone Bank, the Three

Peaks (Whernside and Ingleborough first) make their appearance to the NE, over a slight dip. Here again are some good stopping-places among the many sizeable rocky outcrops, and you have the comforting knowledge that the going is nearly all downhill from here. A zigzag estate track turns away on the left, crossing the Roeburn and aiming for a shooting cabin on Mallowdale Fell. By the time you have bypassed Alderstone Bank and the hill behind (Hawkshead), the views into the Dales are superb. All the Three Peaks stand up superbly, Ingleborough looking every inch a mountain, and many other peaks and groups of fells can be picked out: Buckden Pike, between Penyghent and Fountains Fell; Gragareth and Crag Hill; much further north, the Howgills. To be robbed of this panorama by mist is truly a deprivation.

It may be here, for the first time, that the reality dawns on us: we have truly walked out of one area of Northern England into another. Gone are the views of Pendle, the South Pennines and the Ribble Valley: here are horizons vaster, more open, fascinating to behold. Quite soon, as we proceed, a large section of Morecambe Bay opens up in the NW, with the Lakeland peaks beyond, Black Combe and the Coniston fells prominent. All kinds of potential pastures new offering themselves to walkers who have not yet turned their footsteps in those directions! Does our home ground seem a little humbled, now? Perhaps, but home's where the heart is.

We are now well across the divide, descending quite rapidly, with many trees and much greenery appearing ahead: the little cairned summit of Mallowdale Pike is on the left (actually more prominent, in retrospect, some miles further on). It comes as a bit of a shock when we start to encounter gates again: the first, at (628607), is usually open, the next one - a mile and a quarter ahead, after a greener section of track - will need opening. Further on, the path drops through a little dip to cross Salter Clough Beck, then goes left and slightly uphill. By the time the next gate is passed, High Salter is clearly visible 150yds. ahead as the road bends right. High Salter is the terminus of the public road, and you may have arranged transport from here: the diehards will press on, some four miles still to go. You could consider some paths leaving on the right (map), bound for Wray, which I admit to not having investigated.

The road is typically very quiet, and the abundance of interesting bird life continues. Along a half-mile stretch or so hereabouts I have heard a cuckoo, seen common snipe, redshank and many linnets, in addition to the ubiquitous lapwings and curlews of these moors. Just below Middle Salter you will find an amusing sign, "No through Road to Slaidburn", thankfully of no consequence to the walker. At Lower Salter is the Roeburndale Methodist chapel in a remarkable setting, and just below, after a steepish drop, you encounter the Roeburn at Barkin Bridge, in delightful wooded surroundings, the river gliding over large slabby rocks. Oystercatchers, which have become quite a common sight by northern streams in the last few decades, may well be seen here.

Inevitably, the climb up from the bridge, at this stage of the walk, will seem much more severe than it really is: positively the last climb worthy of the name, though. An easy level promenade ensues, passing isolated farms and pleasant woods: the views of the Three Peaks remain superb, with the extensive limestone pavement below Ingleborough and Ingleton village now seen in addition. A glance behind still reveals the white ribbon of our moorland track, as far as Alderstone Bank, but already becoming lost to sight in that shy, retiring Bowland manner.

When the road begins to drop away in front of you, with a small plantation on the left, a fine wooded stretch of the Lune valley becomes visible, with Hornby Castle prominent further east. Soon you reach a road junction: turn right for Wray (and Wennington, if planning to use the train), keep straight on for Hornby - the "2 miles" here is an overstatement, you will be pleased to hear. How different it all seems now! A pleasant stroll down a quiet leafy lane, a world apart from the watershed moorland, but an enjoyable contrast. Initially the peaks of Lakeland are still quite prominent ahead, and Ingleborough remains very dominant on the right. You pass a wayside memorial seat (a bit late, we ruefully think) with a roadside cross by its side. Very soon, go directly accoss the B6480 which cuts our path, and on into Hornby.

Fifteen miles? It seems all too short, in the end: a glorious kaleidoscope of scenery, wildlife and solitude packed into a few precious hours of our time, a deeply enriching experience. Hornby provides just the right conclusion, as we stop perhaps to look over the bridge onto the Wenning, admire the grounds of the castle or just stroll along the fine main street of this neat, quiet village, recollecting. If you are relying on public transport rather than private arrangement, there should be at least one bus per hour to Lancaster during the day until about 7 p.m. (Monday - Saturday).

I could think of no better walk with which to finish, for here we have truly left the confines of our old map and landed on the doorstep of both the Dales and the Lakes. Like to explore them, now? If those who have not already done so resolve to go on, I shall be well content. For those areas, there is no shortage of guides or guidebooks, and I cheerfully take my leave of my readers. I hope that, though graduating to higher things, you will, like this author, feel an increased affection for the old home ground, and spare in particular a thankful thought for those unknown ancestors who, in centuries past, first trod the Hornby Road.

APOLOGIA

It was inevitable, I suppose, that a sense of omission should finally linger: so many footpaths and much fine walking country remain unexplored. Still, the fact is that a book must end somewhere, and there was never any intention of aiming for a comprehensive list of walks. My principle from the start was to set walkers on their way, then encourage them to find out more for themselves. What I have included is highly subjective, based on personal associations and assessment, rather than systematic. Nevertheless, I believe the walks give, with a broad brush coverage, a picture of the varieties of walking to be found within Landranger no. 103 and on its fringes.

Where I sense particular omissions, though, I make brief mention now, again inviting readers to taste and see for themselves. The Gisburn Forest area, for its extensive lonely vistas and dramatic sunsets; the circuit of Stocks Reservoir - though more interesting in its birdlife to me, the walking a bit too hemmed in; the charm, history and character of Chipping, visited only as an alternative in Walk 18, and its profusion of low-level footpaths, particularly going NE to Whitewell; the many paths on Waddington and Easington Fells, with splendid views, whose extremities only were clipped by Walks 8 and 13; further stretches of the Pennine Way, for instance around Stoodley Pike in the south and the section from Cowling to Airton further north (though arguably of less interest than the stretches we employed); the Rossendale moors - barely touched on Walk 7 - and West Lancashire moors; further walks in the Forest of Pendle. I could go on, but I should soon be writing Book Two!

Errors of commission, too? Of course. A guidebook writer tends to develop a style which radiates omniscience. Pretension! We write at length about what we are virtually ignorant of except through our own few visits and limited reading. Talk to the locals, and you will learn more in five minutes. I have striven for factual accuracy, nevertheless, insofar as I have recorded and correctly understood my sources, and I accept responsibility for any inaccuracies.

Finally - do I really need to say it? - beauty is in the eye of the beholder. No doubt many could wander along the ways described and be unimpressed; I accept that with no grudge. Indeed I can only return to the spirit of my opening remarks, for it is the personal associations that make walking in this area special to me. Nevertheless I firmly believe that I am not alone in finding beauty here, and I willingly add my pen to those who have striven to do justice to the fine scenery of this corner of Northern England, still so little known in comparison to the Lakes and the Dales. Yet rediscovery was the keyword for me, returning to old-familiar surroundings after a major upheaval of life and finding new beauty there. For attempting, however inadequately, to describe some aspects of that newness which so refreshed me I make no apology.

BIBLIOGRAPHY AND ACKNOWLEDGEMENTS

Pennine Way Companion, A. Wainwright (Westmorland Gazette)
A Bowland Sketchbook, A. Wainwright (Westmorland Gazette)
A Ribble Sketchbook, A. Wainwright (Westmorland Gazette)

All three volumes by the old master provide valuable reading. The *"Companion"* gives extra detail for parts of Walks 9, 10 and 14 and, indeed, for the whole backbone of map 103. The other two volumes, much less known, give pleasant background reading - plus the characteristic drawings - on many places visited on our travels in the Ribble and Hodder valleys, Bowland and Pendle.

Walks in Pendle Country, Walks in Hodder Country and Walks in Bronte Country (3 vols.), A. Lawson (Gerrard)

These three paperbacks, full of detailed footpath information, offer a host of walking possibilities in the areas described, generally breaking down into shorter walks than I have given. Alan's enthusiasm and love of his subject are clear at a glance. I have made reference to the first two of the set since about 1970.

Bowland and the South Pennines, J.Gillham (Grey Stone Books)

A very well-compiled collection of walks together with introductory notes and some good photographs. Gillham restricts himself almost entirely to the high moorlands: his descriptions of routes are concise and gradings are given for each walk. Significantly, his experience is that of a former Southerner won over by the distinctive charm of the northern landscape.

Journeys through Brigantia (several vols., especially vol. 8), J. Dixon and P. Dixon (Aussteiger Publications)

A detailed set of studies of Northern England, concentrating particularly on settlements, buildings and local history: altogether a storehouse of information. The walks are woven around the various settlements described.

Bowland and Pendle Hill, W. R. Mitchell (Dalesman)

A well-researched study of the Area of Outstanding Natural Beauty from the early days of its inception, acknowledged by Wainwright in his *Bowland Sketchbook*. Very recently the author has also published a collection of Bowland walks.

Exploring Bowland and the Hodder, R. Freethy (Countryside Publications Ltd.)

This is a booklet essentially for the motorist, a description of five short tours covering the district with recommended places of interest to visit. The same author's monograph on *The River Ribble* (Terence Dalton Ltd.), a detailed geographical and historical study, may also be warmly recommended.

For the story of the Pendle witches, *the* classic book remains *The Lancashire Witches*, H. Ainsworth (Gerrard), a fascinating blend of historical background and fiction. Inevitably many other books have been based on the story, a particularly popular romance being *Mist Over Pendle*, R. Neill (Arrow Books); an interesting and imaginative paperback, fairly recent, is *The Fate of the Lancashire Witches*, A. Douglas.

Two other walking guides which may be mentioned are the Ordnance Survey's compilation *Walker's Britain, vol 1,* which describes the Pudsay's Leap section of the Ribble (see Walk 13) and *Walking the Pennine Way*, A. Binns (Gerrard).

I also consulted: *Walking Roman Roads in Britain*, P. Graystone (University of Lancaster), for the vis-a-vis of the Roman Road and the Hornby Road (Walk 20); *Getting to know Secret Lancashire*, R. & M. Freethy (Printwise Publications Ltd.); *Untrodden Ways*, N. Channer (Ward Lock); *Portrait of the Pennines*, R. A. Redfern (Hale & Co.); and *History of Burnley* (3 vols.), W. Bennett (Burnley Corporation) for information on the Long Causeway and its origins.

Finally, *The Walker's Handbook,* H. Westacott (Penguin) is still a most valuable sourcebook on the practicalities of walking-equipment, maps, compass work, and brief notes on suggested areas to explore.

* * * * * * * * * *

At this moment I look back over what is already an appreciable stretch of time to thank all those who contributed personally to this book - with information, by providing companionship over the miles, with comments on the text, and secretarially. Especially I am grateful to David MacNamee and Linda Blakeman for their willing assistance and extensive knowledge of footpaths, buildings and family history in the Bowland area, notably around Slaidburn. Alan Lawson's companionship and walking experience have been much appreciated, as have his hints on compilation and various items of background. Michael and Kath Walmsley and Kitty Ward have manfully tramped many miles with the author and given much hospitality and encouragement as well as observations on the text; Jon Sharples has similarly accompanied me on many walks over the years. I would also like to give my thanks to Pauline Russell for her faithful production of the first typescript and her cheerful encouragement. Finally I thank Brian Jordan for his skilful reformatting of the sketch maps.

EPILOGUE: THE SHORTEST JOURNEY

Great Harwood and Dean Clough Reservoir (Circular).
2 ½ miles

I could not tell you, with even moderate accuracy, how often I have done this walk. Probably a thousand times would not be an underestimate. Certainly I have done it at all times of the year, in all weathers, and found often enough that even this short outing is subject to the full force of the elements. Despite the changes over the years, it has become a trusty friend, to the point where every step on the way has become familiar. More than that, I look back at my own past, too, so intimately bound up in the old town and its surroundings. This description will therefore have an autobiographical element which I have purposely minimised in the other walks, and I beg my readers' indulgence for that. It makes an appropriate note on which to conclude this volume.

Oh, yes - before I forget - the walk. It's a pretty good one actually, as Great Harwood folk will tell you, though far from being a beautiful one. In microcosm, it exhibits many of the good things that the earlier, longer and more splendid walks in this volume have offered. During an outing of about fifty minutes, you can enjoy some excellent, far-ranging views of up to thirty miles, visit some surprisingly remote-feeling spots - and clear your mind of all manner of insignificant worries. I can say with confidence that I have invariably finished the walk in a better frame of mind than that in which I began: that, to me, is one of the enduring benefits of walking.

Off we go, then, down that familiar rough track. The first section is in a sad state of neglect, nowadays: once a series of neatly fenced, if not always neatly-kept, allotments, with open areas where you could go down to the little stream. Now, though many smart new houses have sprung up in the district, the immediate surroundings are unkempt and the path itself is a bit of a trudge: sodden or hard-rutted in winter, grossly overgrown in summer. But keep going! It gets better. Honestly.

Of course, in *those* days, the stream was the thing! Eager young feet used to tread this way, toy boats in hand, ready to play in the water. How many idle, happy hours passed in that way! Then - listen again - was that the ice-cream van sounding? Just time, then, if you put on a sprint, to get to the corner for your reward, a sizeable cornet for 3d., or if the man was kind, a small one for 2d. Life's little luxuries.

Up we go, climbing steadily, the stream still in attendance. This part of Gt. Harwood is really built up now: there was talk of a new through road here, a few years ago. Thank goodness, it never materialised. Look round, and the view is already opening up, Great Hameldon prominent, and on reasonably clear days, the long, more distant ridge terminating in Boulsworth Hill. Then through a gap in the fence ahead, climbing up the long field following, and quite suddenly the town is left behind: a good retrospect, now, of Pendle and its satellites. A breezy, upland pasture succeeds as we pass the site of the first Clinkham Quarry, long since filled in: the second, across the cobbled lane at the top, suffered the same fate earlier.

On reaching Edge End Lane, I usually pause and look around, in truth it is difficult not to. The town is laid out like a map before you, with much of East Lancashire visible further afield. A very characterisitic landscape. The towns all cling to the valleys, with the fells rising above them - though in earlier times, small village settlements began high up the hillsides, such as Bedlam and Green Haworth above Accrington.

Closer at hand, truly at arm's length as it seems, Great Harwood itself. The sights seem to blend with familiar long-lost faces and sounds, too, as I gaze down. The Town Hall and Mercer Memorial, central, stand up proudly. Look along Blackburn Road, and there's the old Grand cinema. Saturday afternoon children's matinees; the Famous Five, or suchlike. Or, more often, those long, unending Saturday evening affairs, which Mum and Dad seemed to find absorbing; goodness knows why, you thought. Back on Town Hall square, the roller-skating rink. Licquorice assortments, orange juice, home in time for tea, the pre-telly days of the late 1950s. Truly another world, and other values. Look further round, and there's the football ground, floodlights clearly visible. "It's a good 'un!" Yes, I hear that old touchline barracker now. Round further, the old school, unmistakable red-brick, first step - as it proved - on the road to Cambridge. Who could have thought it? Old class-mates, too: Christine, Janice, Scam, Brads . . . where are they now? It would be nice to know. Distant but still potent memories, borne up from below in the mists of time. Just visible, too - certainly in winter - the tower of St. Bartholomews, my first spiritual home, always a welcome place for worship now.

Yes, it can be difficult, some days, to get walking again! Further up the lane, approaching the old farm of Edge Side (1770) and beyond, the distant view, now remarkably good, takes over. From these relatively modest heights, about 750ft. by the water tower at the head of the lane, you can spot many of the places referred to in this volume. Pendle shows its characteristic SW aspect, the main hill rising massively, supported by the twin buttresses of Wiswell Moor and Padiham Heights. Further east and south, the long ridge of the true Pennine watershed, from Boulsworth to Black Hameldon and beyond; to the left of Boulsworth, and further back, the Wolf Stones, a good fifteen miles distant. Further north, look between Pendle and Waddington Fell, right up the Ribble Valley: on clear days appears a grand and inspiring sight, the twin peaks of Penyghent and Fountains Fell at its head. Twenty-five miles! Not bad. To the right of Fountains Fell, on exceptionally clear days, you can pick up Great Whernside, above Kettlewell, about thirty miles. Contrary to some printed claims, though, Ingleborough is *not* visible from here: you must go about a mile down the top road towards Blackburn before its familiar cut-off summit peeps out above Waddington Fell. Overall a splendid panorama.

On reaching Blackburn Old Road comes the least enjoyable section, about a quarter of a mile along the road with the plantation on your right, the site of the old golf course lying across the road. It's a sad reminder that, not long ago, this was strictly a quiet country lane. Now it is a recognised alternative route to Blackburn. You can give the traffic a miss, though, by taking a rather wet path through the woods, turning left after the first section. Either way, at the end of the plantation, the path going down to Dean Clough Reservoir is unmistakeable. Actually, this generally very quiet lane is a place of some notoriety! Some years ago, a body was dumped here, apparently the result of a gangland feud. Nowadays you may occasionally encounter another sign of criminal malaise, the burnt-out shells of cars abandoned or stolen.

Back to the view, which has now opened in the northern arc. Longridge Fell stretches across in front of us, Stonyhurst's green domes being conspicuous. Behind, you will recognise at once the line of Bowland fells from Parlick and Fair Snape to Totridge Fell, the Ward's Stone massif and White Hill further north. We dip down now towards the reservoir itself, which I have seen containing anything from a small muddy puddle of water in the drought of 1976 to overflow (frequent!). Nowadays its volume is strictly regulated: it is used only for back-up supply. This is a fine secluded little valley, often receiving striking sunsets, though buffeted by strong winds. You may encounter almost any number of souls; perhaps no-one at all, on other days a steady stream of joggers, anglers, dog-exercisers and fellow walkers. There's something for everyone here. The wildlife, particularly birdlife, is impressive too: bring your binoculars! Great crested grebe are usually about on the reservoir, terns may be seen on passage, and herons are relatively common. In the woods, I have spotted goldcrest, jays, various tits, tree creeper, owls and sparrowhawk as well as commoner species.

Past the reservoir now, along the well-made rough vehicular track. Numerous cows and sheep to be negotiated here: lapwing and curlew often about in the fields. Pendle again dominates the view ahead, with the quaint Bowley Hill, a grand viewpoint in its own right, much closer. On the last lap, now, as we leave the track altogether and meet Goldacre Lane, with a stiff little climb following just when you thought the hard work was all done. Again the transition seems sudden as you find yourself back on Blackburn Old Road in the outskirts of Gt. Harwood. We're still very much in the breezy uplands here, as any frequenters of the cricket ground (Cliffe Park, now passed on the right) will tell you. I have known rain to stop play up here when it was bone dry down in the town!

On winter days it may be dusk by now, the row of neat bungalows and old stone terraced houses at the top of Cliffe Lane looking snug and inviting.

Now we are come to the sun's hour of rest:
The lights of evening round us shine.

In a few minutes, the round trip will be over. The feet turn in at the front door, and after those visions of remote and romantic places all seems rather tame once more. But the walk has enriched us, in a score of ways we can hardly express in words: we are sensible of that as we quietly relax at home afterwards. On that old round, familiarity never breeds contempt for me. Enjoy your walking, too, for what it is, wherever you may find it.

About The Author

Andrew Stachulski was born in Blackburn in 1950, the son of a Polish father and English mother, and grew up in nearby Great Harwood. He was educated at Accrington Grammar School, Lancs, from 1961 to 1968, when he gained entrance to read Natural Sciences at Fitzwilliam College, Cambridge. He graduated with first-class honours in 1971 and, after winning a senior scholarship, remained at the college to work for a Ph.D. under the supervision of Prof. Alan (now Sir Alan) Battersby. Following the completion of his doctorate in 1974, he held postdoctoral fellowships with the Medical Research Council and at Jesus College, Oxford until 1978.

There followed a long period of employment in the chemical industry, firstly with Beecham Pharmaceuticals (later SmithKline Beecham) and then Ultrafine Chemicals, Manchester. In 2001 he achieved a long held ambition by returning to academic life at the University of Liverpool, where he is now a senior lecturer.

Walking has always been a great love of his life, beginning in the Ribble Valley and Pendle country of his native Lancashire. In the mid 1970s he completed many of our long distance footpaths, the Pennine Way, Offa's Dyke Path and Coast to Coast Walk in particular, accompanied by college friends. Subsequently he climbed most of the fells of the Lake District, where he often returns, and from 1981 began to tackle the Scottish Highlands. In 2003 he completed the circuit of all the Munros, the separate Scottish mountains of 3,000 ft. or greater height.

His first walks were planned with a one inch Ordnance Survey 'Blackburn and Burnley' map, and that is truly his home ground. It was particularly following his return to the North in 1991, living in Greater Manchester, that this book came to be planned. Old walks familiar from childhood in the South Pennines, Ribble and Hodder valleys, Pendle country and the forest of Bowland were revisited and built on and many new walks were added. From these the twenty walks featured in this book have been selected, walks which appeal personally to the author through their beauty or special associations, or which in his opinion speak most clearly of the characteristics of the area.